Against Indifference

PUBLIC CATALYSTS

Manuel Bailo Esteve

Lent

Intensitat

Amor

pp. 25 0 **Introduction**

1_ **Reasons**

29 1_1 Between two moments
33 1_2 Work process. From transitory urbanism to the laboratory of indifference
39 1_3 What is proposed? Public catalysts

2_ **Previous References**

47 2_1 Werner Hegemann. The classification of public space
51 2_2 Camillo Sitte. The construction of the public space according to artistic principles
59 2_3 Edmund N. Bacon. The public space of the second man
66 2_4 Philadelphia_Rome_Troy
78 2_5 What do we get from all of this? A methodology
81 2_6 Bohigas' Model
85 2_7 Barcelona Playgrounds
109 2_8 Transitory public space

119 3_ **Indifference**

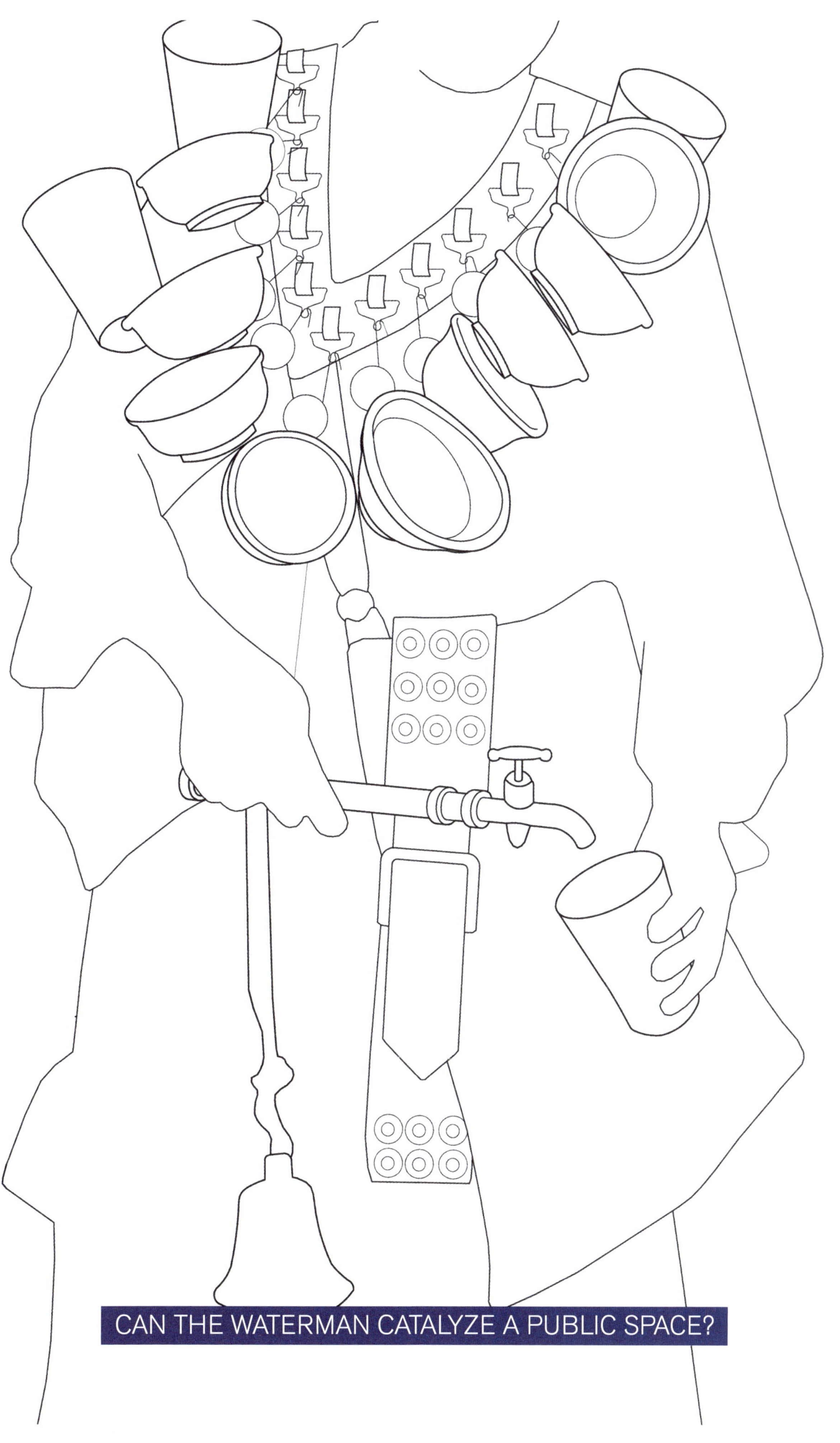
CAN THE WATERMAN CATALYZE A PUBLIC SPACE?

DOES A FRUIT CART CATALYZE A SQUARE?

CAN THE UNSTABLE SHADOWS
JUMPING OVER THE STAIRS FORM A SPOT
FOR PEOPLE TO MEET?

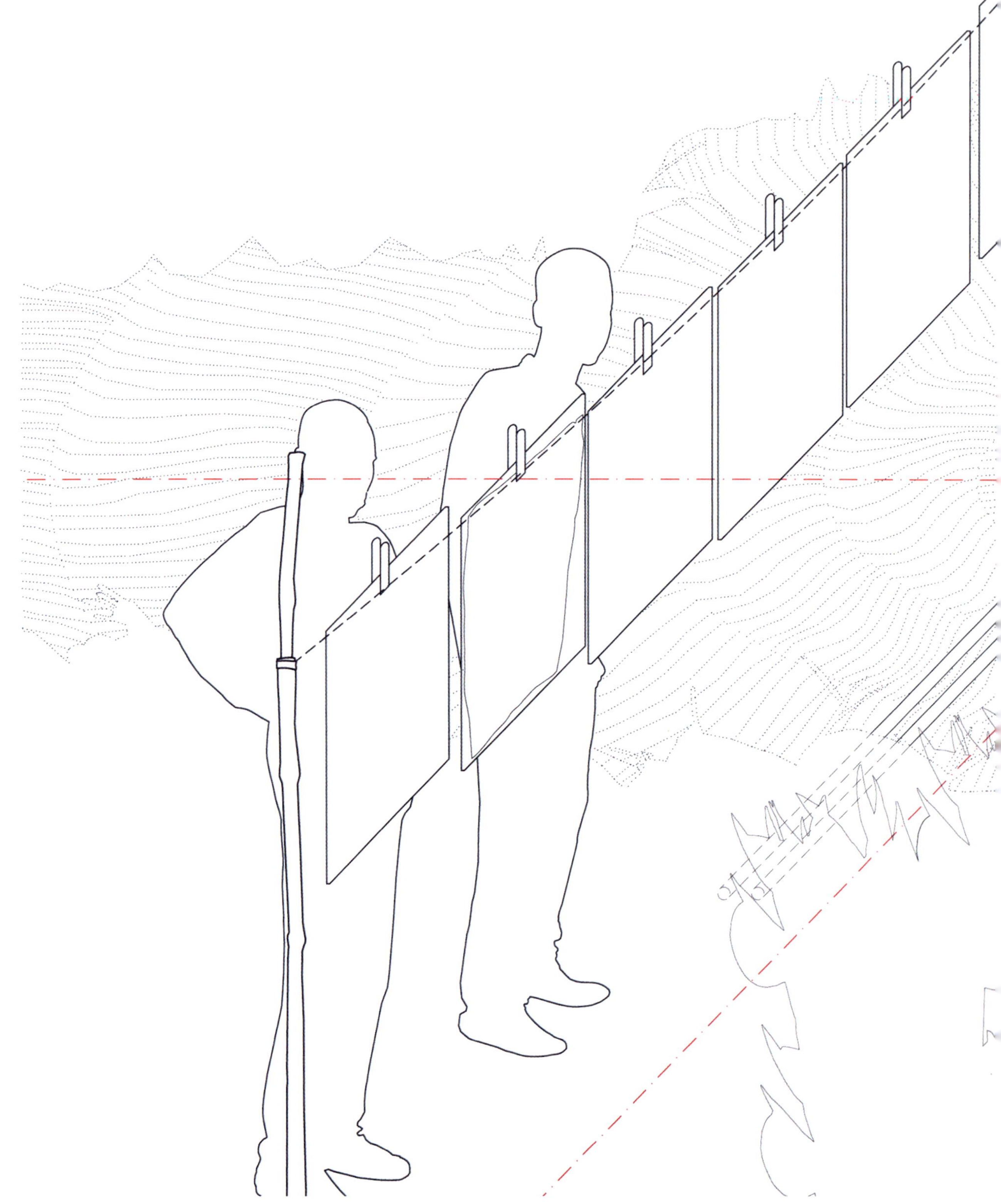

CAN CLOTHESPINS ACTIVATE A FOREST
BY HANGING JOURNAL PAGES FROM A TREE?

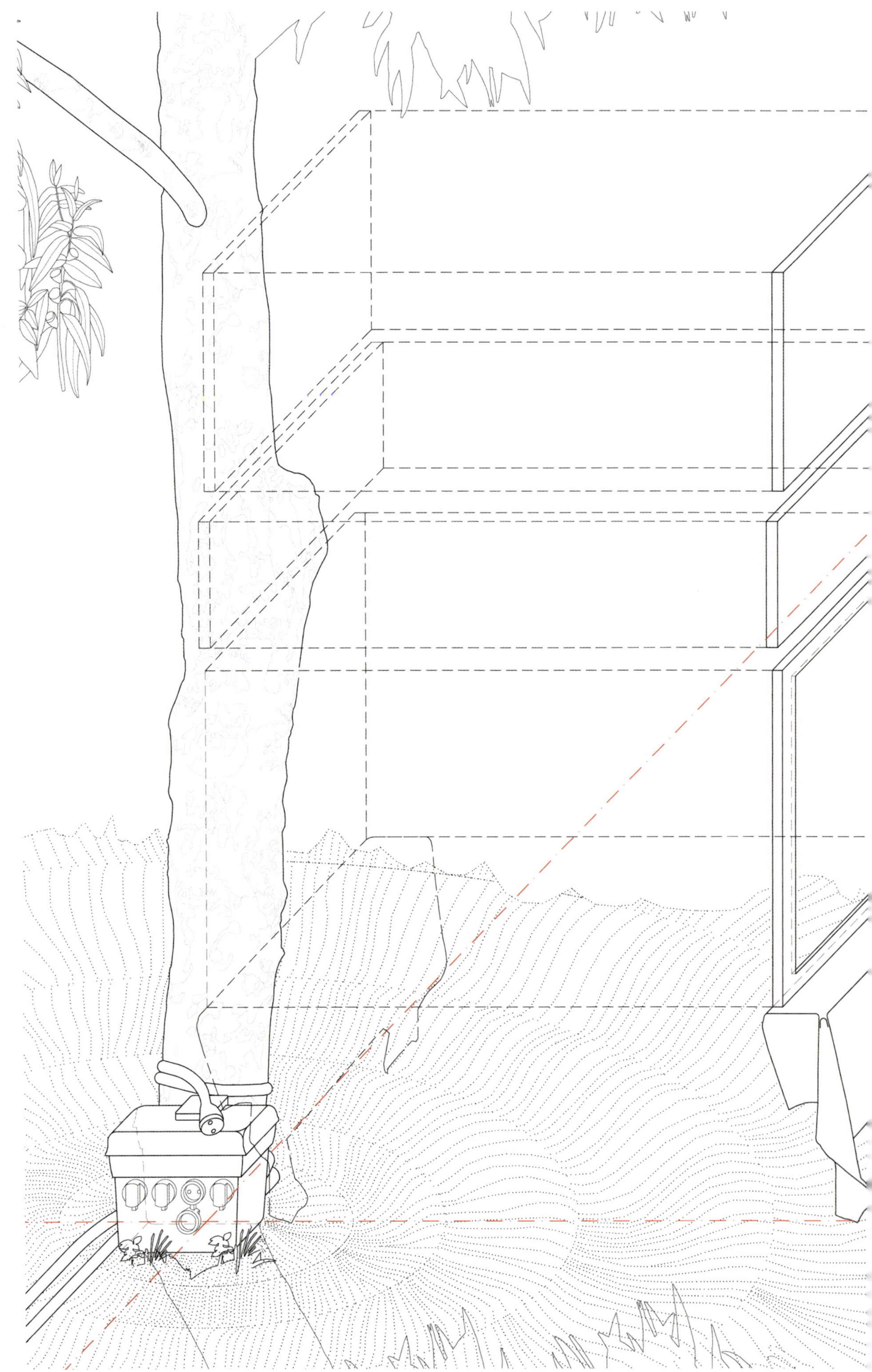

WHAT ABOUT A BARBER?

CAN THE ACCIDENTAL ESCAPE OF WATER FROM A FIRE HYDRANT CATALYZE A STREET?

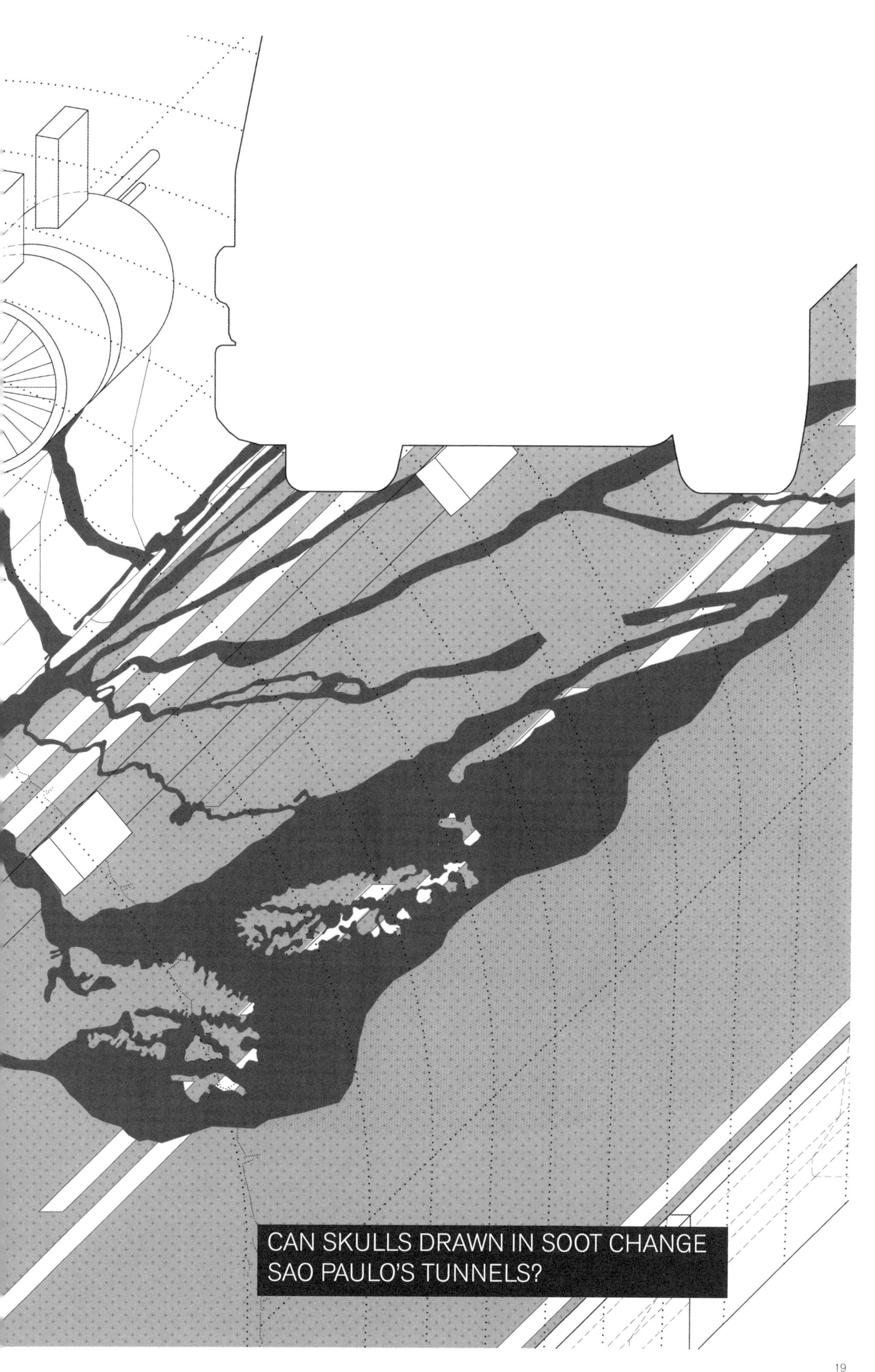

CAN SKULLS DRAWN IN SOOT CHANGE SAO PAULO'S TUNNELS?

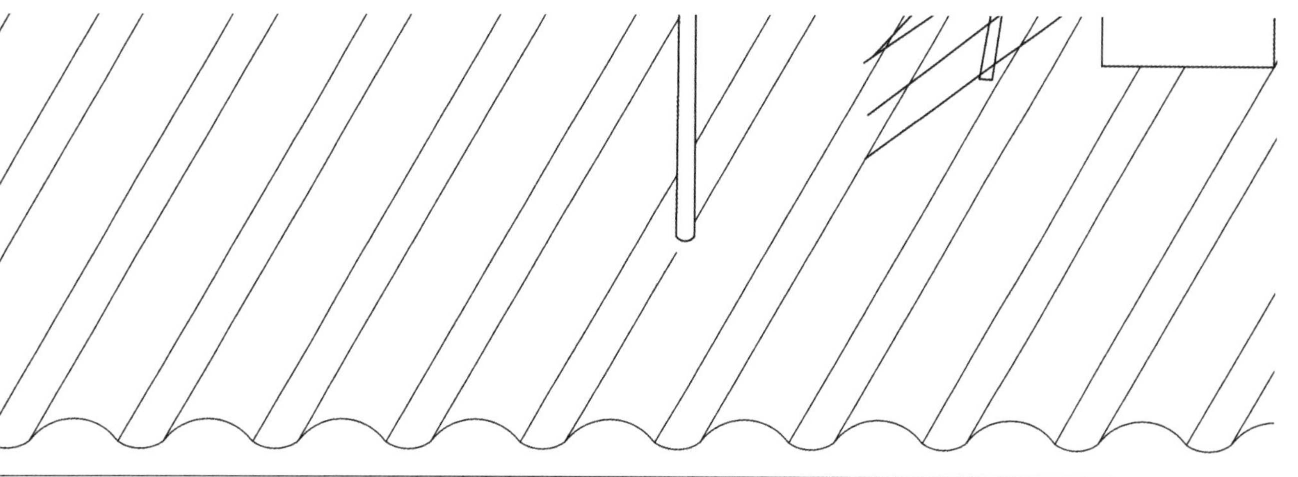

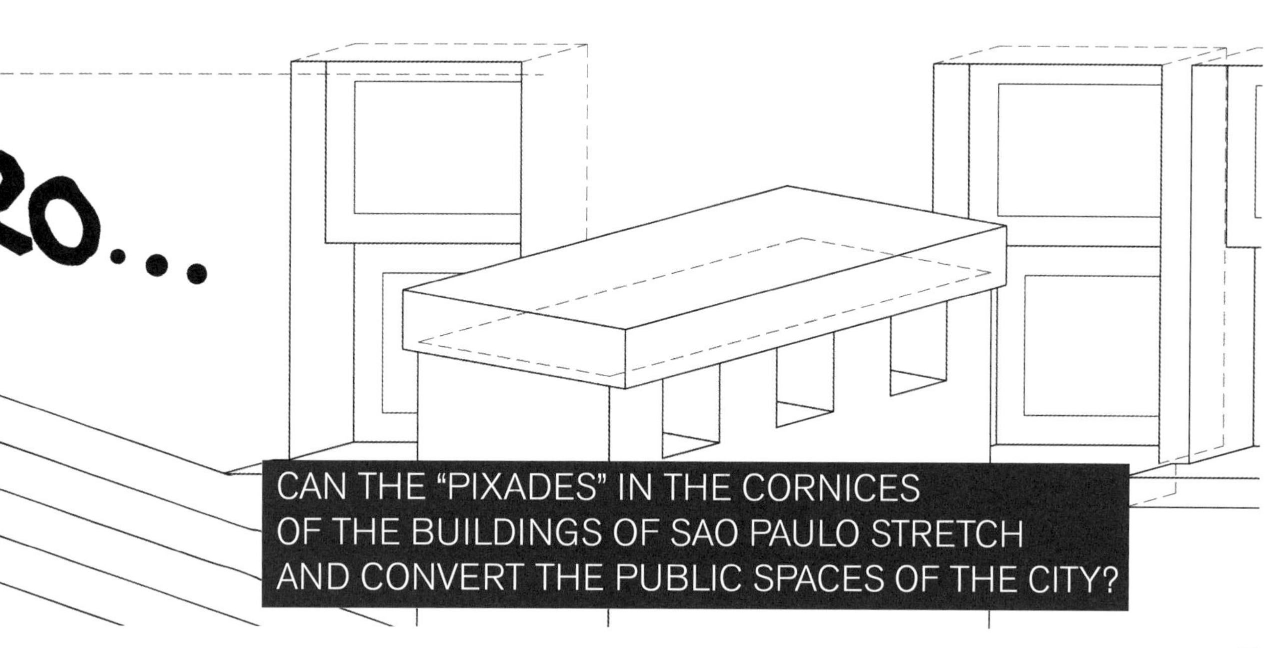

CAN THE "PIXADES" IN THE CORNICES
OF THE BUILDINGS OF SAO PAULO STRETCH
AND CONVERT THE PUBLIC SPACES OF THE CITY?

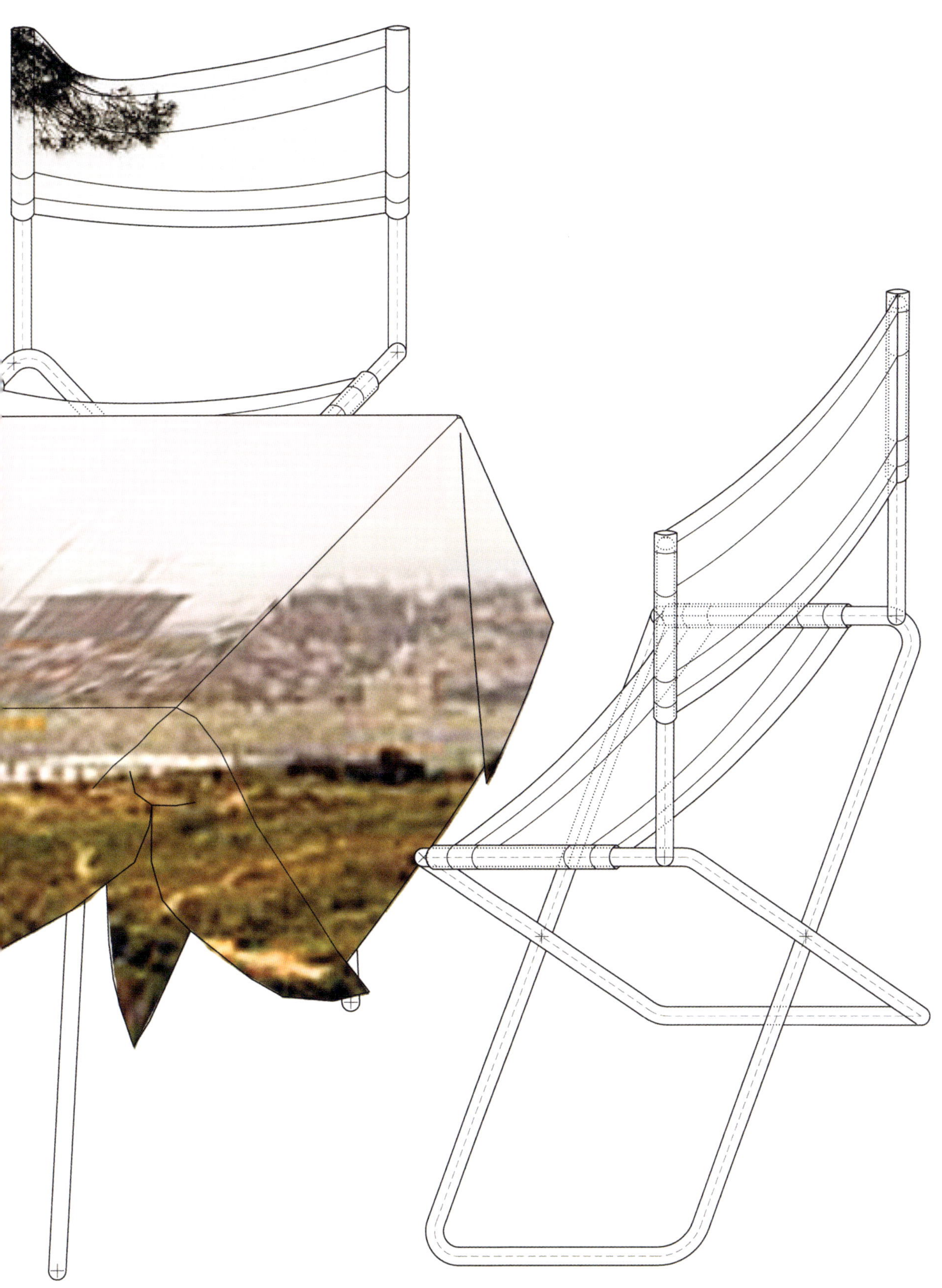

DO CHAIRS, FOLDING TABLES AND TOWELS CATALYZE AN INDIFFERENT FORGOTTEN SPACE?

Blaugrana celebration. Canaletes Fountain Barcelona

Why are the blaugrana supporters gathered here, in this space? Why does Barça celebrate their victories at the Canaletes fountain? Does the water have some kind of special power that attracts fans? Why is the celebration at an intersection and not at the very middle of Plaça Catalunya? Why not somewhere else? What makes this odd spot become such a thrilling place? What is the trigger of this public space?

The Canaletes fountain is the spot where the supporters of F.C. Barcelona, the football club also known as *Barça*, celebrate the team's victories. These people are called *culés* or *blaugrana* supporters; this last one referring to the team colors, blue (*blau*) and maroon (*grana*).

Research and experience

This book evolved out of delicate research and curious experience with public space. The work explores the construction of urban spaces throughout history, initiated by an interest in what makes a public space become a place of relation between people.

The transformation of public space in my own city of Barcelona led me to recognize the importance of empty space in a city. This study works to infiltrate the recreational dimension of cities, revealing their unwritten and hidden laws. It is open research, not limited to the study of Barcelona but rather looking to understand the origin of a broader range of public spaces within many cities.

Transitory intensity

Public Catalysts: Against Indifference is an atlas of public urban situations. In a moment where cities and landscapes are being gobbled up by an indifferent and generic urbanism, I would like to reveal the value of intensity as a reference for building identity spots. This is a non-exclusive endeavor to track down the uncertain and transient boundaries of this urban intensity.

"Skin is the deepest."
"Everything takes place in the surface, where life's events and thoughts of the individuals lie."[1]

"The street, this field where the nature of every urban thing ends up accomplished, made of shining sparks and ephemeral focal points."[2]

This book does not propose a futile discussion between formal or informal attitudes, a dilemma between confronted architectural options, but rather looks to discover the capacity of transformation of what anthropologist Manuel Delgado calls the "aesthetics of the event."

"Not in vain, the differentiation, central here, between the city and all urban related things is analogous, recovering classic architectural concepts, to the one that Giulio Carlo Argan established between structure and decoration. The first one refers to the city in terms of long time periods: big configurations with an estimable length of decades or centuries; the second one, refers to an hour-to-hour changing city, from minute to minute, made of images, sensations, mental impulses, a city that we could stare at and would place us in the very border of the aesthetics of the event.
"Therefore, urban anthropology should be presented more like the anthropology that defines the urbanity as a way of life: made of dissolutions and simultaneities, made of cold and minimalist negotiations, made of weak and scarce bonds connected to each other to the infinite, but in whom the short circuits are always present. This urban anthropology would be mostly similar to public spaces anthropology."[3]

In this work, we investigate the catalysts of all urban things. We search for the aesthetics of the event. We archive a meticulous and hyper-realistic study that recognizes and grants the actual transformation value capable of activating each public space.

Small scale

We bring urbanism to the smaller scale, focusing our attention on apparently insignificant situations. We discover the power of catalyzing both the designed and the spontaneous public space with lighthearted actions.

Hyper-realistic and obsessive drawing

The key to this study is the act of measuring and drawing the true urban importance of seemingly irrelevant elements and actions that convert the public spaces of cities. We have been able to discover the transcendence of these evasive situations by representing and fulfilling them in an obsessive, precise and hyper-realistic way.

1_ José G. Moreno, "Nietszche y Deleuze: encuentros", in J. Montoya, *Nietszche, 150 años* (Cali: Universidad del Valle, 1995), 307.
2, 3_ Manuel Delgado, *El animal público* (Barcelona: Anagrama, Coleccción Argumentos,1999), 183.

We study the non-muscled part of architecture and public space.
This is similar, with its differences, to the study that the master Richard Sennett proposes in his book *Flesh and Stone*:

"When Lewis Mumford wrote *The city in History*, he recounted four thousand years of urban history by tracing the evolution of the wall, the house, the street, the central square – basic forms out of which cities have been made. My learning is lesser, my sights are narrower, and I have written this history in a different way, by making studies of individual cities and specific moments – moments when the outbreak of a war or a revolution, the inauguration of a building, the announcement of a medical discovery, or the publication of a book marked a significant point in the relation between people's experience of their own bodies and the spaces in which they lived".[4]

4_Richard Sennet, *Flesh and stone: the body and the city in Western civilization* (New York, London: Norton & Company, 1996), 21-22.

FIG. 1/ View of St. Peter's Square in Vatican City from the Dome, 26 /01/09. MBE.

1_ REASONS

1_1 BETWEEN TWO MOMENTS

Bernini sculpts the Saint Peter's Square in Vatican City

Rome's St. Peter's Square and Sao Paolo's Pixades. Two images. Two cities. Two urban spaces executed in very distant moments.

On the one hand, Saint Peter's Square in Vatican City, Rome, (fig. 1) designed by Gian Lorenzo Bernini (1598-1680) in the year 1656.

The construction of a baroque public space for our imaginary reference. A historical urban space, densely formalized by the sculptural work of an artist. He constructs the square by shaping it with stone; a public space in which the repetitive pace of the heavy columns' shade constitutes a picturesque space.

Heinrich Wölfflin explains how Baroque architects inherited and developed Renaissance technologies to construct their own projects in his book, ***Renaissance and Baroque***[5] published in1888. Wölfflin suggests that the use of lines and geometry to control space in the Renaissance turned into the use of blot and shade to construct sensations in the Baroque.

Wölfflin calls this more sensual way of thinking of architecture, in which architects look to formalize emotions, "picturesquism".

5_Heinrich Wölfflin, *Renaissance and Baroque*, 1982 in *Science Observed*, ed. K. Knorr et M. Mulkay (Sage, 1983), 141-170.

FIG. 2/ *Pixaçaos* at Sao Paulo's downtown, Brazil, 26/01/09. MBE. The *pixaçaos* stretch the public space and define a new dimension of the city.

Pixades[6] at Sao Paulo

On the other hand lies the image of the urban interventions of the pixadores in the city of Sao Paulo (fig.2). These urban actions invade the private property of the skyscrapers of the city, activating the upper stories of outdoor space *by painting* the public space cornices. These installations requalify the squares and streets of the city despite their fragile and transitory nature. The encoded dialog of the paintings defines a new level of urban activity. Walk along the streets of Sao Paulo, take a look towards the last floors of the buildings, try to understand the pixadores drawings.

This becomes a new way of living the city: the pixades, which are mainly characterized for being placed in the highest spots of the buildings, make the public activities developed at the street level split and change to a new level of public connection.

The pixadores move and stretch the public space of Sao Paulo, increasing and extending it from the sidewalk up to the cornices of the buildings, transforming the city's civic space with intensity.

6_ Pixades. Abstract Graffiti at the highest spots of the buildings in Sao Paulo

The work that I present here is a journey between these two images, a research work that has been developed during the last ten years, while teaching urbanism at the ETSAB (University of Architecture of Barcelona), with Enric Serra and Maria Rubert de Ventós; also at the project classes in the University of Architecture of Alicante, with Josep Mª Torres Nadal; and at the Washington University of Saint Louis, with Kathryn Dean and Adrian Luchini.

Disasters and public space

I emotionally remember listening to Maria Rubert explain that the origin of many public spaces is in catastrophic event. She showed the class a disturbing panoramic black and white image of a blurry Barcelona filled with smoke columns after an air raid of the Italian troops allied with Franco. Other examples include the church burnings of the Tragic Week in Barcelona. Many of the urban gaps in Barcelona were caused by the bombs of the war. On many occasions these ravaged spaces proceeding from a tragedy are gradually consolidated into new public spaces of opportunity for the city.

I remember that moment in the classroom that was the first time I asked myself: "what is the origin of public space?"

FIG. 3/ *Campidoglio's Square*, 23/06/1995. MBE. The square without the equestrian statue of the emperor Marcus Aurelius. Michelangelo designs a unique pedestal for all the different sculptures of the square.

FIG. 4/ *Djemaa el Fna's* Square, 31/01/2004. MBE.
At noon, more than a dozen mobile restaurants lay the table and start cooking all kinds of Moroccan gastronomy dishes in barbecues.

FIG. 5 / *Djemaa el Fna's Square*, 01/02/2004. MBE.
Lamb celebration "Aid Al Adha". There are no carts, nor street markets, nor restaurants, nor itinerant funfairs. The square is a waste ground made of asphalt and empty ground.

Public formal space or public informal space

I wanted to discover what made the catalyzation of a public space possible. What is present in an extraordinary spot like Djemaa el Fna's square in Marrakech that makes it such an alive space, so full of activity. The absence of an architectural project seems to be the key to its formation. Is it possibe to concieve a square without architecture?

Do the Campidoglio square in Rome (fig.3) and the Djemaa el Fna's square in Marrakech (fig.4) have something in common that turned them both into active public spaces? The first square was projected and drawn by an artist, and the second one was the apparent result of a spontaneous action. How is it possible that two urban places with such different origins and historical processes are both excellent reference models of public spaces? How could two almost opposite urban spots, in terms of form, be so similar? The Campidoglio square becomes a formal reference model, and Djemaa el Fna's square is an example of the capacity of commercial activity to construct public space. Which one of these two squares is a better reference model from which to project contemporary public space?

Today, the value and capacity of formal architecture is constantly questioned. Public space without form, such as Djemaa el Fna's square, which is constructed through spontaneity, action and trade, has become a good tactic to think about today's public spaces.

We live in confusing times where it is common to put expressive architecture on an equal footing with expensive and capricious architecture; or intense architecture with excessive and unnecessary architecture.

It is a moment in which the economic crisis provides pessimistic and destructive arguments that erroneously justify the exaltation of mediocre architecture. We are living through a period in which the destructive and sterilizing reasons of architects and disillusioned critics allow the perfect conditions for the indifferent and banal architecture to appear.

To simultaneously study the Djemaa el Fna's square and the Campidoglio square is the expression of a non-exclusive attitude. This is an attitude that understands that good architecture is neither formal nor informal, not excessive or even minimalist. This is an attitude that realizes that in order to exist, architecture must always be intense. (fig.5)

Perhaps the form is not so important to project a contemporary public space? Is it better to design unfinished public spaces? Must we conceive of public space as an indefinite open process that will contruct itself with the passage of time? Must public space be produced informally? Must we think of public space as its action or as its form?

1_2 WORK PROCESS FROM TRANSITORY URBANISM TO THE LABORATORY OF INDIFFERENCE

Transitory urbanism

In *Transitory Urbanism*, an early essay within this project, we tried to demonstrate the importance and convenience of thinking about the condition of transience when designing a contemporary public space. We criticized the trend to design public spaces as finished objects and denounced the impermeable attitude of many architects. Over time, however, we came to realize that this position was too simple.

Transitory Urbanism appealed against the lack of attention to the world of open processes in the design of public spaces. We highlighted the non-physical characteristics linked to public space, including activity, trade, and the transforming capacity of the people's actions. It proposed a much more informal attitude towards development of projects; a trust in the constructive value of all that is transitory, of the formless action. It discouraged the definitive value of deaf and invariable objects. The new attitude understood and understands architecture as a non-definitive result of a process in which the provocation of randomness is mixed with the logical, sensitive wand intelligible reasoning. It claimed a way of conceiving the civic space of cities in which instability and transience were considered catalysts, capable of enriching and improving the projects in an arrhythmical way.

We wanted to recover the fundamental value of transience for the construction of the public space. Why have many contemporary public space projects forgotten the condition of transience? Transitory Urbanism questioned the loss of transience and to the loss of the value of the ordinary aspects in the current public space.

Is it possible to conceive of a public space starting from lightness? Is it possible to establish it through action and trade? Of all spaces, shouldn't public space best exemplify the character of an unfinished and open process? Public space is, by definition, a project without a unique property and therefore a space for everyone, an anonymous space. For this reason, shouldn't it be a space without form, in which all of its fundamental value is transitory? (fig.6)

FIG. 6/ *Xavier Ribas, Sundays, n. 15* from the *Barcelona Pictures series*, 2002. 26 C-Print,120 x 140 cm, edition of 6.

"Walking along Barcelona's outskirts on a sunny Sunday, we find a strange landscape. Between the roads and the apartments blocks, the industrial estates, the malls, the sport complexes, the natural parks and the theme parks (all a part of contemporary urbanization), we will find marginal areas where groups of people gather every weekend to spend their leisure time. Why do these people transform these residual spaces into the center of their leisure activity?"

Xavier Ribas, *Perfect Distraction* (Salamanca: Ediciones de la Universidad de Salamanca,1998)

FIG. 7/Xavier Ribas, *Flowers, n. 7 from the Flowers series*, 1998-2000 10 C-Type printed to 89 x 106 cm. 6 units edition. According to Xavier Ribas, the presence of flowers "fills the space with meaning and incorporate this space to the symbolic universe of a limited amount of persons".

FIG. 8/ Xavier Ribas, *Sanctuary, n. 7 from the Sanctuary series*, 2002. 8 C-Type printed to 110 x 130 cm. 3 units edition.

Why are those flowers placed there, next to the road (fig. 7)? Who has put them there? Why? Is this place someone's property? Or is it a possible beginning of the construction of a public space? What is that chair doing beside the road (fig. 8)? Where is the person who normally sits here right now? Will this person return?

If we could know how to gather this delicacy at the moment of constructing a public space, we would surely be able to save the spot's charm from disappearing. Transience and ordinary-ness are forgotten values in the design of the contemporary public space today – by capturing these values in design, we can stop this loss of identity.

To revalue transience would help us reconsider the current egalitarian and homogenized treatment of the public space. It would also allow us to check the often excessive attitude of the overbearing architect, who often does not pay attention to what it is not easily visible, such as lightness, memory, customs, sensuality, and pleasure. He does not acknowledge the transience of ordinary local values.

Productive schizophrenia

Throughout our work on *Urbanisme transitori* (Transitory urbanism), we tried insistently to find arguments that could justify the convenience of designing today's public spaces from transience.
In the subsequent development of the research, my curiosity shifted towards understanding the total capacity of historical public formal spaces for urban transformation. Throughout was a growing suspicion that contemporary public space shouldn't be proposed only from transience.

Formal and informal

Despite my personal interest in the research and production of open processes and informal strategies in design and my intense experience at the University of Architecture of Alicante as referential cultural focus of transience, it became clear that it was also necessary to analyze the public formal spaces in order to find the focus of the study of the public space.
This was a schizophrenic and productive attitude.

We took on an attitude of simultaneously supporting two opposite points of view as a research method. In order to be able to be supported and, in spite of the absolute conviction of not having a first-rate intelligence, we needed the permanent aid of F. Scott Fitzgerald's appointment:

"The test of a first-rate intelligence is the ability to hold two opposed ideas in the mind at the same time, and still retain the ability to function".[7]

This research analyzes formal projects and informal projects of the public space in parallel. Therefore, it cannot recommend an attitude in opposition to other one. Rather, we discovered common values between two unequal architectures, common conditions between different spaces capable of transforming the places into real urban, spaces.

7_Francis Scott Fitzgerald, *The Crack up* (New York: *Esquire*, 1936).

Give me a laboratory and I will raise the world

We have always had in mind Bruno Latour's article *"Give me a laboratory and I will raise the world"* (1983)[8]. Latour's article offers a reference framework that confirms the importance and the need to develop a laboratory in order to elaborate a rigorous research project. In this article, Latour explains the importance of the laboratory as a reference space that exemplifies, due to its conditions, the evolution that modern society has experienced. The French anthropologist describes the laboratory as a place where three exercises take place, capable of turning what was invisible into something visible.

The form in which people work at a modern laboratory as described by Latour, has been a reference guide during all this research time.

Limits dissolution

According to Latour, the activities in a modern laboratory lead to the dissolution of the border that separates what is inside and what is outside. Latour thinks it is necessary to go out to gather information and then be able to return to the laboratory in order to isolate and analyze this information in a different context.

During the research, we were constantly aware of the need to personally experience the urban spaces to be able to study them. We never trusted a rigorous research work on a public space that denies fieldwork as a fundamental source of information.

8_Bruno Latour, *Give me a laboratory and I will raise the world*, 1982 in *Science Observed*, ed. K. Knorr et M. Mulkay (Sage, 1983), 141-170.

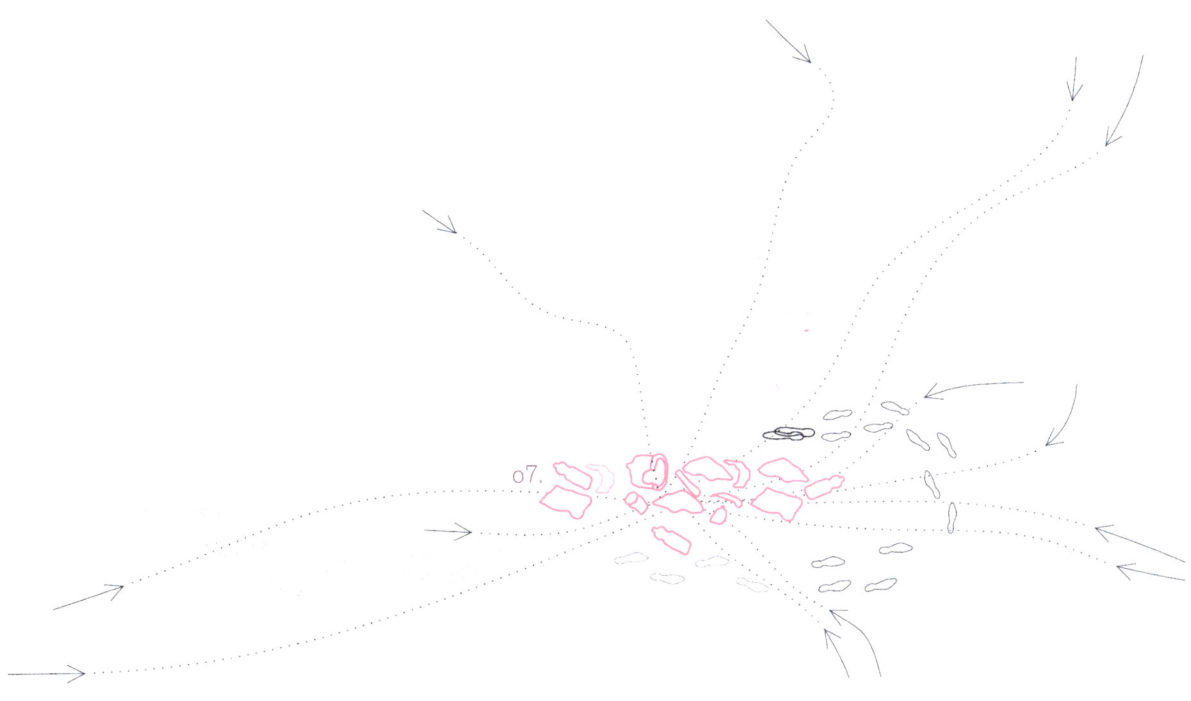

FIG. 9/ "Mon Oncle" 1958 by Jacques Tati.
Tati discovers how the garbage and the dustman can turn into the real driving force behind a square with the capacity of qualifying and modifying the space.

micro MACRO micro

Modern laboratories are an exercise in scale dissolution: a constant non-linear work that passes from micro to macro and from macro to micro.

To Latour, the work of scale inversion is capable of obtaining macroscale transformations from microdiscoveries. The laboratory invented by the scientist Louis Pasteur exemplifies the model of modern laboratory that Latour imagines. Pasteur's microdiscoveries made (before then invisible) microbes that were responsible for many contagious diseases visible. There have been many scientific advances that work from the microscale but have direct impact on the macroscale. These discoveries, though tiny in scale, are capable of intervening on the society and transforming it.

Our laboratory trusted in research without scale as a method to explore microscale decisions are as important as macroscale decisions in order to construct a quality urban place.

Processes of inscription

Another fundamental exercise for a successful laboratory is the definition of the processes of inscription, as Latour calls them. The aptitude to transform and improve of a modern laboratory does not only depend on the quality of the discovery, turning something invisible into visible. It also hinges on how those things that were unknown until the present can be shown and explained, and of how that new knowledge is transmitted and communicated.

In our laboratory we have trusted in the precise and detailed drawing as a key to explain everything we were discovering. The accomplishment of a few simple but meaningful drawings reveals, by layers, complex situations, often with a falsely banal appearance.

We draw the initiator of a public space formation. A hyperrealistic drawing allows us to measure and to slightly revalue each architectural situation. (fig. 9)

Laboratory of Indifference

Our laboratory is the "Laboratory of Indifference". In this laboratory, experimentation turns into a fundamental work method. The necessary conditions are constructed to provoke and to play without resigning to chance. The laboratory creates a research space where the surprise of the random and the meticulous work of procedural research coexist.

Taking Latour's laboratory as a reference model, we reconstructed the conditions of the modern laboratory. It became a space where we could investigate without scale. We developed precise exercises of observation in order to recognize minimal actions, customs, or economic activities – 'insignificant' things capable of provoking transformations in the urban space. At the Laboratory of Indifference we worked without the limit that separates the interior from the exterior. We investigated traditional public spaces as well as uncertain spaces between the public and the private.

And in the tradition of Latour, since a research laboratory must also transmit and communicate that which has been discovered – we proceed to illustrate: ***the public catalysts.***

The work elaborated in the laboratory was also a personal work. We have lived in these different places, and through those personal experiences we discovered what makes them similar by means of the confrontation and the comparison of apparently unlinked situations. It was a dialectical and personal exercise that allowed us to reach the essence of the public space, captured through a non-habitual way of observing things.

It was an intense, multiple and opened work, recognizing the value of apparently superficial things through a modern and personal laboratory. This work lead us to discover and demonstrate the hypothesis of this work:

The existence of minimal elements, that we will call public catalysts, that are the driving force behind the construction of the public spaces of the past and the present.

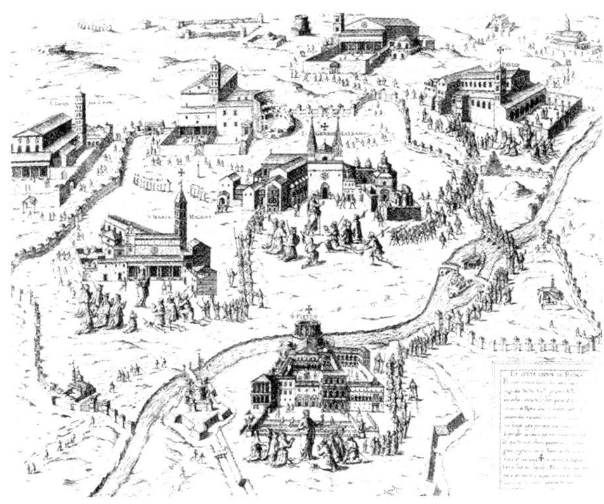

FIG. 10/Antonio Lafreri, Vedutte delle Sette Chiese di Roma, 157 in *Urbanism*, June 1959 in Edmund N. Bacon, *Design of cities.* In the draft pilgrims come from around Europe to visit the Seven Churches outside the very degraded urban area of Rome.

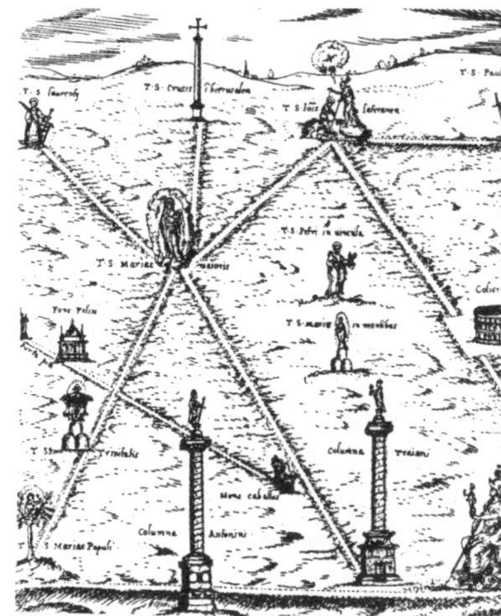

FIG. 11/ G.F. Bordino, Veduta Schematica del Piano Stradale Ideato da Sisto V, 1588, in *Le Piante di Roma*, Vol. II. Ed. Amato Pietro Frutaz, Instituto di Studi Romani. Rome, 1962. in Edmund N. Bacon, *Design of cities*
The plan of Sixtus V arranges the mess shown in Lafréri's above sketch. The routes appearing in the drawing weave through the famous obelisks system.

1_3 WHAT IS PROPOSED? PUBLIC CATALYSTS

To understand the new public space defined by the pixades in Sao Paulo, we cannot keep it in isolation. We rather compare it with a historical public space, widely documented and theorized. In order to understand the pixades of Sao Paulo, it is better to study their opposite – Renaissance and Baroque formal public spaces that were fruit of the strict control of the form.

Perhaps by doing this type of exercise we will manage to clearly explain this confused (and surely precipitated and wrong) intuition, which suggested the convenience of designing the contemporary public space only from transience.

The informal Baroque

The Renaissance was a resurgence of the interests and forms of classic art. Renaissance architecture arises at the beginning of the 15th century as a response to the disorder and informality of Gothic architecture. Baroque architecture was conversely a response to the rigid simplicity of the Renaissance. (fig. 10)

If, at the Renaissance they worked with lines, in the Baroque they worked with the masses; if in the Renaissance they worked with plans, in the Baroque they worked with space; if at the Renaissance they worked by means of the definition of frames, at the Baroque they worked by means of the definition of spots and shades.

Swiss historian Heinrich Wölfflin (1864-1945), specialist of the fifteenth through the eighteenth centuries, explains the transition from the Renaissance architectural style to the Baroque in his book, *Renaissance and Baroque* (1888).[9]

Wölfflin describes the Renaissance as a precise art that reaches a state of calm by means of the wise use of geometry, lines, and perspective. The historian then explains the Baroque as its opposite – a picturesque art. According to Wölfflin, the Baroque is the art of sensations, impact, and emotions. It is the construction of infinite and unlimited spaces. Wölfflin's Baroque is at its essence an informal art. (fig. 11)

9_WÖLFFLIN, H., *Renaissance and Baroque,* 1982 in *Science Observed*, ed. K. Knorr et M. Mulkay (Sage, 1983), 141-170.
Wölfflin's hypothesis confirms the value of the informal in the design of public space. The Baroque focuses on the construction of atmospheres rather than the construction of objects. The construction of relationship systems take precedence over the construction of isolated objects. As "any mentioned word always wakes the opposite ones" (Goethe); the study of the Renaissance and the Baroque must lead us, with no doubt, to deeply study and know opposite strategies.

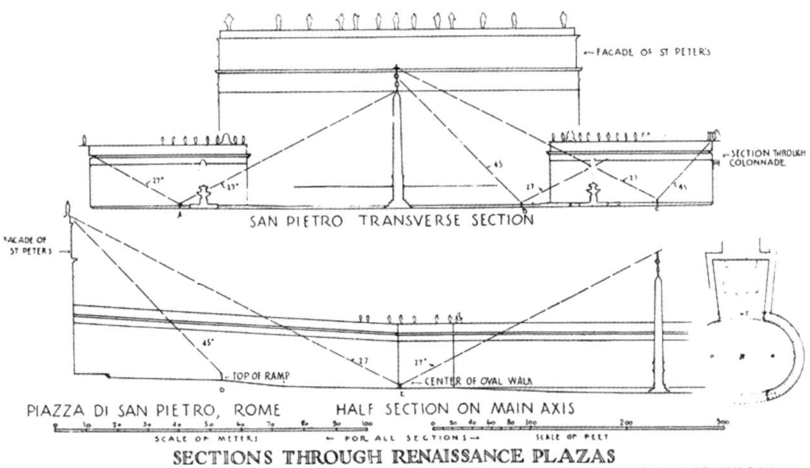

FIG. 12/ J. Gros, Sections through Renaissance plazas. Roma, 1612 in Werner Hegemann and Elbert Peets, *The American Vitruvius: an Architects' Handbook of Civic Art* (New York: The Architectural Book Publishing Co., 1922)
Objects and public space.

Saint Peter's Square in Rome was designed and executed by Gian Lorenzo Bernini (1598-1680) between the year 1655 and the year 1667.
It is a public space with Baroque character – a square constructed with formal expressions that construct a picturesque urban scenery. The square is an emotive public space and a dense and porous space of reference.

Saint Peter's Square is not only Baroque. It is also a key piece of the history of Renaissance urbanism.
The space is a lynchpin in a strategy of urban reform based on a formal and spatial plan of Rome according to the geometric Renaissance principles. (fig. 12)

In 1585, Sixtus V began his reign as Pope of Rome. The new Pope had experienced the precarious condition of Rome, riddled with buildings in ruinous conditions. He knew that the current city sat in terrible urban conditions of hygiene and health. At the age of 64 years, Sixtus V, advised by the architect Domenico Fontana, orchestrated the arrangement of the chaotic city of Rome.

Conscious of his age, Sixtus V designed a system of urban reform that would ensure his legacy by forcing his successors to continue the program after his death. His reign lasted only five years, but his plan lived on.

"As just a dowser, [Sixtus V] placed obelisks at the spots where the most important squares would be urbanized in the following centuries."
– Giedion[10]

Sixtus V's strategy of urban acupuncture solved a problem. Two hundred years earlier, the temporary transfer of the Holy See to the French city of Avignon set off the steady depopulation of Rome. The return of the Vatican to Rome sixty-eight years later gradually attracted a return of tourism to the depopulated city.

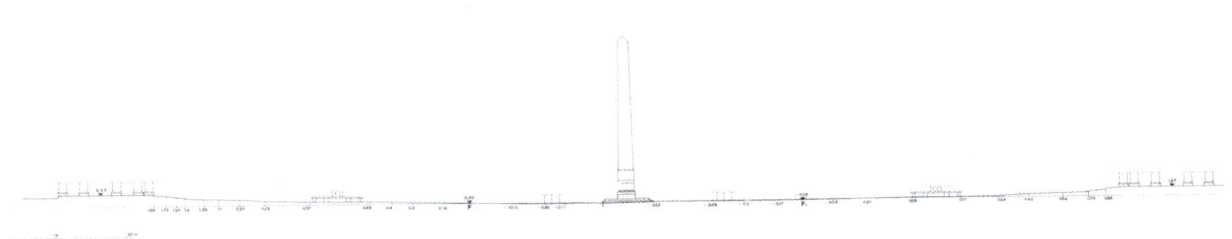

FIG. 13/ Section of Saint Peter's Square in Vatican City. Bernini.
Like a needle, the obelisk pricks the public space and depresses the square's surface.

With this combination, Rome turned into a decadent and dangerous city. The rising number of tourists looking to remain permanently in the city and the periodic floods of pilgrims for celebrations became a potential source of resources and money for Rome. The distribution project of Sixtus V marked the future interventions of the city with obelisks while also organizing the confused strolling of the lost pilgrims.

In the Laboratory of Indifference we studied the different drawings realized by Bernini for the Saint Peter's Square in Rome (fig. 13). Layering the different versions of the floor plans in top of each other, we discovered that all the projects always had a common element, despite their radical floor plan distributions. Though it was minimal element of small scale, with a fragile appereance, easily detachable and transportable. Despite its smallness compared to the large proportions of the square, this was an element full of significance, with intensity and strategy. This was the obelisk.

The re-drawing by the Laboratory of Indifference of all the versions proposed by Bernini is proof of the magic force of the obelisk. (fig. 14) Each floor plan maintains the axis between the obelisk and the front façade of Saint Peter's Basilica as a geometric reference. In almost all of the designs the axis of the obelisk with Saint Peter's front facade is used as a line of symmetry in the construction of the floor plan. The intense magnetic attraction of the obelisk marks the intersection point of the two ellipses in the final design of the square.

The obelisk turned into a spatial order reference node and became the center that spatially structured the whole project. Bernini takes the obelisk as the point of intersection of the two axes that define the elliptical floor plan.

10_ Sigfried Giedion, *Space, time and architecture; the growth of a new tradition* (Cambridge: Harvard University Press, 1954).

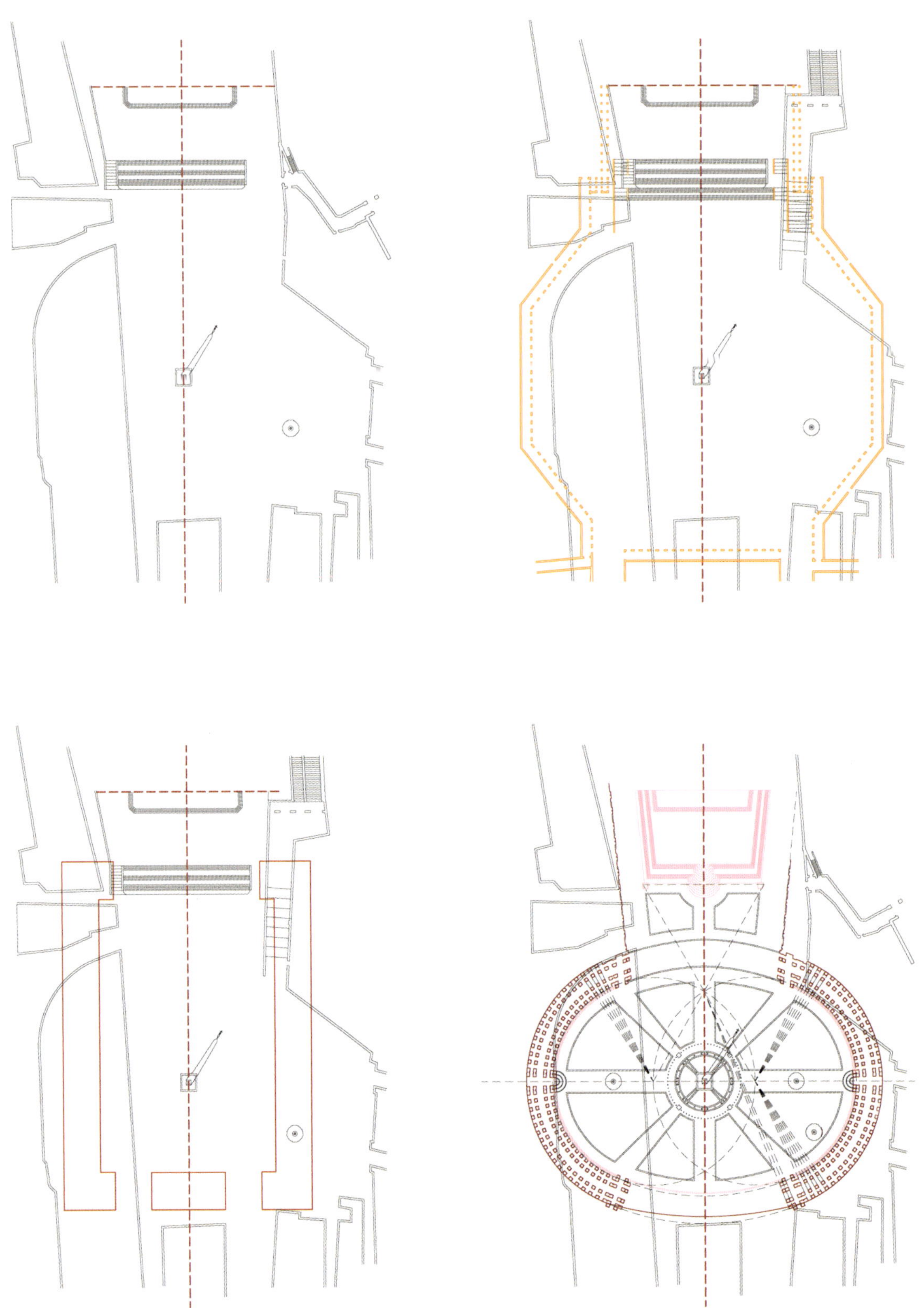

FIG. 14/LABORATORY OF INDIFFERENCE. (LAB IN)

Overlapping of all the plans for Saint Peter's Square in Vatican City, 2009. From left to right and from top to bottom, original state of the square, Francesco Reinaldo's project, Gian Lorenzo Bernini's first proposal, the second proposal, definitive proposal and superimposition of all the proposals. The overlapping allows us to discover that the axis defined by Saint Peter's facade and the obelisk is the only common order that all the proposals have.

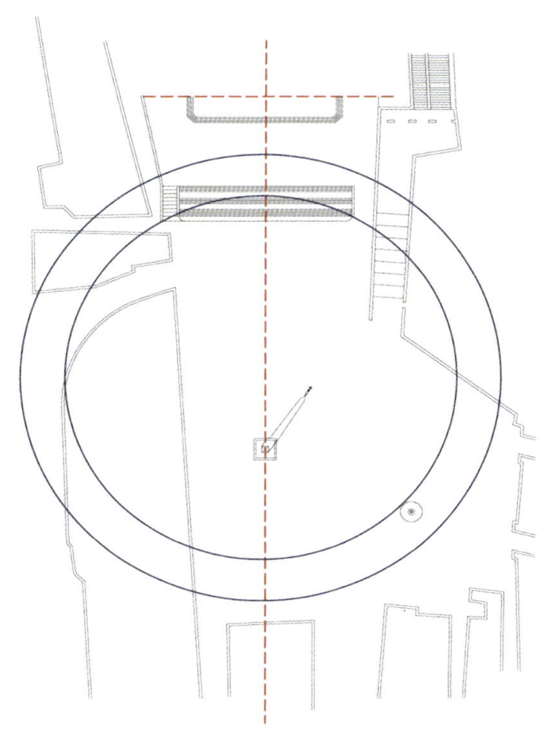

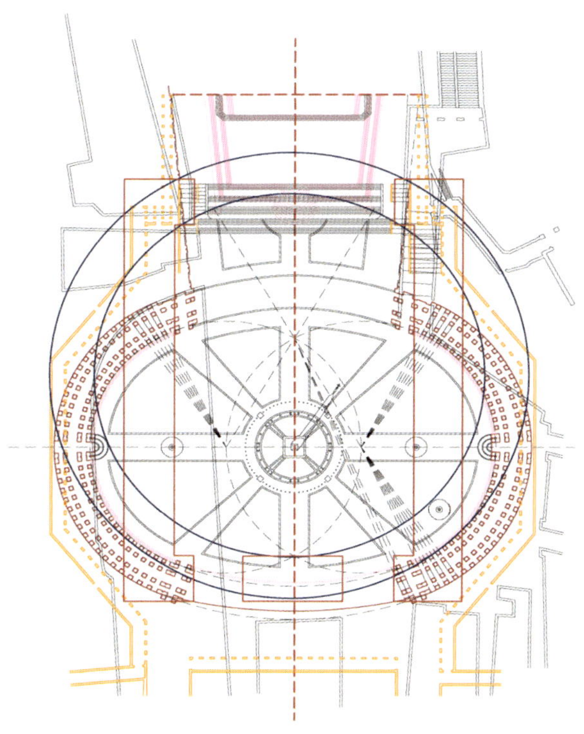

FIG. 15/ Colonnades of Saint Peter's Square in Vatican City, Rome, 1995. MBE.
The heavy columns constitute a dense filter between the square and the outside that prevents the visitors from seeing Saint Peter's facade until they access to the square.

FIG. 16/ Saint Peter's Square in Vatican City, Rome, 1995 Picture taken facing the ellipse's long axis. MBE.
The fountains and the obelisks cover the only permeable view of the colonnade. This way, the only boosted axis of the square is the axis aiming towards the basilica's facade.

It organizes the square through a different visual treatment of each one of these axes, pivoting around the obelisk.

The dense colonnade of the square's lateral facades constructs a porous (fig.15) filter that allows the people to walk and move through it while simultaneously blinding their vision of the streets that end at the square. The strategic placement of the overlapping of four rows of thick stone columns along the curved guideline of the ellipse allows the sight of the front facade of Saint Peter's Basilica alone. This view coincides precisely with the short ellipse axis, defined by the basilica and the obelisk.

The long ellipse axis, parallel to Saint Peter's facade and perpendicular to the short axis, fundamentally reinforces the scenographic construction of the square and avoids any possible distraction from the view of the cathedral.

Bernini fragments and disables the only alternate view that was geometrically possible according to the floor plan organization. He constructed a duplicate of the existing off-axis fountain and placed the pair on either side of the obelisk along the long ellipse axis, assuring that this axis would always be a visually fragmented and secondary axis. By obstructing the view along the secondary ellipse axis, Bernini guaranteed that the view of Saint Peter's Basilica would be the only visual protagonist of the square. (fig.16)

As seen in the section of J. Gros in *Civic Art,* the placement of the obelisk in Saint Peter's Square (fig.12) is tied to its treatment in section: Bernini depresses the pavement in order to slightly depress the obelisk. The height of the obelisk and its placement in the center of the square determines the height of the whole design. The height of the rising water from the fountain also follows this composite logic – each is determined by angles of 27° and 45° from the height of the obelisk.

The exercise to understand transience by means of the study of the public formal spaces had driven us to involuntarily exclude every slight thing that was forming part of this kind of public places. Had we had an excessively automatic attitude? The will to demonstrate the convenience of designing the transitory had wrongly led us away from the minor things within formal spaces.

FIG. 17/ *Pixades* in Sao Paulo, Brazil, 2009. MBE.
The *pixaçaos* prick the sky.

Pixades and obelisks

This project reoriented during a messy conversation on the plane back from Brazil (fig. 17) with Jordi Sardà and Lluís Alejandre Casanovas, three of us hovered over seatback tables. The different versions of the floorplans proposed by Bernini for Saint Peter's Square that I had redrawn and the pixades at the cornices of the high buildings of Sao Paulo's downtown suddenly had something in common. We realized that the monumental force of the colonnades of Saint Peter's Square had blinded us. The radical control of the project and the stunning perfection of the space prevented us from seeing Saint Peter's own essential transitory elements.

In the places where order wraps and overwhelms you, is it possible to find minor elements catalyzing the space? Is the force of the heavy order the one that made Saint Peter's Square such an active and alive space or was it thanks to other lighter motives?

What did the images of Sao Paulo and Rome have in common that had suddenly reordered the direction of the project? Both spaces have some fragile elements, isolated and of small scale – ephemeral, permanent or somewhere in between. These are apparently minimal, secondary elements; the stone obelisk of Egypt of Saint Peter's Square or the paintings on the skyscrapers of Sao Paulo. These elements, despite the fact that they are so different, achieve the same thing – catalyze the public space.

The obelisk of Saint Peter and the paintings of Sao Paulo are two catalysts that have qualified and transformed the space and the environment where they have been placed.

Public catalysts

All the research work realized up to this moment led us to discover that public spaces, whether they have a formal or a transitory character and whether they are recent or historical public spaces, always need minor scale elements in order to be activated. They need what we call "public catalysts".

This research focuses on demonstrating the hypothesis that the public catalysts transform indifferent public spaces into different public spaces; against indifference.
We want to verify how public places, in order to be living and active spaces, inevitably need reflections on a minor scale. We see that it is not sufficient to design a public space only from afar. We argue that in order to construct public spaces it is not enough to take compositive or geometrical character decisions, as so often happens in architectural projects. We investigate and demonstrate what is necessary to design apparently light elements that activate the public space. These are elements that, despite their minor visibility and ephemerality, are fundamental to form quality urban locations. These are the public catalysts.

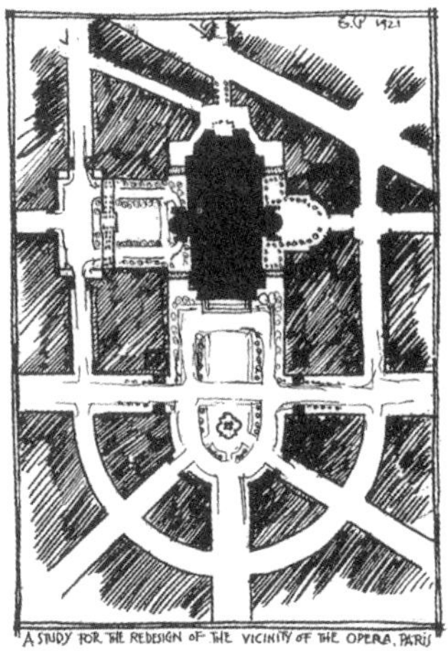

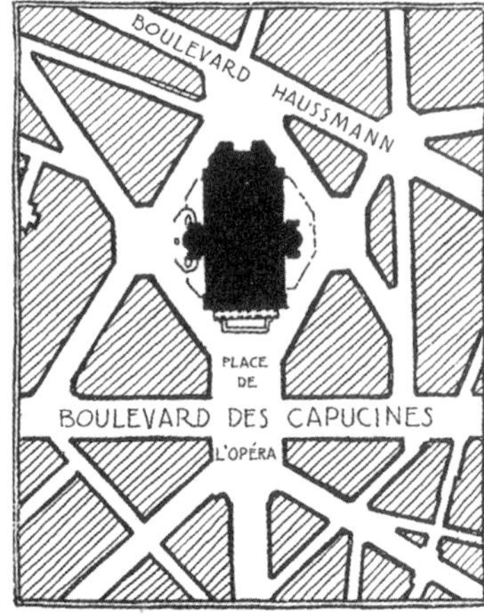

FIG. 18/ Charles Garnier, Opera's Surroundings and the new proposed location. Paris, 1861 in Werner Hegemann and Elbert Peets, *The American Vitruvius: an Architects' Handbook of Civic Art* (New York: The Architectural Book Publishing Co., 1922)

Drawings and picture of the Opera's location. Urban planning proposal by Garnier, consisting of demolishing the existing buildings and tracing new streets and public spaces in order to adapt his building.

2_ PREVIOUS

INTENSE PUBLIC SPACE OR STANDARDIZED PUBLIC SPACE

Architectural explorers

As an architect, I am more of an explorer than an erudite. This project, therefore, developed fundamentally from curiosity and personal experience. It is a document primarily compiled with graphic content to explain, justify and exemplify our hypothesis through drawings and photographs. Often the examples are illustrated with my own photographs. We hold the conviction that the best way to explain the city and its architecture is to experience it and to draw it.

Nevertheless, we have continually consulted books and articles related to public space during these years of research. There are many books that have been written about public space, but among all the consulted books, three were essential to our hypothesis:

_ *The American Vitruvius: An Architect's Handbook of Civic Art*, by Werner Hegemann and Elbert Peets (1922)
_ *City Planning According to Artistic Principles*, by Camillo Sitte (1889)
_ *Design of Cities*, by Edmund N. Bacon (1967)

2_1 WERNER HEGEMANN THE CLASSIFICATION OF PUBLIC SPACE

In 1861, the French emperor Napoleon III asked the architect Charles Garnier (1825 - 1898) for his opinion of the urban plan by the engineer Georges-Eugène Haussmann (1809-91), in which they would site Garnier's new Opera building. (fig18)

Garnier, who was at that time designing the Opera as one of the most representative Beaux Arts style buildings in the history of architecture, complained about the triangular and irregular form that Haussmann had given to the housing blocks around the Opera. Garnier begged for Napoleon's urgent intervention. The emperor, in turn, demanded Haussman correct his design of the public space that surrounded the building. Haussman ignored these changes and proceeded with his original plan.

Several years later, in 1878, with the building and the urban plan successfully constructed, Garnier wrote the following protest letter on Haussmann's lack of attention to his suggestions: (fig. 19)

"I don't know any ancient or modern monument placed in an environment with such deplorable surroundings as the Opera! Some of them ended up hidden, others are hard to see, others are in sloping areas or in hollow depressions; regardless of their emplacement, each one of them has been saved from fighting against irregular surroundings, houses of bigger size, close-up perspectives, wings and backsides composed by vulgar buildings, wrongly placed or interlaced, and facing open spaces too small to install the exempt monument and too big to introduce stairs! Anyway, the Opera sinks in a hole, buried in a quarry! And frankly, if I were not an admirer of Haussmann's big conquests, I would feel a furious anger against him. But since I had time to calm down... I find some consolation in the thought that in a few hundreds of years, Paris will have a prefect (as we have today) willing to disembarrass the Parisian monuments of those times, and he would have the inspiration of digging out the Opera by cleaning the whole area! [...]

Whatever the future Paris will be, the present Opera is wrongly placed, it's built in an area that is narrow at the front side and at the backside, with a widening in the middle part that, respected by the fence that follows the perimeter, makes this one look like the handles of a cobble-paving machine... And last but not least, the land has a lateral slope that inevitably leads to a lamentable hindrance that is not associated to anything, and instead of framing the monument, it reminds a crooked picture placed in the in the center of a lounge's wall."[11]

11_Werner Hegemann and Elbert Peets, *The American Vitruvius: an Architects' Handbook of Civic Art* (New York: The Architectural Book Publishing Co., 1922), 9.

FIG. 19/ Paris' Opera. 2010. MBE.
The Beaux Arts building by Garnier doesn't have a public space to be located on it.

FIG. 2—CAOS.
Dibujo procedente de *Architectural Review*, 1904.

FIG. 20/ Drawing appeared at Architectural Review in Werner Hegemann and Elbert Peets, ***The American Vitruvius: an Architects' Handbook of Civic Art*** (New York: The Architectural Book Publishing Co., 1922)
According to Hegemann, this picture appeared in a magazine of his time exemplifies the chaos prevailing in the contemporary city.

Thus begins Civic Art, a self-proclaimed thesaurus of public space compiled by Werner Hegemann, German architect and planner, and Elbert Peets, American landscape architect and planner. Hegemann, the senior collaborator on the project, was a well-educated and widely travelled scholar of architecture. Upon its publication in 1922, Hegemann had studied architecture, urbanism, art history, economics, and political science at the University of Berlin, Charlottenburg Technical School, l'Academie des Beaux Arts in Paris, and the University of Pennsylvania in Philadelphia. He completed his doctorate in economics in Munich in 1908 and went on to a career contributing to the rise of modern urban-scale planning.

His career as an architect was driven by his worry for the messy, out of control growth of cities during his time. Hegemann presents his book as an atlas of harmonic architectural solutions of ideal models to guide disoriented architects. The book promises an imaginary trip to clients with no architectural instincts.

It is a catalogue of examples to be wielded in the face of the chaos of the modern city as a manual for the way forward:

"Only in very special circumstances, an exquisite work will stand out while joining the chaos; the charm and the fine manners are absurd when compared to the persistent offensive imbalance of the surroundings. If we trust that the good quality work will stand out because of being different from its environment, we are deceiving ourselves.

The commotion that several orchestras playing different melodies at the same time generate in the political parties, perfectly symbolizes the architectural physiognomy of a modern city's typical street.
Even though one of the orchestras would be performing a Beethoven symphony, this fact does not remove the chaos. In this chaos, harmony and honesty have been lost." (fig. 20)

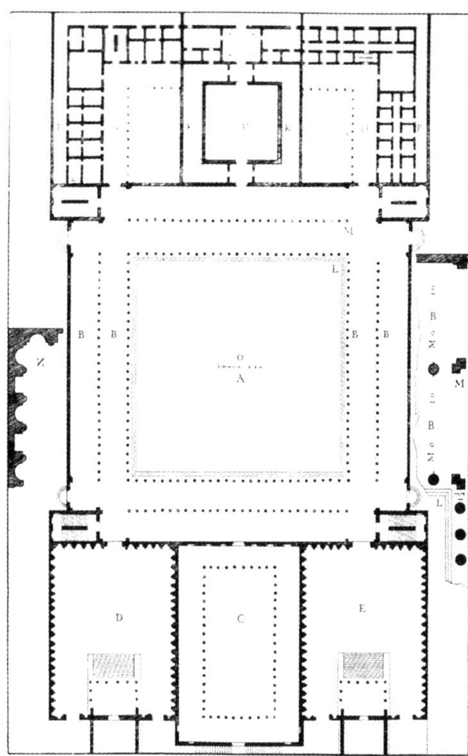

FIG. 21/ Andrea Palladio., Ideal floor plan of a Greek piazza. Rome, 1612 in Werner Hegemann and Elbert Peets, *The American Vitruvius: an Architects' Handbook of Civic Art.* Public space understood as an architectural object. A lesson in Beaux Art composition.

Civic Art. A Beaux Arts public space catalog published in 1922

Hegemann published his *Civic Art* in open defiance of his contemporaries as architects and theorists published the first writings on modern urbanism. In 1925, Le Corbusier published *Urbanisme*[12] and, two years later, in 1927, Ludwig Hilberseimer wrote *Large Town Architecture.*[13] It is no accident that Werner Hegemann, a restless intellectual, decided to write an atlas full of ideal models and exquisite urban compositions. He writes with total confidence in the architectural form defined by the classic criteria of Beaux Arts construction. (fig 21)

Despite its unfashionable timing, *Civic Art* had and continues to have a strong influence that is still recognizable in many contemporary urban projects. Hegemann's delicate book asks questions that are incredibly relevant today.

Civic Art sets out the problems of public space treatment and solves them through the construction of a landscape of architectural objects. The Beaux Arts principle of the connection of the parts with the whole becomes an integral solution.

Civic Art **was the manual that tried to classify the situations of urban space. It is a catalogue of solutions and a historical reference model: a book of precise recipes of public spaces for architects needing to face the disorder and "chaos of the modern city".**

12_Le Corbusier, *Urbanisme* (Paris: Crès, 1925).

13_Ludwig Hilberseimer, *Large-town architecture* (Stuttgart: Julius Hoffman,1979).

Drawing by Camillo Sitte, 1889.

Google Street View 2010.

FIG. 22/ Camillo Sitte, Perspectives: Berne -Tour de l'Horloge- and Verona -Piazza Erbe, Piazza dei Signori- in Camillo Sitte, *City planning according to artistic principles.* Permanent Public Space.

2_2 CAMILLO SITTE THE CONSTRUCTION OF THE PUBLIC SPACE ACCORDING TO ARTISTIC PRINCIPLES

Hegemann devotes the first chapter of his *Civic Art* to Camillo Sitte. The work *Construction of Cities According to Artistic Principles* – in which it was criticized the construction of the city according to the hygienists principles of the urban engineers and the space of the urban phenomena, from a sensitive look close to the artistic imaginary, was claimed – represents for Hegemann a fundamental base for the elaboration of his book. Nevertheless, in spite of the declared admiration for Sitte's work that he demonstrates in his book *Civic Art*, the two architects represent two very different ways of looking at how to project the public space.

Sitte had been, for the majority of intellectual of the beginning of the 20th century, an upright figure, one of the most influential thinkers of urbanism history. His book quickly turned, from the first edition, into a theoretical reference model with an unquestionable value. Despite the common interest of Sitte and Hegemann to theorize about the growth of the city, the importance of Sitte's work in Hegemann's book seems a forced quote to justify the recognition and rather than testimony to a common ideological reference model.

In his book, Sitte directly criticizes the flat and rational proposals of the urban engineer's urban tracings, a critique that also affected to the physical relation of the city objects with the environment that this city should have produced. His meticulous study realized for 30 years allowed him to write a book full of examples that justified his ideas. (fig. 22)

Construction of cities according to artistic principles is a reference model in terms of the organization and reasoning of a research work. In the book *Camillo Sitte: The Birth of Modern City Planning* by George R. Collins and Cristiane C. Collins, Sitte's work is included, quoted in a press release that appeared in a Chicago newspaper explaining the way Sitte used to work in order to write his book:

"Sitte's study of the cities, especially the medieval ones, had an encyclopedic dimension, and furthermore, the program that he used to follow when visiting an unknown city had a nice proposal, referring to its extension in a practical sense, but also in the way it posed a certain savoir-vivre. When he arrived to the station, he used to order the chauffeur to immediately take him to the main square. There he used to ask for the library and when he would arrive, he would arise three questions: first, which was the tower from where he could have the best sights of the city; the second one, which was the best map of town; and third, the hotel with the best meals. Later on, after having cut the map in manageable small squares just in case it would get windy, he used to go up to the panoramic tower, spending several hours analyzing the map of the city. Later he used to closely study and sketch the cathedral's square, the market's square, and probably of some other important point of the city.In 1889, after 30 years of these researches, he wrote about the matter".[14]

Sitte posed his book with the attitude of an explorer: he wanted to know the cities and their significant public spaces in the flesh. His book is important as a critique of the hygienic and abstract planning of the modern engineers of that time, but also because it represents a new research model. By gathering tangible proof, Sitte proposes new urban explanations.

14_ George R. Collins, Christiane C. Collins, *Camillo Sitte: The Birth of Modern City Planning* (Mineola: Dover Publications, 2006).

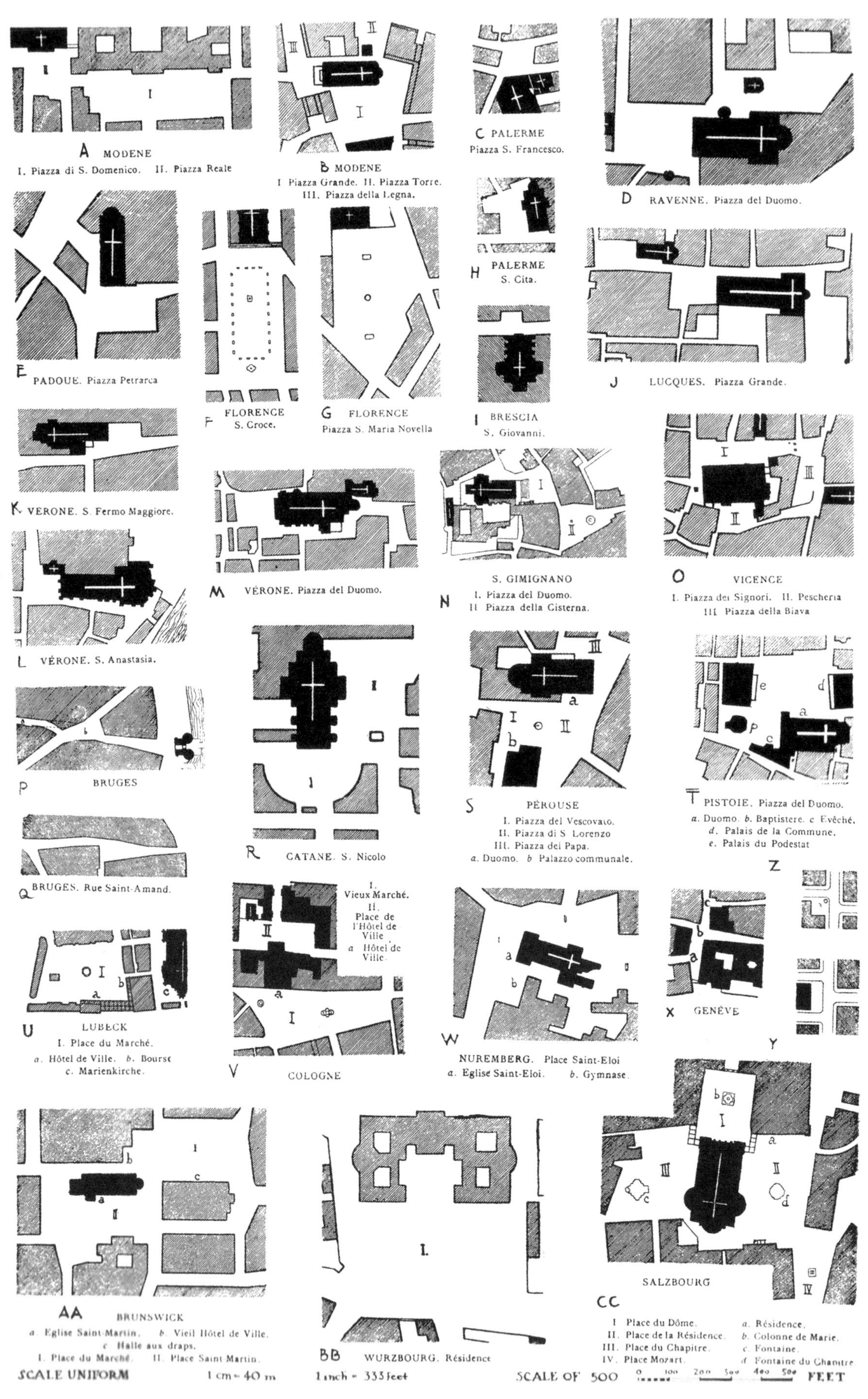

Fig 23/ Camillo Sitte, Plans in Camillo Sitte, *City planning according to artistic principles* (London: Phaidon Press, 1965).
Sitte draws all the floor plans of the public spaces that he visited in the same scale.

Sitte's systematic and repetitive method, in which he redraws the built squares in black and white plans, while sitting in the most significant public spaces of the city, compiles information to capture the environment and the specific character of each one of these places. After 30 years, all these research documents became material in Sitte's personal laboratory. Unusual graphic documents that are authentic proofs to certify and to exemplify his thinking, a systematic research method that allowed him to weave his own argument, step by step. (fig 23)

The space and the city

Sitte wished to bring urbanism closer to the human scale, exemplified by his delicate, personal freehand drawings. All of the plans that appear in the book are always in the same graphic scale in order to improve the reader's comprehension, to give an impression of size. These urban perspectives, in which human figures usually appear, explain the city with space and the people. Sitte's perspectives are a manifesto to take urbanism from the engineers and return it to the architects, explaining the city from space, from public space.

Error, time and city

Sitte understands the city as a process of formalization that accepts game and opportunity. He sees the growth of the cities as personal; in which error is a value capable of providing them with more complexity and quality, an attitude that understands the city in a procedural way in which the passage of time conglomerates urban differences. Sitte proposed a non-purist urbanism, alternative to the hygienist criteria of the modern engineers. Sitte declares his opposition to the modern hygienist proposals of isolating the singular buildings from their contexts. He supports his claims wielding his extensive compilation of plans of Italian churches attached to their neighbor buildings.

In chapter II, "Why the center of the squares must always remain empty", Sitte explains how the discovery and the bad use of geometry led modern architects to wrongly occupy the center of the squares with objects and exclude buildings:

"The rule of keeping the center open is valid not only for monuments and fountains, but also for buildings, especially for churches, which today are almost invariably located in the middle of plazas, in radical contrast to the older custom. Close scrutiny of the situation teaches us that in former times, particularly in Italy, churches were not erected as free-standing edifices. In Italy we find that interesting plazas result from churches being fused to other structures on one side or being encased by them on two or three sides. This is to be the subject of our inquiry.

The result is indeed astonishing, since from amongst 255 churches:

Churches with adjacent buildings in one side:	41
Churches with adjacent buildings in two sides:	96
Churches with adjacent buildings in three sides:	110
Churches completely surrounded	2
Isolated churches	6 [15]

15_ George R. Collins, Christiane C. Collins, *Camillo Sitte: The Birth of Modern City Planning* (Mineola: Dover Publications, 2006).

Drawing by Sitte, 1889.

Google Street View 2010.

FIG. 24/ Camillo Sitte, Venice Perspectives in Camillo Sitte, *City planning according to artistic principles* (London: Phaidon Press, 1965).
Permanent public space.

Sitte's documentation of the city as an alive, complex and open system allowed him to demonstrate that the theories proposed by the modern engineers of an abstract, flat and purist city would inevitably lead them to a dehumanized city. Sitte had a working method that Bruno Latour[16] might identify as a modern laboratory, capable of documenting and demonstrating ideas through empirical analysis. (fig. 24)

Hegemann's alternative

Hegemann proposes a very different way of thinking the city. He argues that the modern city had lost the coherence and homogeneity of the ancient cities and posed the recovery of order as an instrument to plan and to construct a controlled and harmonic growth of the cities.

Although he declared himself a follower of Sitte's method, Hegemann observes chaos in modern cities. Perhaps subconsciously, *Civic Art* becomes an alternative urbanism book to Sitte's *City Planning According to Artistic Principles.* Where elements of Sitte's city were constructed from error and opportunity over the passage of time; in Hegemann's city requires control and the Beaux Arts order to obtain a formal result.

***City Planning According to Artistic Principles*, by Camillo Sitte, and *The American Vitruvius: An Architects Handbook of Civic Art*, by Werner Hegemann, constitute two treatises of urbanism based on artistic principles. In the first case the artistic principles are recognized in the entrusting of the action, of the opportunity and of the passage of time; in the second case, the artistic principles are recognized in the control and the order of its objects.**

16_ Bruno Latour, *La vivienda en un laboratorio. La construcción de hechos científicos* (Barcelona: Alianza Editorial. 1995.

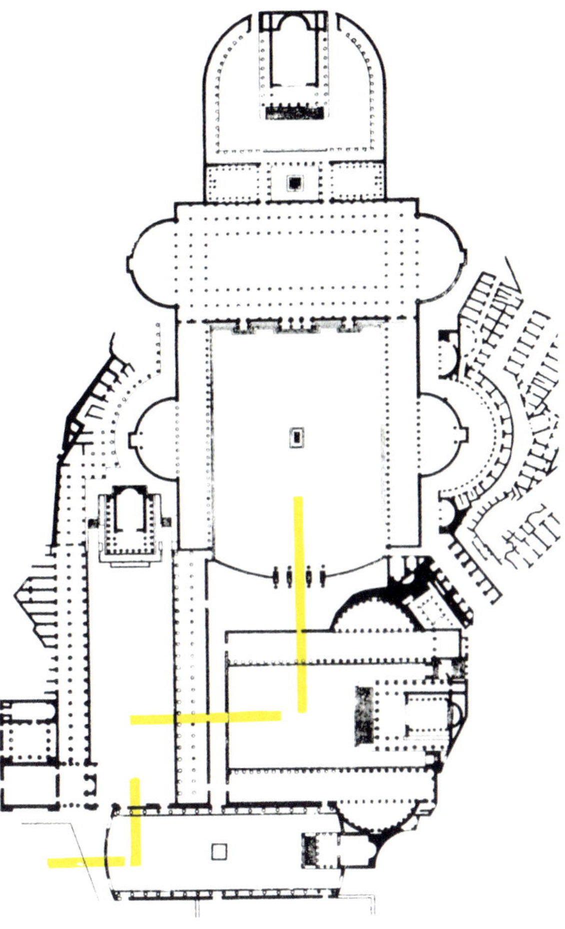

FIG. 25/ A.V. Bunin, *History of the Art of Urban Planning* (Russian edition), Moscow, 1953 in Edmund N. Bacon, *Design of cities* (New York: Penguin Books, 1974).
Public space built as a route of linked axis.

The public space as finished buildings

The Beaux Arts studies that Hegemann received in Paris formed his classical architectural character. According to Hegemann, art was the expression of visual reflection of order. This order was to be obtained through the precise application of the geometric rules of centrality, hierarchy and symmetry.

These Beaux Arts principles led him inevitably to propose the public space as finished architectural objects, public space-buildings, harmonic and compound. The references that Hegemann chooses to include in the manual *Civic Art* demonstrate this inclination to classic solutions.

The construction of public space in the Roman period was based on the gathering of public infrastructures arranged symmetrically and hierarchically. The example of the floor plan of an imperial forum in Rome conveys how the classic public space was planned from the coordination of principal axes of symmetry. (fig. 25) The sensation of the spaces is constructed through the serial gathering of small tied public spaces along an axis of organization. Roman public spaces were executed as if they were buildings. Hegemann references a Roman public space model that was enclosed by blind walls. Inside these enclosures, the blind walls that separated inside from outside were reinforced with porch galleries, creating an interior outdoor space. Hegemann does not wonder what happened outside of those blind walls that defined the public enclosures. Was the public space just an interior space? What were those 'empty' spaces outside the enclosures, were those not the true public spaces?

The compilation of exquisite examples that Hegemann selects repeatedly demonstrates that Hegemann imagined the public space as an architectural finished object. That Hegemann incorporates classic references not only from the Roman period but also from the Renaissance and the Baroque, demonstrates his interest in the public buildings-spaces as isolated objects.

Hegemann also includes Leonardo Da Vinci's drawings of a symmetrical and central building arranged on horizontal and vertical axes; suggesting Hegemann's interest in interpreting and moving the objectual order to the hierarchical public space that he proposed.

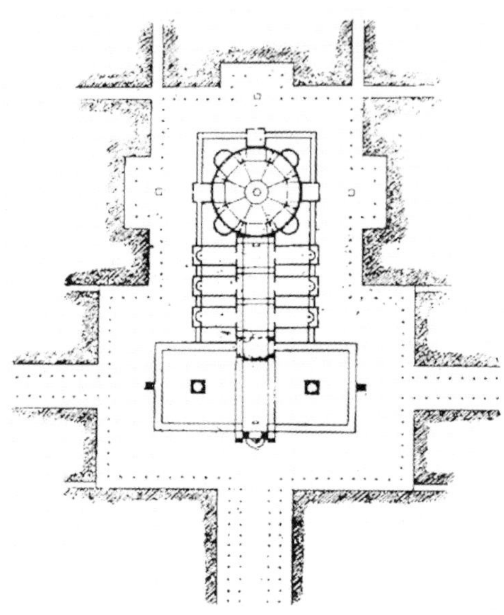

FIG. 26/ K.M. Heigelin, Floor plan of a church and its urban framework. Rome, 1830 in Werner Hegemann and Elbert Peets, *The American Vitruvius: an Architects' Handbook of Civic Art* (New York: The Architectural Book Publishing Co., 1922), 66.
Case-type public space.

Egg cartons and public space

Hegemann illustrates K. M Heigelin's proposal for a square placed around a church in which the public space surrounding it is adjusted and deformed reproducing the exact tracing of the church's floor plan, as a reflection. The free space follows the heartbeat of the interior space by reproducing the interior chapels on the exterior facades.

Hegemann imagines this as his ideal public space: symmetrical, in balance, controlled, defined with geometrical accuracy and completely finished. It is a public space designed as if it were a cabinet, in which every object finds his own space where to place and where to be protected. This "egg carton" public space fits its contents exactly, as the structure of an egg carton fits an egg. (Fig. 26) Hegemann's inclusion of these examples demonstrates his desire for *Civic Art* to be a manual of examples for architects.

City Planning According to Artistic Principles, by Camillo Sitte, and *The American Vitruvius: An Architect's Handbook of Civic Art*, by Werner Hegemann, became two fundamental books in the history of urbanism. Today, these works infiltrate, almost unconsciously, our way of thinking and seeing cities. Both books now constitute an important part of our formation as architects. The two documents are so deeply assumed that, just for this reason, it is often difficult to recognize their transcendency in our urban culture.

Sitte misinterpreted

Sitte's proposal to bring urbanism closer to the architects and to recover a sensitive look on the urban questions was too often misinterpreted in his era of engineered sterilization. Though his work is an example of methodological rigor, many readers understood it as a proposal of reinterpretation or even an indiscriminate copy of the ancient city.

Wisely anticipating this future misinterpretation of his message, Sitte makes clear at several points that his slightly reflexive and picturesque approach will no doubt attract criticism. To these future criticisms he responds by emphasizing the highly methodological approach of his drawings, though they may seem "artistic" on the surface.

FIG. 27/ Catalyst Exercise Urbanism Master Mexico DF 2011. Some pieces of chalk activate, in an informal way, the city's public space.

"Working in the assumption of creating a new arrangement in an exclusively decorative way, a new magnificent and picturesque sight, as if its only aim would be the glorification of the city, it is not possible to achieve this with our rigid alignment: to obtain those affections, those colors must be used. It would then be necessary to foresee in the floor plan all kinds of curves and angles, that is, permission to the force and intentional coincidences. But is it possible to invent and construct as they did along the history? Could they be spontaneous and fresh this stilted naivety and artistic naturalness?

The infantile happiness is denied to a civilization in which the construction without rhyme or reason doesn't exist anymore, a civilization that rationally studies everything on paper. Neither the life nor the modern construction technology allows an exact copy of the former urban planning, and it is necessary to admit it in order to avoid falling into infantile phantasmagoria. The beautiful works of those masters must continue existing otherwise that by a servile slightly reflexive imitation. Only if we investigate the foundation of these works and we manage to discreetly apply them to the modern circumstances, we will manage to obtain a new seed from the sterile ground.[17]

In spite of misinterpretations and early incorrect translations, Sitte's key message of looking at the city as artistic phenomena is intensely relevant to the present moment. Sitte's *City Planning According to Artistic Principles* continues to be an especially relevant historical reference model to design the informal public space. (fig. 27)

17_ Camillo Sitte, *City planning according to artistic principles* (London: Phaidon Press, 1965).

Nouvel - Garnier. The construction of the emplacement

We introduced Werner Hegemann with Charles Garnier's 1878 letter demanding a new public space for the Opera of Paris (fig. 28); we return to this proposition with the presentation of another – in 1984.

In 1984 the city of Nimes organized a restricted competition for the construction of a mediatheque in the historical center of the city. The city invited several architects of international reputation to submit proposals for a very delicate location adjacent to the Maison Carrée, a Roman building with high historical value. I would like to draw attention to Jean Nouvel's proactive and provocative proposal; setting aside Norman Foster's winning project, which posed a subtle exercise of dialog between new and historic objects.

One hundred years after Garnier's letter asking for an intervention from the Emperor to correct the site of the Opera of Paris, Nouvel's attitude in the proposal of Nimes' Mediatheque reminds us of Garnier's request.

Nouvel's attitude in 1984 is exactly opposite to Garnier's in 1878. Garnier wanted a whole environment to be reformed in order to leave his building perfectly framed. In other words, he proposed the construction of a public space replacing ancient buildings so that it could adapt to the architecture of the Opera.
Instead of designing a new building, Nouvel proposed a new site for the Maison Carrée. Nouvel's project was not an object-based proposal, but rather a buried mediatheque, a building without presence. This non-building would be a new square for the Maison Carrée. A building without form, hidden. A deep public space constructed by the overlapping of different layers. It would be a public building-space in which the light and the reflections would construct a new place without time, in transition. A site with no end. (fig. 29)

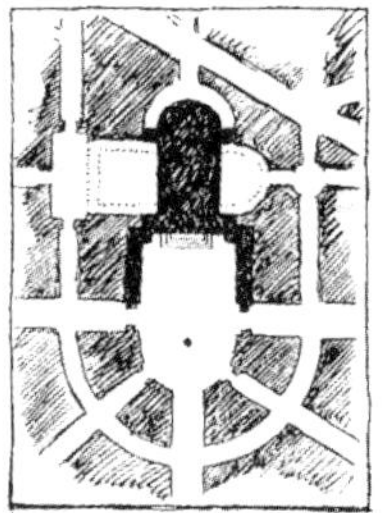
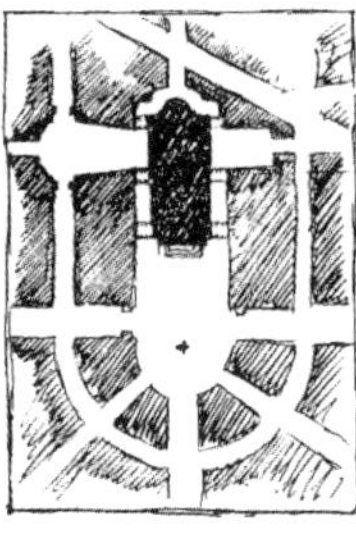
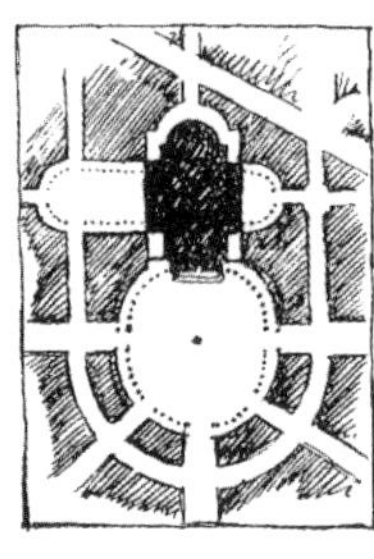

FIG. 28Chalres Garnier, Three studies of the Place de l'Opéra's shape. Originally in Charles Garnier, Le Nouvel Opéra, in Werner Hegemann and Elbert Peets, *The American Vitruvius: an Architects' Handbook of Civic Art.*

Studies for the location of Opera's building. Urban planning proposal by Garnier, consisting of demolishing existing buildings and tracing new streets and public space in order to adapt his building.

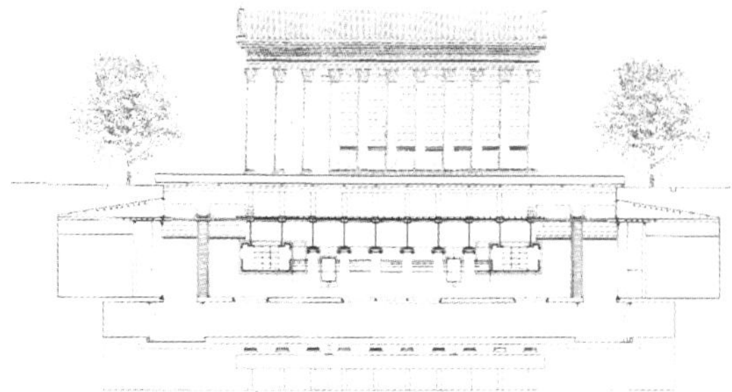

FIG. 29/ Atelier Jean Nouvel, Mediatheque competition in Nimes. Cross section, 1984. in Jacques Lucan, "Jean Nouvel: presentació de l'obra", *Quaderns d'arquitectura i Urbanisme*, n. 181-182 (Barcelona: Col·legi d'Arquitectes de Catalunya, 1989).

The mediatheque sinks to give importance to the Maison Carré. Nouvel built a new location, square, at the roman temple.

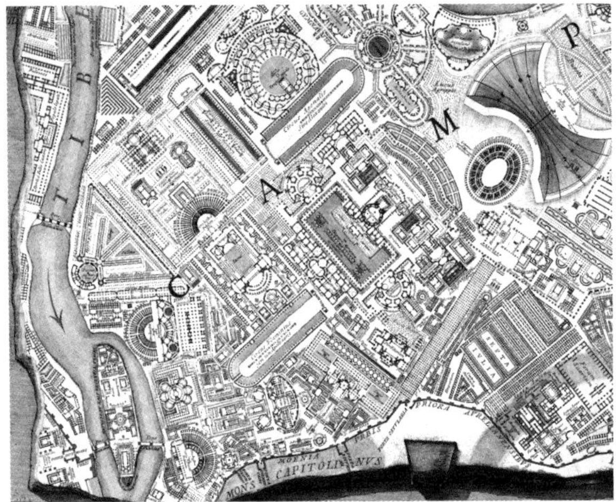

FIG. 30/Giovanni Battista Piranesi, Campo Marzio, Rome, 1762. At Piranesi's Campo Marzio, the public space is the interior of the buildings and not the streets.

A drawing where the Genius Loci and the Genius Seculli coincide, according to Peter Eisenman.

FIG. 31/ Atelier Jean Nouvel, Mediatheque competition in Nimes. Model, 1984 in Jacques Lucan, "Jean Nouvel: presentació de l'obra", *Quaderns d'arquitectura i Urbanisme*, n. 181-182 (Barcelona: Col·legi d'Arquitectes de Catalunya, 1989).

A new location for the Mediatheque.

To occupy the empty space

Nouvel's project poses an alternative to the spaces imagined by both Garnier and Hegemann. Taking the Roman model as a reference, Hegemann proposes the construction of public space as the composition of different public objects. (fig. 30)

This leads to absent-minded and disconnected public spaces constructed as finished objects, arranged and balanced. Thick enclosures segregate and forget the empty space outside. Hegemann, as in many public Roman constructions, doesn't bother with the space between the public buildings. The gaps between these public objects (often streets) are understood as residual geometric spaces between the different autonomous pieces. According to Hegemann, places without form and without interest.

The design of Nouvel's Mediatheque in Nimes proposes to construct the building in those forgotten spaces. (fig. 31) Unlike Hegemann and the Romans, Nouvel occupies the residual empty space.. Nouvel proposes to construct a space within that public space between the public objects. He proposes to construct a Mediatheque that occupies the squares and the streets.

2_3 EDMUND N. BACON
THE PUBLIC SPACE OF THE SECOND MAN

Camillo Sitte's porous influence is present in another fundamental text about the public space written in the 20th century. In 1967, Edmund N. Bacon published the book *Design of Cities*. Bacon was an American urban planner, educated at Cornell University and the Cranbrook Academy of Art, and a disciple of the Finnish architect Eliel Saarinen.

Bacon explains his treatise in this way:
"My hope is to dispel the idea, so widely and uncritically held, that cities are a kind of grand accident, beyond the control of human will, and that they respond only to some immutable law. I contend that human will can be exercised effectively on our cities now, so that the form that they take will be a true expression of the highest aspirations of our civilizations". [18]

Bacon, as Sitte, understood the city as a work of art:
"True involvement comes when the community and the designer turn the process of planning and building into a work of art." [19]

Bacon sees the city as the result of the decisions of the people:
"The city is an act of will."

18_ Edmund N. Bacon, *Design of cities* (New York: Penguin Books, 1974), 13.

19_ Edmund N. Bacon, *Design of cities* (New York: Penguin Books, 1974), 23.

FIG. 32/ Francesco Guardi, *Architectural Capriccio.* Ink drawing. Victoria and Albert Museum in Edmund N. Bacon, *Design of cities* (New York: Penguin Books, 1974). Spatial and phenomenological study of Public Space.

The man and the city

Bacon, like Sitte, brings city planning closer to the architects. In the same way that Sitte studied the spatial conditions of the city in his book through repetitive and delicate work of his urban perspectives, Bacon proposes to understand the city as a phenomenological experience. According to Bacon the city is especially a spatial experience. It is from this architectural perception that the new city should be designed.

In a careful study of Francesco Guardi's (fig. 32) drawing, Bacon searches for the keys to intense urban experience. He analyzes the relationship between the buildings and the sky, the relationship of the buildings with the land, the pointillism of space, the recession of the planes, depth, convexity and concavity and the relationship to man. This clearly demonstrates Bacon's attitude of moving away from the abstract urbanism, decontextualized and dehumanized.

At the first pages of *Design of Cities*, Bacon quotes John Wood the younger's words, author of the Crescents of Bath:

"In order to make myself master of the subject, it was necessary for me to feel as the cottager himself... no architect can form a convenient plan unless he ideally places himself in the situation of the person for whom he designs."

FIG. 33/ GUARDI, F., Architectural Capriccio. Ink drawing. Victoria and Albert Museum a BACON, E.B., Design of cities.
Bacon draws the squares including tables and pavements.

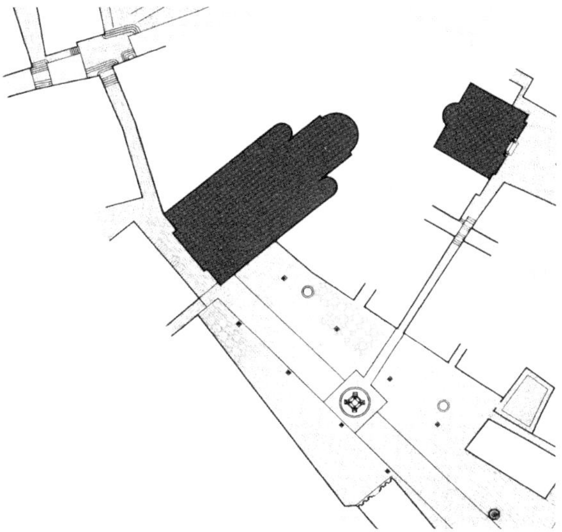

John Wood's words are a clear testimony of Bacon's opinion; he thought that in order to be able to design the city it was necessary to experience the place in a phenomenological way.

Greg Heller, current president of the Ed Bacon Foundation and a collaborator in Bacon's last publications, explains in his doctoral thesis how his teacher elaborated his books.[20] According to Heller, Bacon's method always began with a search of graphic information and images that supported Bacon's own intuitions and experiences. Once the images were compiled, they were extended on a table, as if they were a card game, meticulously arranged to set up a game of associations. Once the images were organized, he filled the empty spaces with the text that related them.

The way Bacon elaborated his books as a composition of empty and filled gaps explains the architectural nature of his theoretical work. The architectural character of the graphical design of *Design of Cities* complements and reinforces Bacon's idea of explaining the city as a spatial experience.

In the book, besides the exquisite and suggestive selection of images that demonstrate Bacon's ideas, the series of delicate drawings executed by the same author that complement and radicalize the book are very surprising.

The small scale as space catalyst

Bacon's drawings are thrilling due to their precise pedagogic force. His text are always full of intensity and preciosity when describing his elegant drawings. His careful observations illustrate the scrupulosity and the wit of his analysis. His look is intense, capable of focusing in the small urban scale and trusting that the minor intervention would also be a real catalyst of the public space.

"The drawing of the previous pages was intended to show the series of squares and Piazza San Marco as a concatenation of linked spaces, each comprehensible only in relation to the others. This drawing demonstrates specifically how the paving pattern, the placing of the steps, bridges, enriched facades of churches (shown in gray), wellheads, monuments, and flagpoles, and indeed the very placing of tables in the cafes (blue) and accompanying potted plants (green), all contribute to the unity of the experience, and frequently link one part with another."

Bacon was the first to draw the importance of the contribution of private area to public space. By drawing the cafés and terraces against the arrangement of the pavement and the stores (fig. 33), Bacon shows us the importance of the interaction of the shops in the public space. What seems to be superficial is actually capable of transforming the city. The vendors of Venice understand that the commercial activity can turn a public space into comfortable and active. They propose intense symbiotic relations between the private and public areas, knowing that this association will undoubtedly result in economic gain.

20_ Gregory Heller, *The power of an Idea,* Wesleyan University, 2004.

FIG. 34/ Piazza della Santissima Annunciaziata Florence.
Public space and time. Brunelleschi's rhythm still remains and arranges.

FIG. 35/ Drawing of the Piazza della Santissima Annunciaziata. Florence, by Giuseppe Zocchi, 1744

As Solà Morales enunciates in his book *De Cosas Urbanas*:

"The good city is the one that manages to grant public value to the private things. Therefore, a good city is the one composed of good houses, good shops, good bars and good private gardens, as well as it is constructed with public walks, representative monuments or buildings. And, therefore, the quality of the individual things is the condition in order to generate a collective wealth, by being semantically collectivized".[21]

21_ Manuel de Solà Morales. *De cosas urbanas* (Barcelona: Gustavo Gili, 2008).

The Principle of the Second Man

Enric Serra and Joaquim Español both pointed me towards this key book of the history of urbanism. The reference stemmed from my interest in analyzing Renaissance and Baroque formal public spaces. Of particular interest was Bacon's study of the square of the *Santissima Annunziata* in Florence, and his subsequent theory of the "Principle of the second man." (fig. 34)

Design of Cities is organized chronologically and separated into two big blocks. The first block is formed by lessons that exemplify urban historical projects of European cities. In the second block, he writes about more recent urban projects, both modern and future designs. (fig. 35)

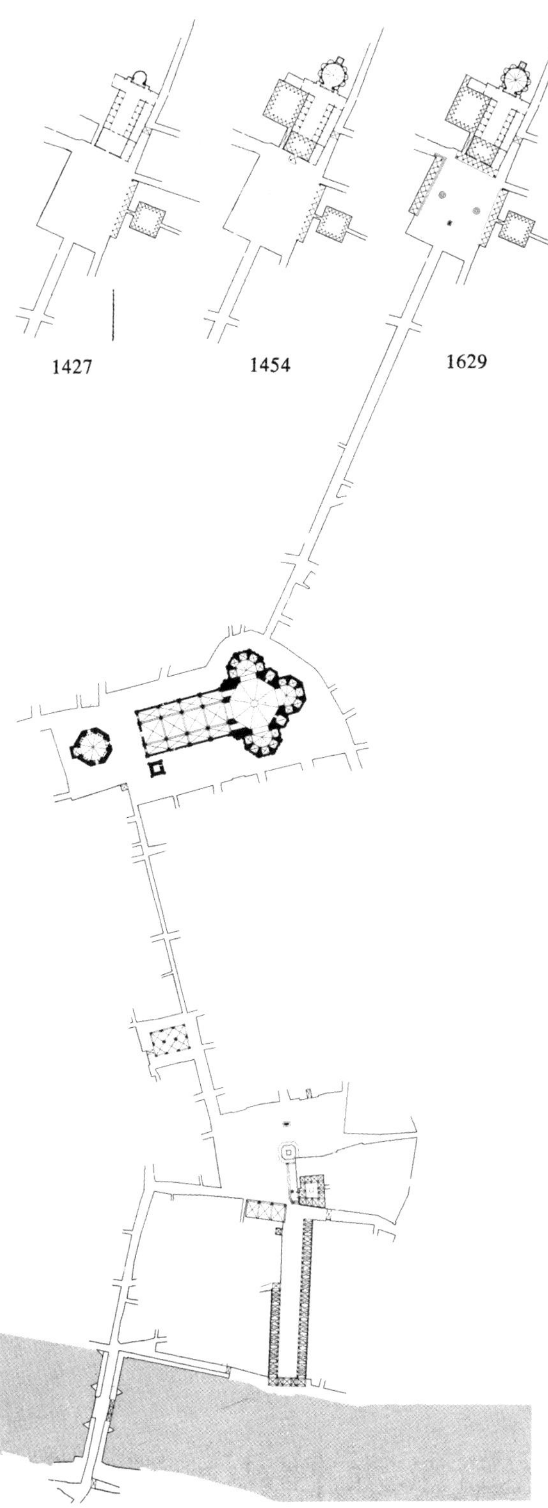

FIG. 36/ A.K. Strobl, Piazza della Santissima Annunziata in Edmund N. Bacon, *Design of cities* (New York: Penguin Books, 1974) Principle of the second man. A public space built in 202 years.

In the first block, when the criteria that justifies the work of the book have been revealed, Bacon explains the importance of experiencing the city personally, and exposes how the architects are capable of defining the urban form. The urban planner initiates a narration of examples of historical urban projects. It is surprising to recognize the coincidence between the books of Bacon and Sitte, two books written with 78 years of difference. Both refer back to ancient historical reference models to illustrate their ideas about contemporary urbanism. When in 1889 Sitte wrote *City Planning According to Artistic Principles*, he needed the historical reference models of Italian cities in order to illustrate his ideas and to be able to criticize the hygienist urbanism.

In one of the first chapters dedicated to the study of the Renaissance city and taking the *Annunziata's* square in Florence as a reference, Bacon discreetly and emotively reveals the Principle of the Second Man.

According to Bacon, the *Annunziata's* square, (fig. 40) designed and constructed over the course of 202 years, from 1427 to 1629, is an exceptional example of the construction of a harmonious and unitary public space. (fig. 36) A small part of the importance of this urban place belongs to the first architect, Fillippo Brunelleschi, who began the square by constructing the Foundling Hospital (l'Ospedale degli Innocenti). However, Bacon explains, that the biggest responsibility resides in Antonio da Sangallo the elder, the last designer to intervene. This is because Sangallo adopts the "Principle of the Second Man", an attitude of self-control so that the Foundling Hospital building remains the protagonist of the space. Sangallo prioritizes Brunelleschi's harmonious composition in the square, without introducing a new personal architectural order. Bacon declares that it was Sangallo who intelligently decided to prioritize the public space in the square. Though he restrains from imposing his own personal brilliance and character, Sangallo is responsible for the final quality of this public place of the city. If Sangallo wouldn't have resigned his personal brilliance and would have constructed a non-respectful building in the site, today the *Annunziata's* square would not be such a significant harmonious public space of reference.

Bacon's "Principle of the Second Man" highlights the importance of the passage of time in the construction of public space. He explains how the intense public space can be thought of as a strategic open project, with connected decisions over a span of even 202 years.

THE BETTER PHILADELPHIA EXHIBITION

. . was conceived by the Citizens' Council on City Planning and the Chamber of Commerce . . . sponsored by the City of Philadelphia . . . designed by Oskar Stonorov and Edmund N. Bacon . . . administered by Richard A. Protheroe . . . produced by the Philadelphia City Planning Exhibition . . . paid for by the City and civic-minded business and industrial firms.

Key to floor plan shown below

1. Vista of the Better Philadelphia.
2. Philadelphia: Past, Present and Future
3. Everybody Plans.
4. The City Planning Commission.
5. Progress Must be Bought and Paid For.
6. The Six-Year Plan.
7. A Better Downtown Philadelphia.
8. How City Planning Affects You and Your Family.
9. The Redevelopment Authority.
10. School Exhibits.
11. "Magic" Ending.

FIG. 37/ Philadelphia City Plan Commission, The Better Philadelphia Exhibition Catalogue. Exhibition's plan.

FIG. 38/ The Time-Space Machine, 1946 Photograph by Ezra Stoller, ESTO, 1946.

The Better Philadelpia Exhibition

Bacon was in the South Pacific enlisted with the American troops in the last days of the Second World War when he received a letter from his friend and architect Oskar Stonorov. Stonorov invited Bacon and Louis I. Kahn to co-direct an exhibition on the city of Philadelphia.

Stonorov proposed an exhibition with the fundamental aim to convince the citizens of Philadelphia that they could have a better city if they trusted in these architects' ideas. (fig. 37)

The Better Philadelphia Exhibition was inaugurated on September 8th, 1947. It occupied two floors of the Gambels Mall, lent by businessman Arthur C. Kaufman. Only five weeks long, the exhibition confirmed Bacon as a visionary planner of the growing city and secured the confidence of the political leaders of the city.

During the 21 years that followed, Bacon would work as the head architect of city planning of Philadelphia (sharing with Louis Khan competences in the offices of the Town Hall). Slowly, he would watch many of the projects proposed in the Better Philadelphia Exhibition go into actual construction in the city.

The Time Machine

The "Better Philadelphia Exhibition" illustrated both the current Philadelphia of 1946 and how they imagined it would be in 1982, 300 years after the foundation of the city. The exhibition began with "The Time-Space Machine", (fig. 38) an interactive panel formed by several layers of back-lit glass designed by Bacon that served to place the visitors on a plan of their own city. This allowed visitors to see the projects that the architects were proposing in relation to their homes.

The "Time-Space Machine" slowly transformed. It was a dynamic panel in which the different execution phases of the projects proposed switched on and off with lights, inviting the visitors to take part in the exhibition in an active way. The Better Philadelphia Exhibition needed to convince the citizens of Philadelphia that a better city might be constructed, but only with their participation.

FIG. 39/ The city center model, 1946. Photograph by Ezra Stoller, ESTO, 1946.
Bacon was in charge of the south-east quadrant, in which he proposed a new green paths system. Kahn and Storonov designed the downtown, where the so-called "Chinese Wall", a huge rail viaduct of the Pennsylvania's train network, split the city into two parts.

The great model

In the exhibition, there was also another model that focused the attention of the visitors. It was a mutant model of big dimensions (10 meters long and 4,5 wide) that showed how Philadelphia would transform in the next 37 years (from 1946 to 1983). (fig. 39) As the Time-Space Machine, it incorporated time and process as ideas of the transformation of the city. The model, magnificently documented with a few images in black and white of the photographer Erza Stoller, illustrates the productive and exquisite collaboration between Ed Bacon's erudite ideas and Louis Khan's brilliant sensibility.

The model had two faces and was placed approximately a meter above of the floor. It was divided in thirteen pieces, and each of which rotated independently. A voice-over explained the evolution of the city as the thirteen chunks turn automatically, showing the bottom face of the model. One of the faces represented the Philadelphia of 1946 and other one, the Philadelphia of 1983. It was a reversible model that allowed the different fragments of the current Philadelphia and the future Philadelphia to mix. The model demonstrated how the force of the ideas can transform the city through time.

The idea of executing a model that would transform following the orders of a secret voice-over runs parallel to the Principle of the Second Man that Bacon would eventually outline in his book *Design of Cities*. Brunelleschi's voice was the voice-over establishing the order of the Annunziata's square.

The future city would have to be designed with a collection of proposals thought of as a system capable of constructing a complex organism of relations. The city would have to be thought of as an open session that would allow to be reformed and to grow strategically.

Time and space

The title "The Time-Space Machine" from the 1946 back-lit model predicts key ideas that Bacon would develop in his academic and professional future: time and space. Was it possible to think the city as an open system? Was there a way of imagining the city that could strategically define the public space through time? How was it possible to design space in order to be neatly developed through time? The Principle of the Second Man would be one of many answers to his questions.

2_4 PHILADELPHIA_ROME_TROY

FIG. 40/ Giovanni Battista Piranesi., Campo Marzio, Rome, 1762.
Genius loci and genius seculi in the same drawing.

The back-lit model of the Better Philadelphia Exhibition shows the city in layers, represented as if it was a historical European city. The new city is shown superposed on an elder city. The aim was to expose the city in constant transformation, as a complex organism without a finished form. Philadelphia is in transition.

Philadelphia and the Campo Marzio by Piranesi

Within Hegemann's extraordinary compilation of diverse drawings and examples from the history of architecture, we find an exquisite etching by Giovanni Battista Piranesi (1720-1778) of the Campo Marzio of Rome. (fig. 40) Piranesi's map is unique among Hegemann's many examples, adding new value to the manual. Piranesi's map includes transitory versions the city beyond its architectural objects. Piranesi's drawings mix the genius loci with the genius seculi of Rome. The drawing is formed by real and imaginary buildings with and without scale.

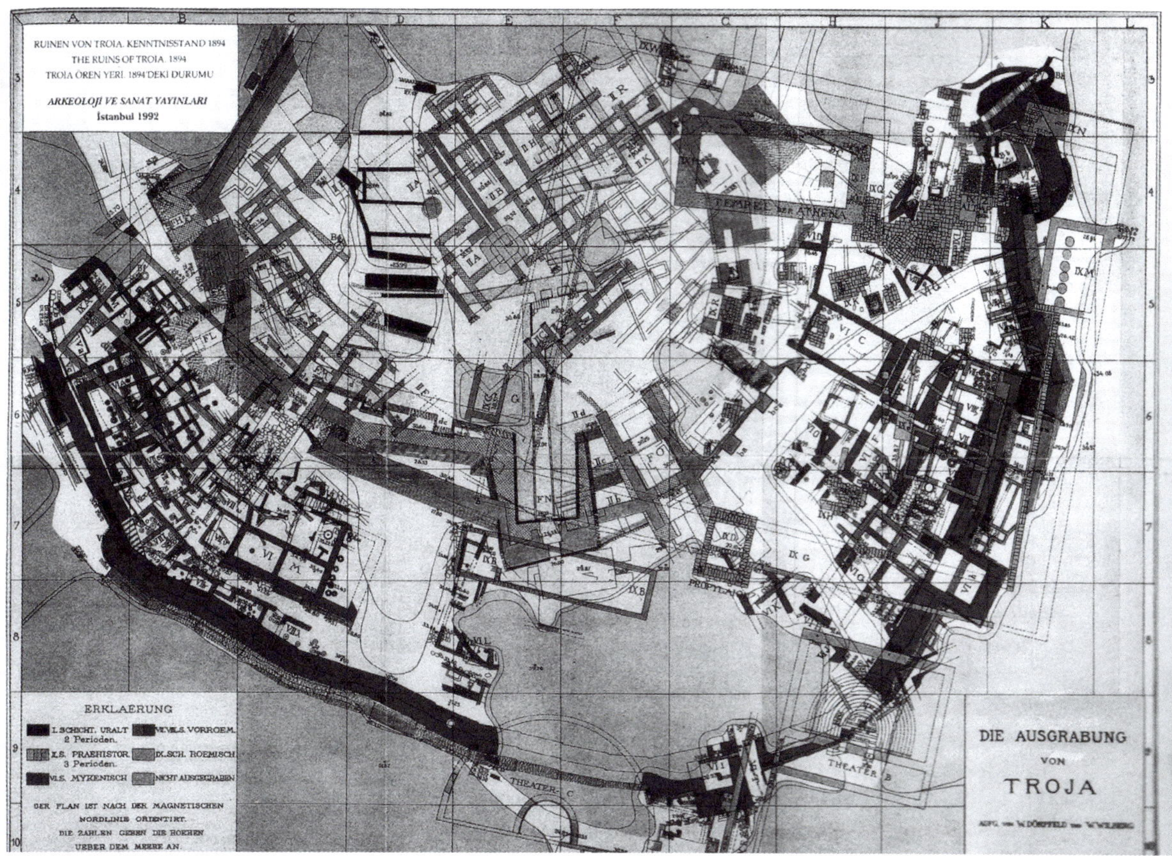

FIG. 41/ Wilhelm Dörpfel, Troy plan.
Troy. Nine superimposed cities. The houses and buildings were built one on top of the other. The streets and the squares, the public space, are the only things that remain the same.

Bacon did not include a reproduction of the map of Campo Marzio in his *Design of Cities.* Despite this, Bacon undoubtedly knew the renowned sketches. Robert McCarter, a historian at the Washington University in St. Louis and author of one of the most complete and recently edited monographs on the Philadelphia architect Louis Kahn, writes about Kahn's fascination with the drawings of the Campo Marzio. These drawings were so hypnotizing and absorbing, McCarter writes that Kahn would remain hours and hours observing in detail the original size etchings hung in his office.

"Kahn's plans now evolved as axial compositions of these independent, symmetrical entities, quite close to those found in Piranesi's Campus Martius plan; geometric, elemental room-buildings that Kahn composed as if they were pieces on a chessboard."[22]

It could be that Bacon saw Piranesi's tragic and decadent character as incapable of constructing harmonious urban continuity. Bacon's strange omission can be explained by this known admiration that Louis I. Kahn had for Piranesi. McCarter attributes the exclusion of the Piranesi drawing to the Bacon and Kahn's complicated relationship.

Philadelphia and Troy

Though Hegemann saw Piranesi's drawing of the Campo Marzio as an immense orgy of columns, the drawing also expresses the transience and informality of the city. It is a graphic, imaginary construction of uncontrolled residual public space.

Piranesi's romantic map and the stratigraphic model of the Better Philadelphia Exhibition remind us of other moving drawings that explain the city as a process of overlapping layers. During the same years that Camillo Sitte researched his book *City Planning According to Artistic Principles*, German archeologist and architect Wilhelm Dörpfeld researched the archaeological formation and transformation of Troy, thanks to the famous archeologist Heinrich Schliemann. Over twelve years of field research in the city in the Aegean Sea, Wilhelm Dörpfeld revealed that the city of Troy was formed as 9 different overlapping cities. (fig. 41) The work executed by Dörpfeld advanced the technology of stratigraphy, identifying each overlapping layer with an age of formation of the city.

22_Robert McCarter, *Louis Kahn* (London: Phaidon, 2009), 298

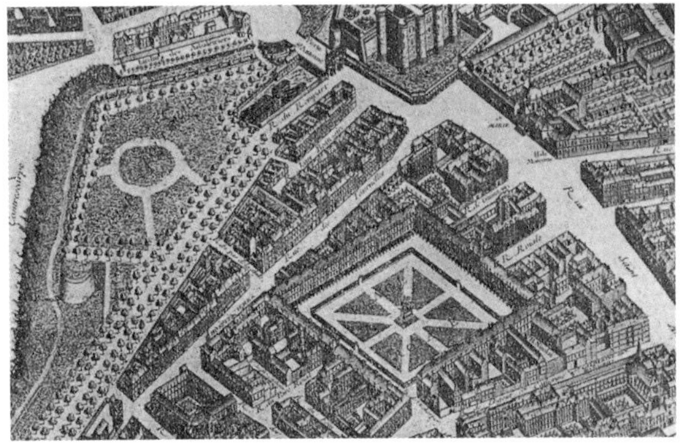

FIG. 42/ Turgot, piece of Paris map. Place Royal (Place des Vosges) in Werner Hegemann and Elbert Peets, *The American Vitruvius: an Architects' Handbook of Civic Art.*

FIG. 43/ Place des Victories, Paris. 05/07/2010. MBE.

Sitte the archaeologist

Dörpfeld and Sitte shared an interest in understanding the historical city. Both architects were employed at the same moment, at the same dates, as archeologists. Both used the same working method. They trusted in scientific research based on fieldwork and methodical and rigorous development, each aiming to discover the laws behind the formation of the city.

Piranesi's drawings of the city of Rome, Bacon and Kahn's mutant model of Philadelphia, and Dörpfeld's topographic drawings of Troy are all magnificent representations of the city understood in layers, immersed in an open process of construction and permanent transformation.

The strength of the landscape: the Delaware, the Tiber and the Seine

Hegemann proposes that architecture is an instrument to organize, rationalize and colonize the landscape. His proposal for the future of public space in the city is based on a classical understanding of architecture as an abstract system that can impose and define limits by the strength of its orders. But what surrounds the buildings in the Campo Marzio sketches? This empty space between these buildings is also a public space, isn't it? A public space different from that imagined by Hegemann, who only sees that which is fixed, finished and controlled by architecture.

In the book *Atlas Pintoresco. Vol 1: el observatorio*, architect Iñaki Abalos revises the borders between architecture, urbanism and landscape. He proposes a new work environment to answer the requirements of a contemporary nomad society. By mixing architecture and landscape, human beings and non-human beings, Ábalos transforms his work. He proposes a new attitude towards public space. Ábalos sees architecture, urbanism, landscape architecture, and landscape urbanism as concurrent and incomplete disciplines that provide knowledge and instruments for our current needs.

He explains this new contemporary public space in this way:

"Central Park in New York, Copacabana and Ipanema in Rio de Janeiro: in the practice, the cities and their inhabitants have relocated the so called public areas into urban areas with a clear landscape profile, partially replacing those representational spaces (squares) ... the transition of the square towards the landscape is not a new phenomenon; from the ascent of the middle class in the nineteenth century, the lounges that had changed their purpose and were places for the people to gather and to go for a walk would turn into complete green areas, which would end up being the ex novo creation of the public parks. Frederick Law Olmstead was fully conscious of the civic meaning of the landscape architecture and, for this reason, from the historical point of view, it is possible to affirm that one of the clear competences of this discipline is research into the modalities by which the notion of public things can be crystallized and expanded in the present."[22]

22_ Iñaki Ábalos, *Atlas de lo pintoresco: el observatorio*, (Barcelona: Gustavo Gil, 2005), 79.

FIG. 44/ SILVESTRE, I., Paris. Place Dauphine, 1652 a HEGEMANN, W., PEETS, E., The American Vitruvius: an Architects' Handbook of Civic Art.

FIG. 45/ Pont Neuf, París. 06/07/2010 Bridge_Square_Equestrian Statue. MBE.

Geography rules

Ábalos and Hegemann take opposite approaches to public space. In the chapter of *Civic Art* dedicated to French royal squares, (fig. 42) Hegemann suggests the French urban model as a precedent for the future city. The centralized squares embody the ideas of order, hierarchy and symmetry that Hegemann illustrated and proposed. However, Hegemann ignores the empty spaces between the buildings that construct the city of Rome in Piranesi's Campo Marzio. In his drawings of Paris' squares, Hegemann does not draw beyond the isolated architectural objects. Hegemann and other Classicists do not acknowledge the empty space between the architectural objects or the landscape as actual values in the construction of the city.

Piranesi's drawings are capable of moving and displacing a view towards an imaginary world of surprising spaces. The drawings of the Campo Marzio include geography and the fluvial force of the river as the real elements that structure and organize the city. But they do not lead Hegemann to discover the power of the landscape. Geographic and fluvial forces go unnoticed by Hegemann under the overwhelming order of the architecture.

When Hegemann analyzes the royal squares of Paris in *Civic Art*, (fig. 43) he does not recognize the fundamental difference between the *Place Dauphine* (1739) and the rest of the royal squares of the city. Hegemann doesn't see, or doesn't consider important, the force of the Seine river, which determines the final form of the square.

Place Dauphine, a bridge-square

The difficulty of imposing a rectangular square into the triangular shape of the Île Saint-Louis forced a transformation and deformation of the original centralized model seen in the Place Royale (1739) and the Place Vendôme (1772) (fig. 44). The force of the Seine River alters the geometric scheme. In the Place Dauphine, the imposition of the tip of the island's triangular geometry provokes a magical effect in contrast to other Parisian squares. It becomes impossible to place the statue of Louis XV in the center of the triangle. Instead, the image of the king moves out of the square onto the adjacent Pont Neuf bridge that crosses the Seine. (fig. 45)

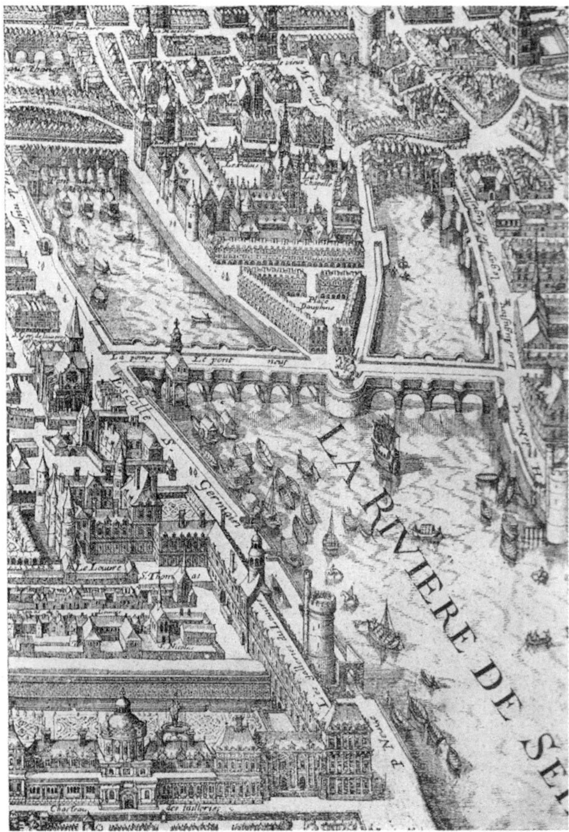

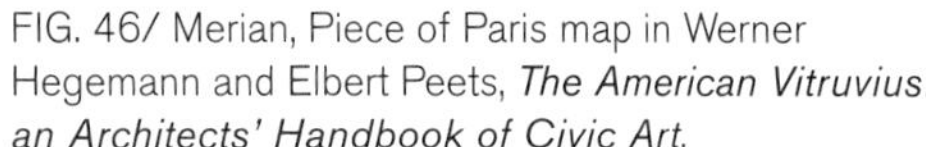

FIG. 46/ Merian, Piece of Paris map in Werner Hegemann and Elbert Peets, *The American Vitruvius: an Architects' Handbook of Civic Art.*

FIG. 47/ Place Royale Pont Neuf Paris. 06/07/2010. MBE. The optical illusion of the statue jumping its way off the square and placing itself over the Pont Neuf builds a new kind of public space Bridge-Square.

This simple operation means that the Place Dauphine is no longer a static square centered around an object, unlike the rest of the royal squares; fluidity becomes a new criteria in the construction of public space. (fig.46) The typical site of a statue in the highly centralized royal squares would be exactly in the center. In the case of the Place Dauphine, this center point was already occupied by a bridge, an infrastructure. This oddity turns the Place Dauphine into a new type of public space.

The Place Dauphine is a bridge-square (fig. 47) that concentrates the qualities of a French royal square while incorporating traffic provided by the infrastructure of the bridge. The public space is both contained and fluid at the same time. The singularity of this square, the form of which is determined primarily by the landscape, is solidified and catalyzed by the sculpture of King Louis XV, an urban element of minor order. The positioning of the equestrian statue in a place with such an urban intensity fills and condenses the site, constructing a living public space.

FIG. 48/ Xavier Ribas, *Flowers*, n.12 from the Barcelona Pictures series, (1998-2000). 10 C-Type printed to 89 x 106 cm. 6 units edition. A bunch of flowers hanging from a guardrail turns an indifferent place into a personal space, a place in which we can feel identified.

Accidents and difference

Manuel de Solà Morales comments in his last book De cosas urbanas:

"To see into their own conflict and confusion, structures, pillars, ramps, stores, properties and domains, movements, barriers, slopes and, over all of them, sights, images and references, which allow to go to the bottom of the urban substance, to the inception of any idea. Because only from the consideration of the enormous signifier of each one of these urban objects as components of a mental cataclysm it is possible to get closer to a urban creativity". [23]

We propose to incorporate landscape and geography as active values to provide fluency, complexity, differences and singularity to the design of a city. To stop understanding the topography as a problem that needs to be corrected as Charles Garnier implored the emperor to modify the topography surrounding the Paris' Opera building. To use landscape and geography to design with a new perspective. An understanding of public space that does not entrust in form and geometry as the only instruments needed to design the city.

To understand the public space as an open process in continuous transformation, capable of flexibility and of incorporating landscape and difference. (fig. 48) To learn to design in an unfinished way using the actions or the minor scale objects as catalysts of the city's civic space.

These constitute the challenges of a contemporary understanding of today's public spaces. (fig. 49)

Action and production of events

Ignasi de Solà Morales, would say that the contemporary public space exercises the condition of emptiness more than it structures the city. It is a place characterized by its particular residual character: a green reserve, a road network, an equipment, etc, and not for its precise aptitude in order to construct the city. Ignasi de Solà Morales argues that the traditional architectural instruments of intervention are no longer valid. It is no longer acceptable to propose solutions based on radical transformation in order to impose, by all necessary means, a new order that would eliminate the original local magic; these attitudes that try to turn the obsolete and abandoned things into something real and effective.

"No intention of exemplifying the new city. No Hypothesis that means the discontinuity with the existing city. Action; production of an event in a strange territory; accidental deployment of a peculiar proposal that is superposed to the existing things; repetition of the emptiness on the emptiness of the city; silent artificial landscape touching the historical time of the city but without cancelling it and neither imitating it. Flow, force, incorporation, independence of forms, expression of the lines that go through them. Beyond the art that shows new freedoms. From the nomadism to the eroticism". [24] (fig. 50)

23_ Manuel de Solà Morales, *De cosas urbanas* (Barcelona: Gustavo Gili, 2008) 75.
24_ Ignasi de Solà Morales, "Terrain vague" in *Anyplace* (New York: Any,1995).

FIG. 49/ Xavier Ribas, *Sundays*, n. 20 from the Barcelona Pictures series, 2002. 26 C-Type printed to 120 x 140 cm. 6 units edition. A refrigerated truck becomes the perfect cooled dining room when it is hot.

FIG. 50/ Xavier Ribas, *Sundays*, n. 12 from the Barcelona Pictures series, (1994-97). 26 C-Type printed to 120 x 140 cm. 6 units edition. A small slope is enough to build the necessary conditions to turn an industrial area into a nice place.

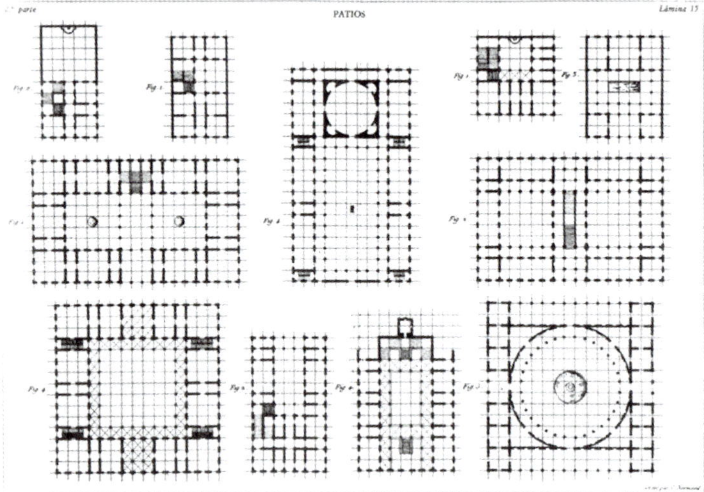

FIG. 51/ Sheet 15 of the Second part of *Compendio de lecciones de Arquitectura de Jean-Nicolas-Louis Durand* (Madrid, Pronaos 1981)

Construction of buildings with patios by means of the disposition of elements on an isotropic plot.

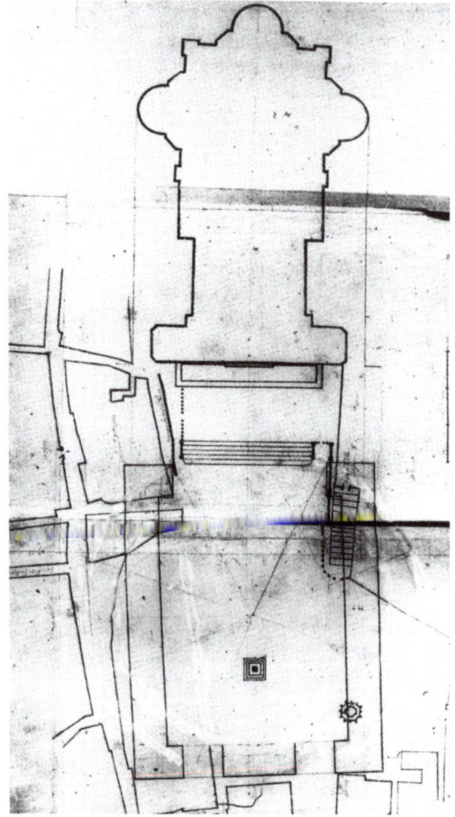

FIG. 52/ BERNINI, G. L., Preliminar proposal for Saint Peter's Square in Vatican city.

Durand surely didn't know that Bernini had already thought a previous project of rectangular square. The obelisk.

Durand and St. Peter's Square in Vatican City

To study the public space proposed by an academician as Werner Hegemann and not to fall in the temptation of rereading his mentor Jean-Nicolas-Louis Durand is inevitable. (fig. 51) As we previously explained, the meticulous scientific work elaborated by Hegemann obeys fundamentally the will of elaborating an aseptic catalogue on the public space, a typified inventory, unprecedented until then, a catalogue that plans all the collective spaces constructed and projected along the city's history.

Durand was a teacher for thirty five years (1795-1830) in the École Polytechnique of Paris where Hegemann himself finished his long academic formation. This coincidence is too evident to not carefully study the strong influence of Durand in Hegemann's work *Civic Art*.

As Rafael. Moneo explains in the prologue of the Spanish edition of Durand's work, *Compendio de Lecciones de Arquitectura. Parte gráfica de los cursos de Arquitectura* [25], Durand's lessons have often unfortunately been misinterpreted. According to Moneo, Durand's proposal is not only a theoretical work on the architectural typologies – Durand didn't invent typologies – but it is mainly a very ambitious proposal that formulates a new system to project the architecture, a system that is based on the composition of the elements on a regular plot, as

Durand himself exemplified: : "... what the words are to the speech and the notes to the music, and without knowing them perfectly it would be impossible to go beyond". [26]

Durand's proposal consisted on a combinatorial system of minimal architectural elements that were capable of constructing the program needed for every building, tidily arranged on an isotropic plot. It was a theoretical work on architecture that tried to be a practical manual for many students and architects, based on the laws of the good composition. Although in his book *Civic Art*, Hegemann never managed to propose a concrete system in order to project the public space in the same way as Durand, the lessons of universal ambition of the latter turned into a clear reference model for Hegemann. *Civic Art* was also, as *Compendio de Lecciones de Arquitectura*, an ambitious book with the noble will of becoming a help manual, a model of book that Hegemann wanted to make extensive a few years later, not just to the architecture, as Durand made, but to the whole city.

25_ Rafael Moneo, *Compendio de lecciones de arquitectura.* (Madrid: Pronaos 1981).

26_ Rafael Moneo, *Compendio de lecciones de arquitectura.* (Madrid: Pronaos 1981), 21.

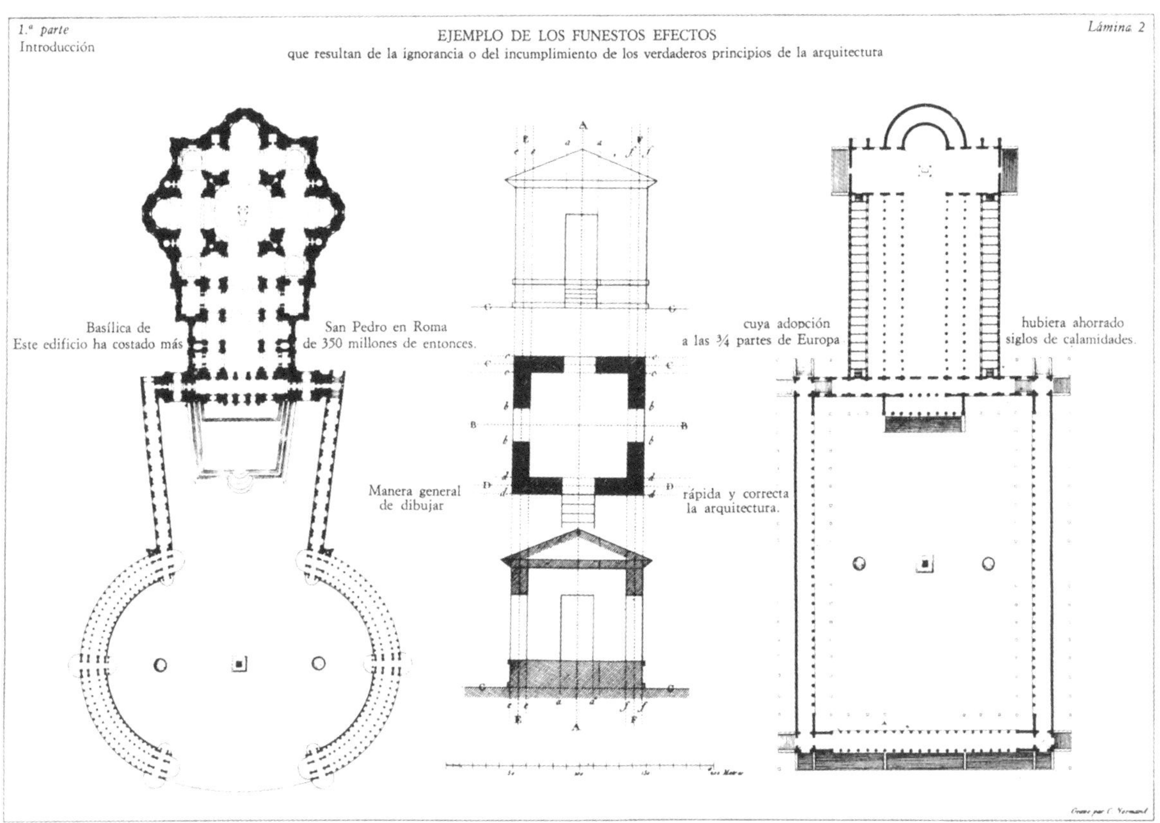

FIG. 53/ Jean-Nicolas-Louis Durand, *Compendio de lecciones de Arquitectura. Parte gráfica de los cursos de Arquitectura.*
The only elements that Durand preserves in his sterilizing sieve process are the obelisk and the fountains.

However, Hegemann compiles from Durand not only his interest to dissect the architecture, but he is also seduced by the force that Durand employed in treating the architecture in such an abstract way. The system that Durand proposed consisted of an abstract composition exercise with minimal elements arranged on an indifferent isotropic plot.

The indifferent treatment that Durand posed in order to project the architecture in *Compendio de Lecciones de Arquitectura* is exemplified in the sheets where he proposed to revise existing architectural works already executed and subject them to a new formalization following the principles of composition and economy that Durand postulated.

Durand and St. Peter's obelisk

In the sheet number 2 of the treatise's lessons, Durand chooses St. Peter's Square in Vatican City to subject it to a purification treatment by applying to it the principles of his indifferent system. (fig. 53) This sheet, graphically arranged in three columns, shows how in the first column the original set of St. Peter's in Vatican City is passed through the second column's sieve, which contains the sterilized doctrine of Durand, to obtain a third column that is the result of a new St. Peter. This entertaining exercise of mutation realized by Durand, which according to the author serves to demonstrate the validity and efficiency of his lessons, is not only a good example that demonstrates that a brilliant theorist is not necessarily a good architect, but it also that Durand possibly didn't know that Bernini had already rejected the option of a rectangular formed square in his first drawings for the project of St. Peter's Square.

Nevertheless, and despite of the admirable demonstration of personal conviction that Durand had in the application of his lessons, the most surprising facts about this sheet are to see how the set of St. Peter is transformed when Durand applies the column of his doctrine and to verify how he extracts a totally different result from the original set. St. Peter's former basilica loses its density and complexity characterized by the different historical interventions and is transformed into a new common church without identity. And Bernini's baroque square surrenders to an erosive process of banalization that erases the whole initial spatial tension that distinguishes it. (fig. 52)

But in this totally mutant process that Durand applied to St. Peter's in Vatican City, it's surprising to observe that there are only three small elements of the original set up that Durand preserves intact in the final proposal. These are three objects of small scale that easily go unnoticed compared to the shocking transformation that Durand proposed; three elements that are redrawn exactly the same way they were in the original set up: we refer to the obelisk and the two fountains on the axes that arranged Bernini's square.

But, why did Durand keep the obelisk in order to explain how St. Peter's Square might have been if his wise advices would have been followed? Why did he take this strange decision? Maybe Durand thought that the obelisk was an insignificant element compared to the total transformation that he proposed, an insignificant object, with no importance? In the case that this would had been Durand's idea, then he was mistaken in its drawing. To keep the obelisk as the only element, together with both fountains, which is not affected by the mutation process of the square demonstrated the opposite. The drawing of the obelisk in Durand's proposal demonstrates that the obelisk was for Durand an indispensable element. And then, how come an apparently non important element suddenly turns into such a relevant and indispensable element?

Maybe because Durand knew that the obelisk is actually the catalyst of the square; the element that distinguishes and identifies St. Peter's public space; an element that is really the responsible for St. Peter's Square to be an actual public space, in spite of its small scale. (fig. 54)

FIG. 54/LAB IN.
Superposition of all the designs for Saint Peter's Square in Vatican city, 2009. All of the proposals reference the obelisk.

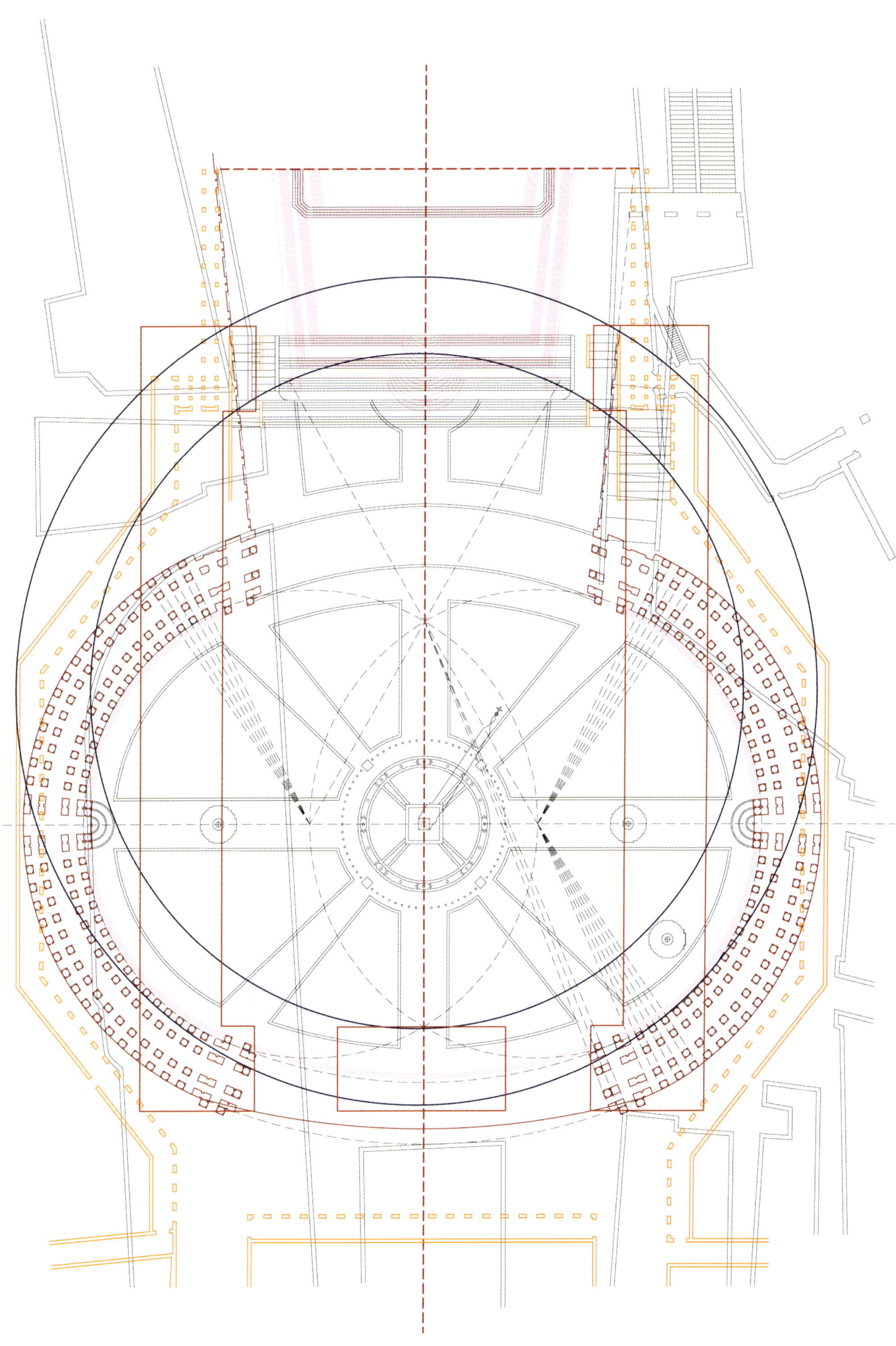

2_5 WHAT DO WE GET FROM THIS? A METHODOLOGY

This book inherits a methodology from Hegemann, Sitte and Bacon. Each of these authors has provided not only a theoretical reference framework to place our work, but also the criteria to organize and structure it.

The research had the fundamental aim to discover the public catalysts. For this reason, one of the main axes of the work at the Laboratory of Indifference has been the collection of a catalogue of cases, with an emphasis on diversity to be representative. The act of drawing each studied example and the extensive fieldwork done is rooted in the work of the authors explained in the previous chapters.

Sitte_ Empirical research.

Sitte's precise and systematic working method based on travelling and experience in his book *City Planning According to Artistic Principles* has been very important to this research. Sitte's research through a personal visit to each place that he analyzed helped us to propose a fundamentally empirical work. Like Sitte, we have also tried to analyze through drawing. Once the public space was visited, the Laboratory of Indifference made the most important decisions of the research graphically, resulting in the drawn conclusions of the Laboratory. We drew the things that made each place special systematically and accumulatively. The precise drawing of slightly visible and minor urban situations helped us to understand the real importance of the things that didn't seem to be transcendental at first glance. The drawing allowed us to discover, measure and legitimize minor objects and temporary conditions that are capable, in spite of their slight condition, of catalyzing the public space.

While drawing the catalysts, we often remembered the wonderful movie *El Sol del Membrillo*,[27] in which director Victor Erice filmed the effort of Antonio Lopez to stop time by painting an impossibly precise picture of a quince tree. By means of precision, these hyperrealistic drawings try to catch the essence, the atmosphere of the artist's backyard.

Hegemann_ An atlas

Hegemann's *Civic Art* is also a fundamental reference for this project. We follow his idea of developing a universal atlas of cases in a catalogue of typified solutions. However, we do not agree with his treatment of public space as a finished and decontextualized object. At the same time, *Civic Art* is an example of a catalogue with a global and timeless character. Therefore, while we are not interested in Hegemann's indescriminate application of pre-established historical solutions, we are interested in *Civic Art*'s universal format, which offers a format to decipher the essential values of contemporary and historic public spaces. This research cannot be limited to the study of recent local cases, but must also spread to analyze distant historic spaces: it must be an atlas.

George Didi-Huberman, curator of the exhibition *Atlas: How to Carry the World on One's Back?* explains how the accumulation of an atlas allows the construction of new relationships, real and imaginary. The discovery of the invisible structures between the images or objects in an atlas reveals their essence.

"When we place different images – or different objects, as the cards of a deck, for example – on the table, we have a constant freedom of modifying their configuration. We can do mountains, constellations. We can discover new analogies, new paths of thinking. By modifying the order, we force the images to take a position. A table is not used for establishing neither a definitive classification, nor an exhaustive inventory, nor for cataloguing once and for all – like in a dictionary, a file or an encyclopedia–, but for gathering segments, division pieces of the world, for respecting their multiplicity, their heterogeneity, for legitimating the relations showed up".[28]

27_*El Sol del Membrillo* [The Quince Tree Sun], dir. by Victor Erice (1992; Facets Multimedia Distribution, 2000).

28_ George Didi-Huberman, *Atlas. ¿cómo llevar el mundo a cuestas? [Atlas: How to Carry the World on One's Back?]* (Madrid: TF Editores and Museo Reina Sofía, 2011).

FIG. 55/ Edmund N. Bacon photographed at the Love Park of Philadelphia.
Pleasure and public space. The experience in order to understand and plan the city.

Fig 56/ 28 October 2002: Edmund N.Bacon skating at the Love Park
Bacon, at the age of 92, supporting the presence of skaters (and here being supported by them) at the Love Park of Philadelphia

Bacon_ Intensity and time

Edmund Bacon understood the importance of designing public space with intensity. His Principle of the Second Man illustrates the city as an open process, in which identity and respect are instruments in design. (fig. 55)

Instead of indifferent public spaces, Bacon poses an attentive open mind in the interest of systems of urban spatial complicities. (fig. 56) Bacon, in *Design of Cities*, revealed the importance of designing the space between the buildings in the construction of a city, an empty space with its own rules of social and urban identity. Bacon's book, in which the city is explained as a complex and unfinished art work composed by buildings, streets and squares; reiterates the fundamental value of time in the construction of the public space. According to Bacon, the city has to be a complex and subtle succession of different linked public urban reference models, empty spaces with their own identity that guarantee the continuity of a qualified urban space, thanks to their exact and pertinent intensity.

In this study, we demonstrate that urban intensity can also have a light character; that in order to construct today's public spaces of identity, it is not necessary to do monumental, singular and finished projects.

The analyzed public catalysts are examples of how a public space of intensity only needs the construction of the minimal necessary conditions for the place to be activated. The passage of time will verify if the proposed conditions have been the necessary ones in order to transform an indifferent place into a public space of identity.

FIG. 57/ Amsterdam covered in snow.
A thin snow layer temporarily transforms the city. Suddenly, game and pleasure fill the street and the empty spaces of town.

Aldo van Eyck_ Barcelona Playgrounds

Aldo van Eyck, the focus of the next chapter, was the real catalyst of this research. His Playgrounds project executed in Amsterdam after the Second World War, illustrates how a minimal and light intervention can transform a whole city. Van Eyck often showed photographs of the city of Amsterdam covered with a thin layer of snow in his conferences and writings. He knew how the city could transform with only a few ephemeral millimeters of frozen water. (fig. 57) The slight layer changes the character of the city, turning it into a new recreational and identity space for the children.

2_6 BOHIGAS' MODEL

FIG.58/ Metrocable in the City of Medellín 2010.
The Metrocable is a public transport system conceived in Medellín. Its cheap construction makes it viable as an alternative to the expensive underground subway. Technology and accuracy flying over the most disadvantaged neighborhoods of Medellín.

Barcelona 1980

In the previous chapters, we explained how Hegemann, Sitte and Bacon provided upright theoretical models in the elaboration of this book. The value of their writings composes the historical and theoretical framework for the research at the Laboratory of Indifference. The study of their works pushed this research beyond a compilation of entertaining experiences from an architecture traveling salesman.

If, like Sitte, we insist on experiencing each of our case studies, there is one city that has influenced this work beyond the others. There is one public space that provoked us to investigate all the others.

The transformative power of the public space project in Barcelona not only improved the quality of many civic places of the city, but also achieved something even more difficult: it created an optimistic and encouraging environment in the daily mood of many citizens of Barcelona. It was an urban project that became social, a transformation that the inhabitants of Barcelona experienced with attention and illusion. Barcelona's citizens took part as users, step-by-step acquiring new quality leisure spaces in the city.

This reform project of Barcelona initiated in the eighties has become a model of urban transformation. In Medellin, Colombia, (fig. 58) the development of a very similar model halfed the index of criminality, which had been one of the highest of the world.

The project began in Barcelona with the energy of a new political phase emerging after forty years of dictatorship. The city trusted the project as a slow and modest, but effective and precise, force to transform Barcelona by means of interventions on the public space.

The project was exemplary because of its strong and contagious strategy, which combined the actual resources of the city with a viable pace and scale of transformation. This effective urban project wisely combined and linked the public and private participation with a common objective. The small interventions began with an investment of public money to finance the recovery of a selected urban space and then the new public space was drawn through private investment. The initial reform of the public space encouraged the rehabilitation of all the surrounding buildings. The combination of these two shifts was essential to the success of the model.

The execution of a great number of small interventions distributed throughout the whole city became an urban scale project that magically transformed Barcelona.

The beginning of democracy at Barcelona's Town Hall

The new democratic time that took place in the eighties in Barcelona had to be seen as a new way of understanding the political future of the country. The overcoming of Franco's dictatorship represented the beginning of a new age in which a brand new political class wanted to urgently recover the lost time and to return the urban, political and social normality to the city.

Forty years of dictatorship left an impoverished country with a poor public investment in the construction of equipments and infrastructures. And Barcelona, as the rest of the Spanish cities in the beginnings of this new democratic stage, was an unattended population without a project of city.

The return of the democracy had to be the opportunity to make clear a new stage of equality between all the persons that lived in the city. It was necessary to make clear that it was no longer an unfair society, full of social differences. For this reason, the best solution was to begin reforming the spaces that are everyone's property, the space where the whole world is equal, the public spaces.

The new municipal government of Barcelona found an administration without public land, capable of receiving new programs of public equipments. The public space projects were the first equipments to be executed in the city, for many reasons: the urgent need to modernize the city and the problem of the lack of public soil, added to the slowness of the process of acquiring land for the construction of new municipal resources. The first public plots that the democratic town was able to acquire in order to transform Barcelona were, precisely, the squares, the streets and the parks of the city.

Oriol Bohigas at Barcelona's Town Hall

The intellectual and socialist spirit of the active political class of Barcelona decided to trust in Oriol Bohigas to assume the responsibility of constructing the new optimistic image of an encouraging future.

The constitution of the new Urbanism Department inside the town hall of Barcelona, with Oriol Bohigas with the person in charge, represented the birth of a new way of understanding the urban needs of the city. The project "Barcelona Model" became a reference model in the field of urban reform, and it also became a sample of how an administration was yielding and entrusting the responsibility of imagining the future city to the architects.

The process of the "Barcelona Model" project started by precising an intelligent selection of the public spaces that were necessary to recover. The chosen public places had to be a few strategic emplacements capable of triggering, in the second phase, the reform of the buildings that were surrounding them. Bohigas' strategy was based on the effect, similar to a metastasis process, capable of transforming the whole city by means of small but numerous public interventions.

Barcelona Model: an "auteur" model

At the beginning of the eighties, the Barcelona Model was characterized as a laboratory where they researched to discover and to test how the public spaces should be projected.

The beginnings of this model represented the opportunity for the Catalan architects to imagine a new type of project that was unknown to them. It was a first stage with the aim of verifying if the conventional instruments used to realize an architectural project were also valid to project a public space. Many of those projects realized during this first stage reacted, due to the disturbing abyss that represented the fact of not knowing how the public space had to be projected, with object architectonic solutions. The result was overdrawn, controlled and formal public spaces. These were public spaces that had been clearly thought with the same conventional architectural instruments, designed as if they were equipment buildings, public spaces in which the town hall trusted in the personal talent of the architects and allowed them to propose, on many occasions, awkwardly singular solutions.

FIG. 59/ Jaume Bach and Gabriel Mora, Plaça Trilla, Barri de Gràcia, Barcelona, 1981-85.

Carpet projects

In this first period of the eighties of the Barcelona Model, characterized by the small formal uniformity of the projects that were realized, they were also executed la Vila de Gràcia square, by Bach i Mora (1982), (fig. 59) and the Plaça dels Països Catalans, by Viaplana-Piñón (1983), which represent the beginning of a new way of understanding the treatment of the public space in Barcelona. Gràcia's squares (fig. 60) and Sants' square represented the first projects that fundamentally understood the public space as an empty space; in spite of the fact that they are two projects that trusted in the design of objects in order to control the public space, as the rest of the public spaces of this first stage. These were projects formalized through a continuous pavement that organized the space and consolidated the land, spaces that gave value to the existing surrounding architecture, yielding the protagonism to the future social activities that would be realized: they were "carpet" projects. (fig. 61)

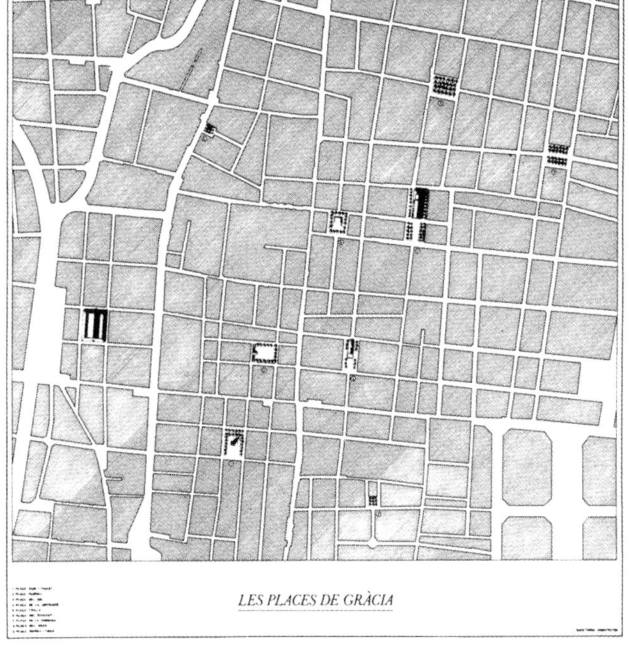

FIG. 60/ Plan indicating Gràcia's squares.

FIG. 61/Granite pavements. Carpet square. MBE.

2_7 BARCELONA PLAYGROUNDS

Oriol Bohigas and Aldo van Eyck.

Barcelona and Amsterdam, two cities with the same project

The similarity between the city plans of Amsterdam and Barcelona is disturbing. The two plans of the two different cities reflect the attitudes of two different architects that shared the same responsibity: to transform the city. The two plans are a testimony to the few projects that intervened in a city by capitalizing on social, economic and urban realities.

In neither of the plans do you recognize the formal gesture of an architect . Both instead explain the city as a complex and alive system, constructed by means of the sum of different opinions and projects. The plans contain an identical strategy to understand the city; both trusting interventions of minor scale to transform a whole city.

The project of the Barcelona Model, initiated in the eighties consisted on the construction of a constellation of small projects spread all over the whole city. Bohigas certainly knew the Playground project by Aldo van Eyck, (fig. 62) initiated in the fifties in Amsterdam, a project of urban transformation of a city, immersed in a postwar period that curiously contained many similar criteria to the ones that Bohigas proposed for Barcelona. (fig. 63)

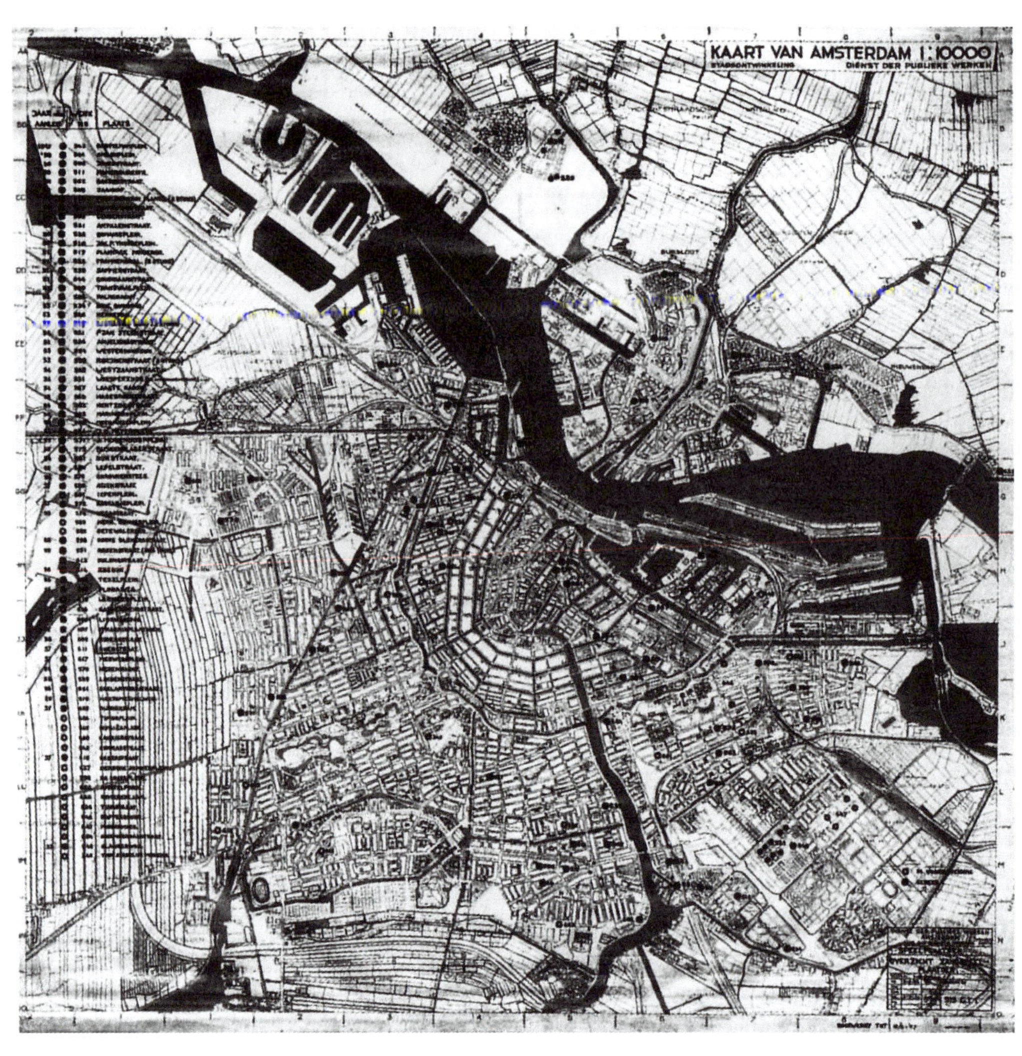

FIG. 62/ Amsterdam and THE PLAYGROUNDS BY ALDO VAN EYCK. 1957

FIG. 63/ Barcelona and THE PUBLIC SPACES BY ORIOL BOHIGAS. 1991.
Two different cities and the same strategy: to transform the city from the small scale.

Aldo van Eyck at the Amsterdam's Town Hall

In the year 1947, Aldo van Eyck was an architect worried about Amsterdam's future. He was actively linked to the Department of Urbanism in Amsterdam, as Bohigas would be thirty years later in Barcelona. Both van Eyck and Bohigas shared the same interest: to design a viable project that would catalyze reform to reactivate their abandoned cities. (fig. 64)

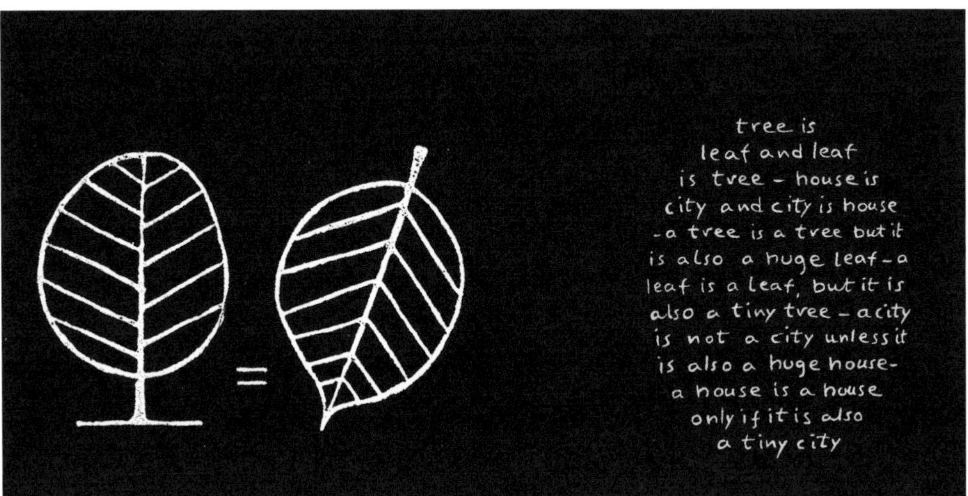

FIG. 64/ Aldo van Eyck, "A tree is a leaf".
The city thought from the small scale and the architecture thought from the city. Van Eyck is a clear reference model that trusts in the transformation capacity of the small scale in order to reform the city.

FIG. 65/ Van Eesteren speaking to the delegates of the CIAM congress that took place from September the 8th to September the 10th at La Sarraz, Switzerland.

The crisis of modern urban planning

The urban planning team in Amsterdam was headed from 1927 by one of the most recognized town planning architects of the modern movement and an active member in the congress of the CIAM: Cornelis van Eesteren. (fig. 65)

When in 1947, Van Eyck joined the group of city planning, he had the opportunity to know an enterprising work team, open to testing the new functionalist ideas of projecting the city, following the criteria of modern urbanism planned by Cornelis van Eesteren. For Van Eyck, working with one of the main ideologists of the new urbanism meant the suitable occasion to be able to verify and question the general and abstract principles that the great masters and theorists of the Modern Movement were postulating at that time.

The ambitious proposals of functional distribution of the new modern city and the utopian abstract principles on which the Modern Movement that Van Eesteren and his team were based on, were for Van Eyck an actual laboratory where he could imagine and confirm the model of urbanism that he would propose later on; an urbanism that would be based on local and concrete urban proposals, capable of changing slowly but effectively, optimistically but in a realistic way, the quality of life of a big city, due to its simplicity and fragility.

During the stage when Aldo van Eyck was working with Van Eesteren's team, he coincided with the town planner Jakoba Mulder. In 1936, leaving the large-scale projects that both architects drew at the planning office, Jakoba Mulder projected a park that surely surprised Van Eyck. Mulder's Beatrixpark of Amsterdam (fig. 66) was a park that avoided the image of the traditional gardens and that tried to propose a new category of leisure public space, a park that wasn't thought as a place for contemplation but as a space for entertainment and action. The Beatrixpark was the first public space in which they used a material that had rarely been used until then for urbanizing purposes: the sand. A park where the sand and the children's furniture constructed a space where they could play in the city. (fig. 67)

FIG. 66/ Jakoba Mulder, Beatrix Park, Amsterdam, Holland, 1937.

FIG. 67/ The Playgrounds were located in residual and ordinary spaces.

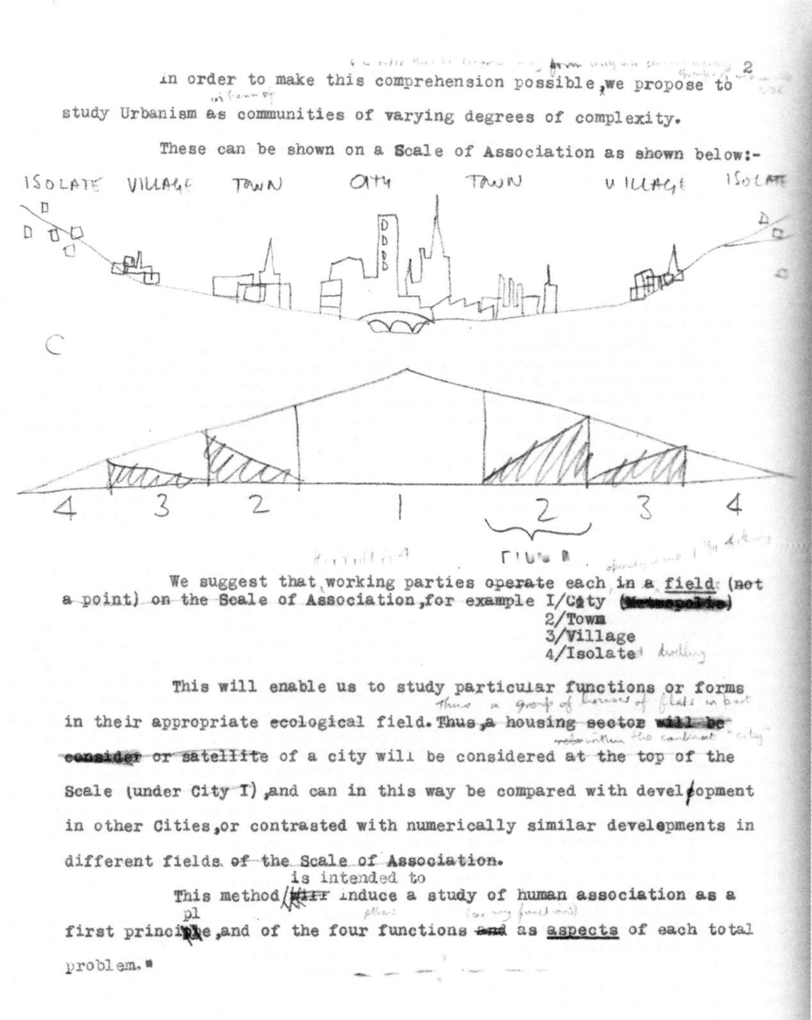

2

In order to make this comprehension possible, we propose to study Urbanism as communities of varying degrees of complexity.

These can be shown on a Scale of Association as shown below:-

We suggest that working parties operate each in a field (not a point) on the Scale of Association, for example 1/City (Metropolis)
2/Town
3/Village
4/Isolate

This will enable us to study particular functions or forms in their appropriate ecological field. Thus a housing sector will be consider or satellite of a city will be considered at the top of the Scale (under City 1), and can in this way be compared with development in other Cities, or contrasted with numerically similar developments in different fields of the Scale of Association.

This method is intended to induce a study of human association as a first principle, and of the four functions and as aspects of each total problem.

FIG. 68/ "Scroll and Valley Section" Alison and Peter Smithson. Dubrovnik 1965. Architecture and landscape. Geography rules and the city just adapts.

Van Eyck and the Team X

In 1953, during the CIAM IX celebration in Aix-en-Provence, Van Eyck, together with Jaap Bakema, George Candillis, Alison and Peter Smithson and Shadrach Woods, founded the Team X. From the formation of the group up to its dissolution in 1981, Van Eyck was one of the most active, lucid and critical members, in the proposals of modern town planners as LeCorbusier, Gropuis, Gideon or van Eestren, founders of the CIAM congresses.

During the CIAM celebration in Dubrovnik in 1956, in which the Team X group of young architects was eventually feeling more confident to expose their opinions in front of the founding masters of the CIAM; it was obvious that the different criterion that existed between the master group of the CIAM and the young group of the Team X were growing bigger. During the conferences in Dubrovnik, where the different congress members explained their projects, the ones from the Team X took advantage of their interventions to expose their distrust in the utopian proposals of functionalist urbanism. On the one hand the Smithsons presented their ordination proposal of "Scroll and Valley Section," (fig. 68) inspired by actual precedent studies of the traditional and popular architecture, in front of the abstract projects of the modern masters. And, on the other hand, Van Eyck took advantage of the congress to present his project of the Amsterdam Playgrounds as example of which, according to him, had to be the way of thinking and reforming the city.

FIG. 69/ Panels 1, 2, 3, and 4 showed by Van Eyck at his presentation at the CIAM congress in Dubrovnik 1956.

FIG. 70/ CIAM Otterlo, 1959.
Van Eyck, Alison Smithson, Peter Smithson and Bakema holding up the sign of Otterlo's congress, Holland 1959, in which they announce with the chalk drawing of a cross and a flower crown the death of CIAM.

FIG. 71/ CIAM Otterlo, 1959.

And pleasure? Had Modern urbanism forgotten pleasure?

Van Eyck, who was already executing several of the Playground projects at that time, used that new urban park model to denounce that functionalist urbanism had forgotten the spaces for pleasure and for children in their grandiloquent city projects. Van Eyck criticized that the urbanism of the great modern masters had forgotten the persons and the small scale when they proposed the future of the city.

The four panels presented by Van Eyck in the congress, entitled "Lost Identity", (fig. 69) were organized in two blocks. In the first two panels of the first block, where the problem of the lack of playgrounds for children in Amsterdam was exposed, the daily character of the images that Van Eyck used was surprising, specially the powerful image of the snowfall in the city, very useful to explain how the city completely transformed with only a slight layer of a few millimeters of snow, capable of suddenly changing the character of the city, which temporarily becomes a playground for children. The second block of the presentation, formed by two more panels, exposed the solution to the problem. For Van Eyck, Playgrounds had to be simple, economic spaces and light as the snow. They had to be spaces capable of providing the city a few new pleasure spaces for the children. In this second block the images reflected free children, playing always alone, are surprising too.

Playgrounds: spaces of freedom and identity.

The polemic congress of the CIAM celebrated in Otterlo in 1959 meant the consolidation of the group of the Team 10 and the end of the congresses of the CIAM. The persistent critique of the group Team 10 to the funcionalist proposals ended up by exhausting the illusion and the arguments of the modern masters who, step by step, accepted, discouraged, the end of the congresses. (fig. 70, 71)

The polemic words pronounced by Van Eyck in the conference of 1959 in Otterlo's congress exemplifies the tense situation that the Team X was provoking:

"There had never been a moment with so many opportunities, because until now we had never had such a disastrous architectonical and urban planning situation".[29]

Van Eyck knew how to take advantage of this tough moment in Amsterdam after the Second World War, to propose the construction of a modest urban transitory project capable of transforming the whole city in a similar way to the one that would be put into practice in Barcelona thirty years later. The Playgrounds project by Aldo van Eyck was one of the most intense, effective and ephemeral projects of urban reform of the 20th century.

29_ Liane Lefaivre, *Aldo Van Eyck: Humanist Rebel* (Rotterdam: 010, 1999).

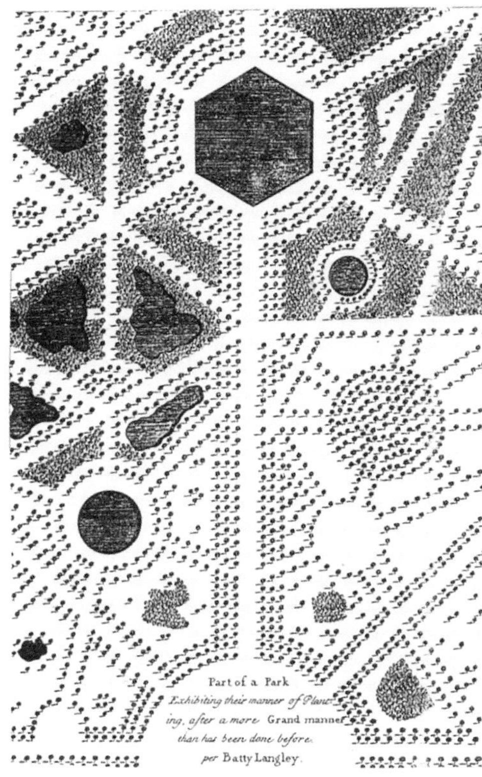

FIG. 72/ Batty Langley Park. London 1728.

FIG. 73/ Paris, location of Louis XV statue. Pierre Patte 1765. Plan from the book *Civic Art*, by W. Hegemann.

The Playgrounds: a polycentric city model

Van Eyck's Playgrounds project in Amsterdam was a different way of arranging the city, very different from the ones used at the beginning of modern urbanism. Van Eyck's project didn't propose to reform the city with big projects that would construct a new city, but proposed a more realistic proposal, based on the execution of small projects that would gradually weave a new network of public spaces that transformed the city. Instead of raising great scale urban development operations, which would make the cities grow in an uneven and messy way, it proposed projects with a more human scale, capable of constructing new nodes of social and urban attraction, a polycentric system, due to its local character.

Van Eyck, as the rest of members of the Team X, raised a non-exclusive working method. He understood the city and the architecture as an open and alive process in which every project had to be able to read the context and to discover the previous local conditions in order to intervene in the most proper way. The Team 10 didn't share the idea of the functionalist architects of the Modern Movement that proposed to initiate their projects by erasing any previous historical track. For the Team X, it was necessary to value, not only the formal or architectural heritage, but the informal or apparently not relevant questions like the customs, the traditions, the nature, etc, because they could, in many occasions, become the key of an urban project.

The Team X trademark of using images from popular culture of daily situations as a way of explaining the projects continues to identify them as a group today. Amsterdam's plan, where the Playgrounds are distributed around the city, remind us of the polycentric English gardens designs. (fig. 72) And Pierre Patte's plan of 1765 that appears in the catalogue Civic Art by W. Hegemann, shows the possible locations for the placement of the statue of in Paris; (fig. 73) it also easily reminds us of the effect proposed by van Eyck in his city.

In spite of being two projects realized within 200 years of difference, Patte's project for the placement of the equestrian statue in Paris and Van Eyck's Playgrounds project in Amsterdam, are two proposals that share the same way of imagining the growth and reform of a city. Patte and van Eyck proposed that an effective way of projecting the city could be from a polycentral system: concrete and precise actions with the necessary strength in order to transform the existing weave and also to form new centers of future growths.

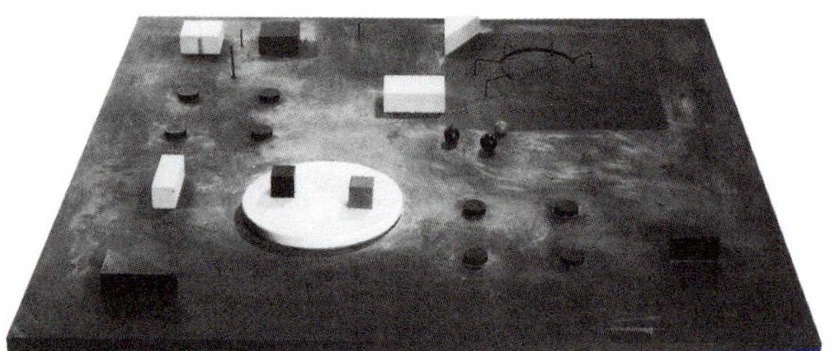

FIG. 74/ Batty Langley Park. London 1728

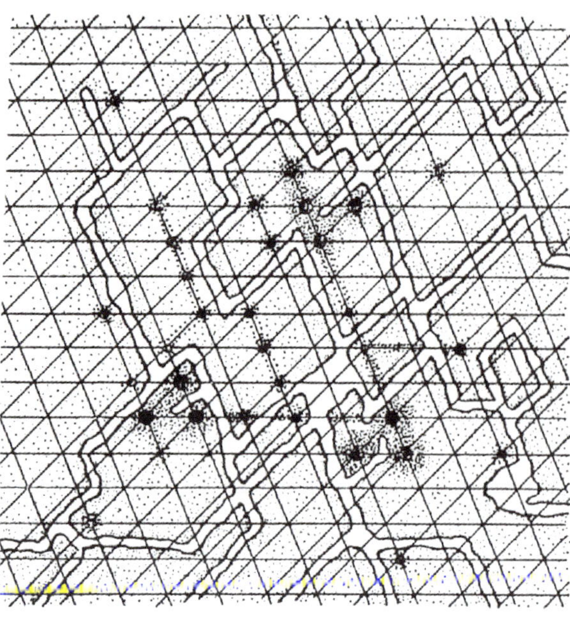

FIG. 75/ Constant, Ambiance de jeu, 1956.

Some situationist Playgrounds

The relation with artists like Piet Mondrian or the theorists Kevin Lynch or Martin Buber gave Van Eyck a strong formal and theoretical support to his works.

The friendship that Van Eyck had with different groups of Dutch artists, as the Cobra group, for which he would design the exhibition at the Stedeljik Museum of Amsterdam in 1949, helped him establish an intense relationship with the architect and artist Constant and with the theorist Guy Debord. A few years later, these two artists and intellectual would form and head the artistic and social current of the Situationists.

Reference: Playground plan

Van Eyck's Playgrounds shared the recreational idea of how the Situationists imagined the city. The Situationists, as the Team X, rejected the functionalist, hygienic, tidy and dead city of the modern town planners. The projects of Constant and Guy Debord wanted to construct a vivacious city that wouldn't be a victim of a mechanical geometry. The Situationists and Van Eyck wanted a city thought from the pleasure.

The ideological and formal mutual influence between the projects of the Situationists and the Playgrounds is so evident. (fig. 74) Constant's proposals, like the project of the Ambiance de Jeu Park, (fig. 75) might have perfectly been a Playground drawn by Van Eyck. And the drawings of the proposals of Constant's New Babylon, who imagined a city in which the individual, his feelings and his perceptions were the principal characters of the project; might have perfectly been the graphical proof of a critical argument made by van Eyck in some of his conferences in the congresses of the CIAM.

Van Eyck and the Situationists' friendship helped to confirm his intuition of raising an urbanism closer to the human scale, instead of a "modern" grandiloquent urbanism based on abstraction, segregation and functionality. The proximity with the Situationists or the meetings with the Team X surely helped van Eyck to confirm that a few modest and simple Playgrounds could really transform the city of Amsterdam. The Playgrounds project was long and slow: it lasted forty years and ultimately represented the construction of 794 projects distributed around the whole city; a city that, due to the Playgrounds, became a city full of pleasure corners.

FIG. 76/Aldo van Eyck, Lost Identity Grid, 1956 and Nigel Henderson, Bethnal Green. Pictures illustrating the panels showed at Dubrovnik's CIAM congress. Which are the ones by Van Eyck?

The kids from Bethnal Green playing at van Eyck's Playgrounds

Van Eyck's Playgrounds project is not an urban isolated experiment. It is the result of the reaction against a worrying postwar situation that was sadly present in whole Europe. The look of the lost children playing around the city of Amsterdam, that van Eyck expresses with his photos presented in the first panel of Lost Identity at the congress of Dubrovnik of 1956, fits exactly with that look of Nigel Henderson when he photographed the industrial neighborhood of Bethnal Green in London. (fig. 76) The optimistic toughness of Henderson's images was fundamental in the formation of the professional beginnings of Alison and Peter Smithson, close friends and partners of van Eyck. Henderson's realistic look, which exposed the post war's life in the streets of London, constituted an essential precedent study in the way of re-formulating the architecture that the Smithson were chasing during the fifties.

The friendship between the Smithson and Henderson initiates in 1952 with the formation of the Independent Group (IG), together with the artist Eduardo Paolozzi, the theoretist Reyner Banham and others. The intense relation and mutual influence between the Smithson, Henderson and Paolozzi becomes clear in the 1956 exhibition "This is Tomorrow" (the same year as the CIAM of Dubrovnik) in which the group realized a pavilion in ruins in order to think about the future, a pavilion in which the footprints, the memories, the time, the process, the sense of touch, the identity, the place and the "as found" will forever become indispensable reference models in all the projects of the future career of the Smithsons, a way of imagining the future with a sensibility that was very close to the Playgrounds of van Eyck.

In 1967, the Smithsons wrote *Urban Structuring*, surely one of the most important treatises about modern urbanism after the *Letter of Athens*, where they were gathered many of the ideas that had been elaborated in the Team 10 meetings and where they explained this new sensitive and intelligent way of projecting the modern city. Significantly, the photos of Bethnal Green by Nigel Henderson were heading and illustrating the introduction of the book. Henderson's images helped the Smithson to synthesize everything that the abstract modern urbanism had forgotten, according to their opinion and Van Eyck's.

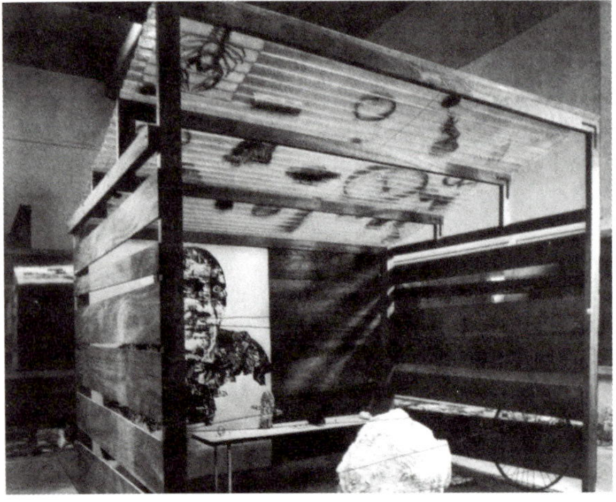

FIG. 77/ Alison and Peter Smithson, Eduardo Paolozzi, Patio and Pavilion. Installation made for the exhibition *This is Tomorrow*, at the Whitechapel Art Gallery, London, 1956. The optimistic and active future, thought from the memories.

FIG. 78/ cA Solar Pavilion. Upper Lawn, 1978. Alison Smitshon paving one part of the garden with stone. The garden is designed as another room of the house.

Paper public spaces. The transparent time

Van Eyck's idea of constructing some public spaces for children in Amsterdam, during the postwar period, was born by the delicate observation of an actual urban problem. Van has a sharp capacity of analysis, which allows him to accurately discover new spaces of opportunity that were hidden until then. It's surprising because he can focus his look on apparently superfluous and non transcendental things –ordinary things– which hide new ways of working, invisible anyone else's eyes. His look is sensitive, capable of waking architectural qualities up beyond the morphologic traditional conditions, is a deep and fragile look at the same time, capable of seeing the past, the present and the future in the same instant.

Van Eyck himself writes in *"The Interior of Time":*

"When the past is gathered in the present and the emergent body of the experience finds its place in the head, the present acquires a temporary depth, it loses its instantaneous acidity, and its razor cut quality. We could say that time is internalized or it becomes transparent. Inside my head I see the past, the present and the future as active continuing. If it is not like this, the appliances that we do would be empty of temporary density, of association capacity".[30]

This way of observing from the dimension of transparent time was surely an attitude that Van Eyck shared, learned and developed together with Alison and Peter Smithson. This look towards the ordinary things is also recognized in the exhibition *This is Tomorrow* of 1956, (fig. 77) in which the Smithsons constructed a ruin in order to explain the future architecture: a courtyard-enclosure realized with a fence covered with a reflective material that erased and diluted the perimeter-location in order to raise in his interior a wooden hut covered with a transparent ceiling full of memories. In this exhibition, the Smithsons proposed to construct the future with old materials, full of history and experiences, instead of using new materials, fruit of the technological research of the moment.

When the Smithsons themselves constructed "A Solar Pavilion, Upper Lawn", (fig. 78) in 1959, this look allowed them to realize an exquisite project of transparent time. The meticulous section (fig. 79) drawing of the project, in which they even reflected the dreg and cracks of the well's wall and the bush over the former and irregular stone fence from the year eight hundred, the dark shade of the different pavements that will inhabit the garden and the immense neighbor deciduous trees, is the reflection of an attentive and meticulous look of what exists in the place: a penetrating and superficial look that wants to catch the pass of time, with meticulous attention.

30_Aldo van Eyck, "The Interior of time", in Charles Jencks, and George Baird, *Meaning in Architecture* (New York: George Brazilier, 1969).

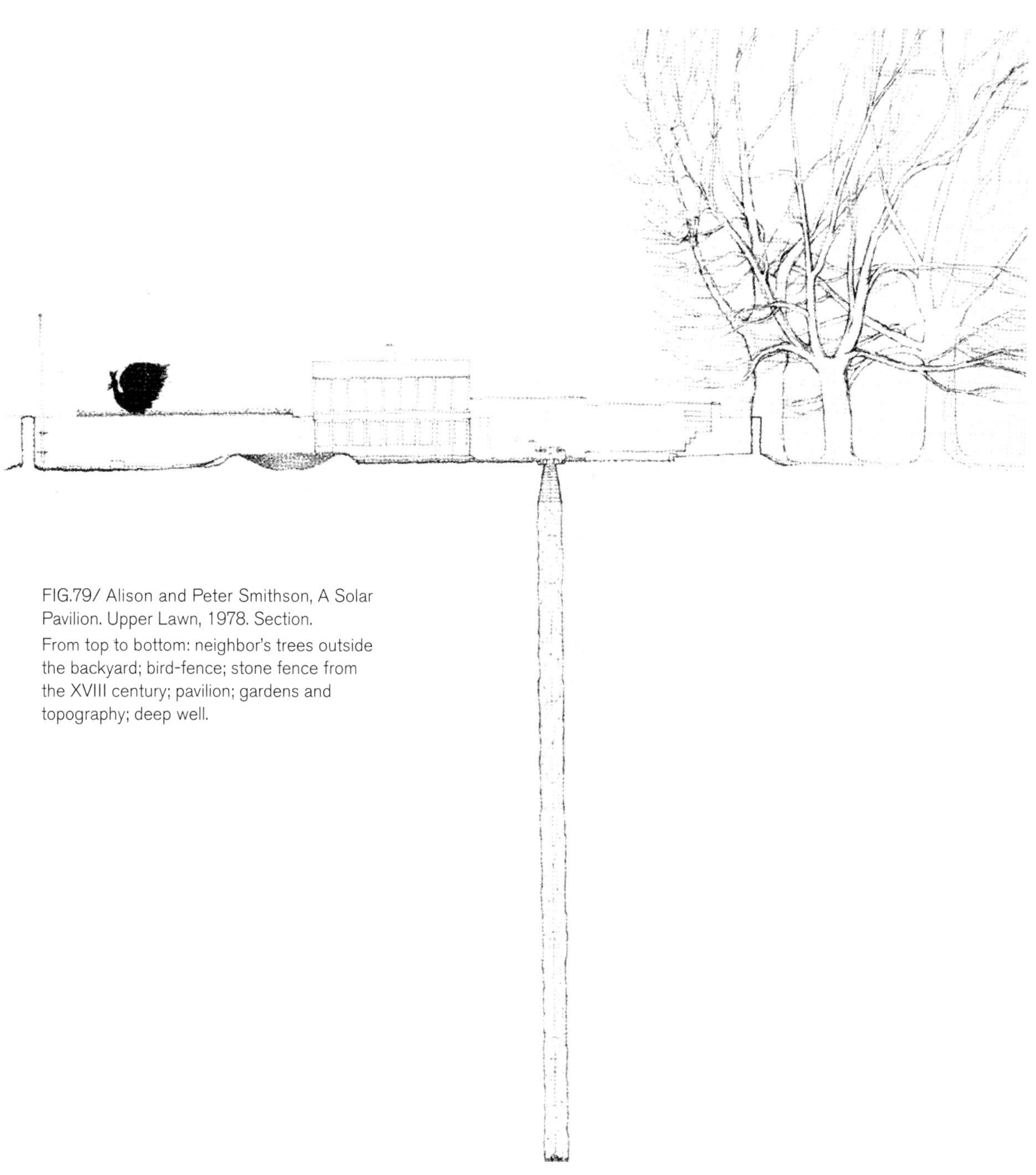

FIG.79/ Alison and Peter Smithson, A Solar Pavilion. Upper Lawn, 1978. Section.
From top to bottom: neighbor's trees outside the backyard; bird-fence; stone fence from the XVIII century; pavilion; gardens and topography; deep well.

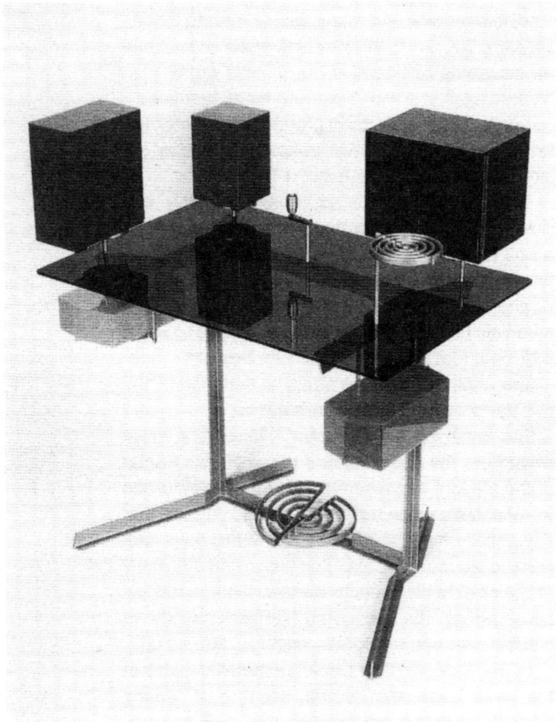

FIG. 80/ Alison and Peter Smithson, Collector's table and fish/ water lily desk, Tecta Catalogs, 1986.
Levels, objects, shadows and reflections floating.

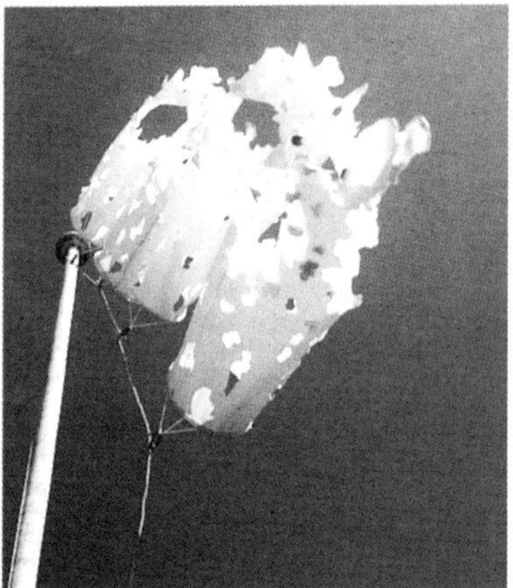

FIG. 81/ Photograph by Peter Smithson, A Solar Pavillion. Upper Lawn.
Time and lightness.

In the project "A Solar Pavilion, Upper Lawn" the deep look by means of temporal strata helped them to position themselves in front of the remains of the past and to recognize the sympathy for the sincerity of ancient things. For this reason, the best strategy is to turn the housing into a pavilion in order to make the weight of the past more evident and to therefore construct an ephemeral architecture, without past or future. But this project also proposes to construct the housing not only as a suspended pavilion on the year eight hundred's fence, but as a housing that is also a plot in which the rooms are flowerbeds of the garden: exterior rooms constructed with existing or new pavements, in which the irregular shades of the stones' joints demonstrate the density and weight of history strata.

The Smithsons' interest to project by superposing strata is not only recognized in their architectural or urbanism projects, but it is also a way of thinking that they use when they project small scale objects. The tables designed by them are a clear example of a complex thought that acquires density by superposing layers. (fig. 80) The tables are not only some horizontal planes with legs, but they are the opportunity to think some deep furniture: tables in which the objects float above and below a neutral glass plan where the reflection takes care of constructing the indeterminate and volatile space of the furniture.

This complex and light look is also recognized in many of Peter Smithson's unusual photographies: the images of the cut outs of colored paper stars flying in the sky, or the photographies of the line of shade that measures and separates the strip of snow that slowly melts by the effect of the sun's heat. They are images that reflect the interest to try to catch the transitory effects of the passage of time, images of Peter Smithson that try to capture the transparent time. (fig. 81)

FIG. 82/ Aldo van Eyck, Taijiri exhibition. Amsterdam 1967. Before and after. Taijiri blowing up the exhibition

An interest that allows us to understand the ephemeral montage materialized with paper for the exhibition that Van Eyck realized in Amsterdam in 1967 for the sculptor Tajiri. Van Eyck, (fig.82) which maintained a constant relation with different artists of the moment, facing the violent sculptures of Tajiri's metal monsters, decided to realize a fragile paper scenography. The choice of a traditional material to construct the places of the sculptures, contrasted with the futurist image of the exposed works. The montage of the exhibition consisted of two transparent paper cylinders, hung from the ceiling and tightened from the floor, which were grouping the sculptures and organizing the exhibition by modifying the existing space of the gallery. But the surprising fact about the exhibition's montage is not only the paper choice or the coincidence with the Smithsons' stars, but the action that was performed before it. Once the paper cylinder walls were well tightened, Tajiri himself blew them up by kicking them and modifying the space of the exhibition. The installation, which finished with the performance of the sculptor, concluded with the transparent paper cylinders torn apart and wrapping Tajiri's aggressive sculptures.

These are images and projects of the Smithsons and Van Eyck demonstrate their interest in trying to find the way to transform the value and the force of an action into a project. A concern about discovering how to turn the transparent time into an architectural project.

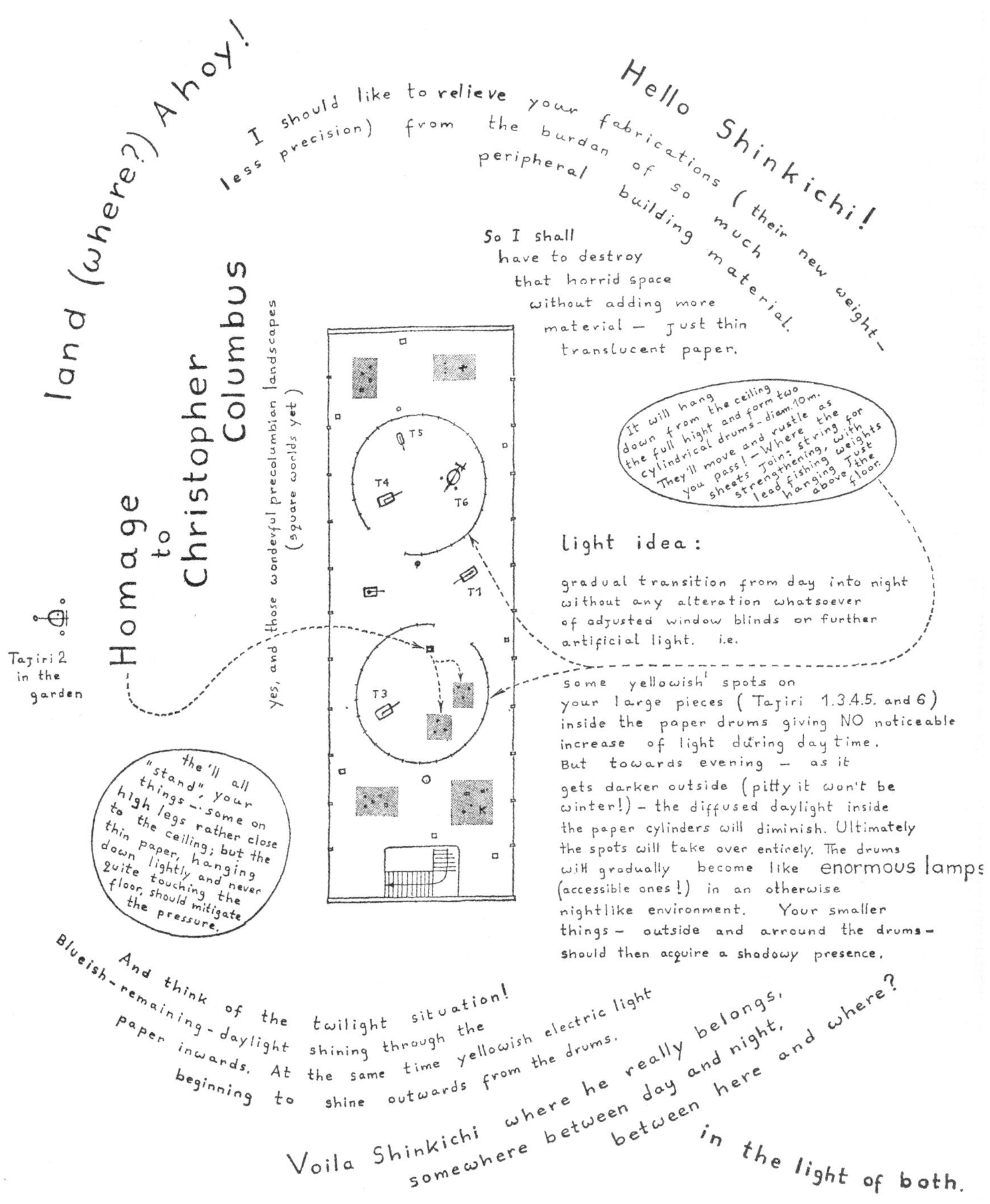

FIG. 83/ Aldo van Eyck, Cristoper Columbus, exhibition. Instruction Plan

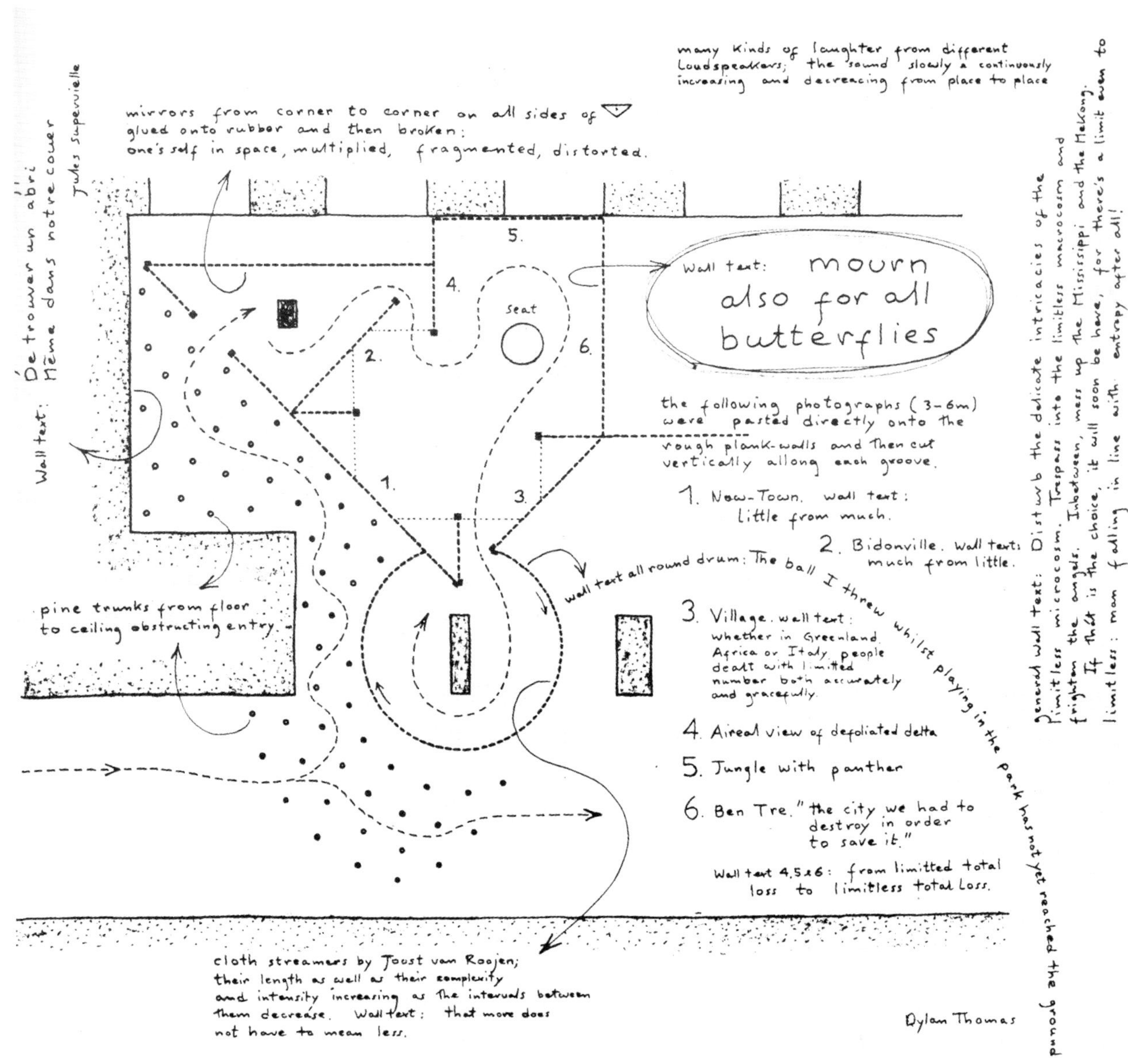

FIG. 84/ Aldo van Eyck, Exhibition Instruction Plan

Instructions plans

The plans that Van Eyck realized for his artistic montages projects were some handmade drawings full of annotations and numbers, explaining the ideas of the exhibition and how they had to be executed. (figs. 83, 84) They were plans that looked like drawings of a manual of instructions and not like some conventional plans of an architectural project; some plans had texts where the words and the phrases were used to construct the space of the project. It's highly possible that a few years later, these drawings could have been the source of inspiration for Georges Perec to write his poetical book *Espèces d'espaces* (1974). (fig. 85) They are plans that Van Eyck wrote with lines, points and arrows that explained the movement of the people walking along the project, texts that tried to draw what the visitors would do during their visit to the exhibition. To walk, to stop, to look, to turn, to cross; this was the way in which the peoples' movements around the space were organized. All these montages that Van Eyck realized were works that were interested in projecting how the visitor would take part in the exhibition and in imagining which would be the personal experience that would be lived by the visitors, and not in designing a final nice form.

ESPACIO
ESPACIO LIBRE
ESPACIO CERRADO
ESPACIO PRESCRITO
FALTA DE ESPACIO
ESPACIO CONTADO
ESPACIO VERDE
ESPACIO VITAL
ESPACIO CRÍTICO
POSICIÓN EN EL ESPACIO
ESPACIO DESCUBIERTO
DESCUBRIMIENTO DEL ESPACIO
ESPACIO OBLICUO
ESPACIO VIRGEN
ESPACIO EUCLIDIANO
ESPACIO AÉREO
ESPACIO GRIS
ESPACIO TORCIDO
ESPACIO DEL SUEÑO
BARRA DE ESPACIO
PASEOS POR EL ESPACIO
GEOMETRÍA DEL ESPACIO
MIRADA QUE EXPLORA EL ESPACIO
ESPACIO TIEMPO
ESPACIO MEDIDO
LA CONQUISTA DEL ESPACIO
ESPACIO MUERTO
ESPACIO DE UN INSTANTE
ESPACIO CELESTE
ESPACIO IMAGINARIO
ESPACIO NOCIVO
ESPACIO BLANCO
ESPACIO DEL INTERIOR
EL PEATÓN DEL ESPACIO
ESPACIO QUEBRADO
ESPACIO ORDENADO
ESPACIO VIVIDO
ESPACIO BLANDO
ESPACIO DISPONIBLE
ESPACIO RECORRIDO
ESPACIO PLANO
ESPACIO TIPO
ESPACIO EN TORNO
TORRE DEL ESPACIO
A ORILLAS DEL ESPACIO
ESPACIO DE UNA MAÑANA
MIRADA PERDIDA EN EL ESPACIO
LOS GRANDES ESPACIO
LA EVOLUCIÓN DE LOS ESPACIO
ESPACIO SONORO
ESPACIO LITERARIO
LA ODISEA DEL ESPACIO

la página

J'écris pour me parcourir
Henri Michaux

1

Escribo...

Escribo: escribo...
Escribo: «escribo...»
Escribo que escribo...
etc.

Escribo: trazo palabras sobre una página.
Letra a letra, un texto se forma, se afirma, se consolida, se fija, cuaja:
una línea estrictamente h
o
r
i
z
o
n
t
a
l
se deposita sobre la

FIG. 85/ Georges Perec, Texts from the book *Espèces d'espaces*, 1974

The Playgrounds were projects thought as a system that didn't want to take total control of the final form of the park, as the artistic montages. The Playgrounds were practically not drawn and it's exactly for this reason that, today, some of the plans of the 794 interventions that they managed to realize all around the city don't exist. Van Eyck, using a simple geometry constructed by elementary figures, such as circles, squares, triangles etc, placed his projects in empty places of the city, in residual spaces. Crossings, abandoned spots, empty plots between buildings... spaces "inbetween" that became "places of opportunities" to construct his projects. Van Eyck designed a catalogue of children's furniture in order to urbanize the Playgrounds. He projected his small parks only by combining the pieces from the system that he had designed, by playing. The Playgrounds were the response to all his interests to propose a urbanism closer to the people and at the same time, to effectively solve the problem of the lack of public places for the children to play in the city: a magic catalogue composed by light and simple solutions that, as the snow, economically and poetically resolved an actual problem of the city, a recreational and pleasant project that crystallized what Van Eyck himself called the "transparent time".

Inbetween space

The choice of the projects' locations was not a municipal decision imposed by Van Eyck, but the place where the Playgrounds would be constructed was the result of a participative process initiated by a group of neighbors that requested a public space for their sons to play to the Town Hall.

The Playgrounds were one of the first projects that Van Eyck had the opportunity to execute. Therefore, in spite of being novice and innocent, it was a project that already contained many of the interests that van Eyck would eventually develop during his career. Van Eyck was one of the first architects who projected the empty space between the buildings; a space that Van Eyck himself would call "inbetween space". The zones of transition, of dialog, of crossing; the indeterminate places became the spaces of pleasure with which Van Eyck played during all his provocative and delicious career. All his works (architectural works, interior and montage design, or the urban planning works), were exercises that reflected how the "inbetween space" had to be projected. (fig. 86)

Bohigas and Van Eyck:

two very different / similar projects

Though the strategy of Bohigas' project in Barcelona to recover the city is very similar to the proposal of Van Eyck in Amsterdam 30 years before, there are also clear differences between the two of them.

The project of the Playgrounds is conceived as a system based on the repetition of a park model, a project in which the standardization criteria of the urbanization solutions and serial production of a children' street furniture that would be placed repeatedly in each of the parks, would ended up turning the Playgrounds proposal into the construction of a catalogue of urban repeatable solutions, and not a specific park project for every concrete location. (fig. 87)

The Barcelona Model is raised in a completely different way. Every public space is thought as an unique and singular project. Every proposal is a finished and unrepeatable project of public space.
While Van Eyck's Playgrounds incorporate time and transience as strategic values of the project, Bohigas' Barcelona Model appears as a series of closed and finished projects. (fig. 88)

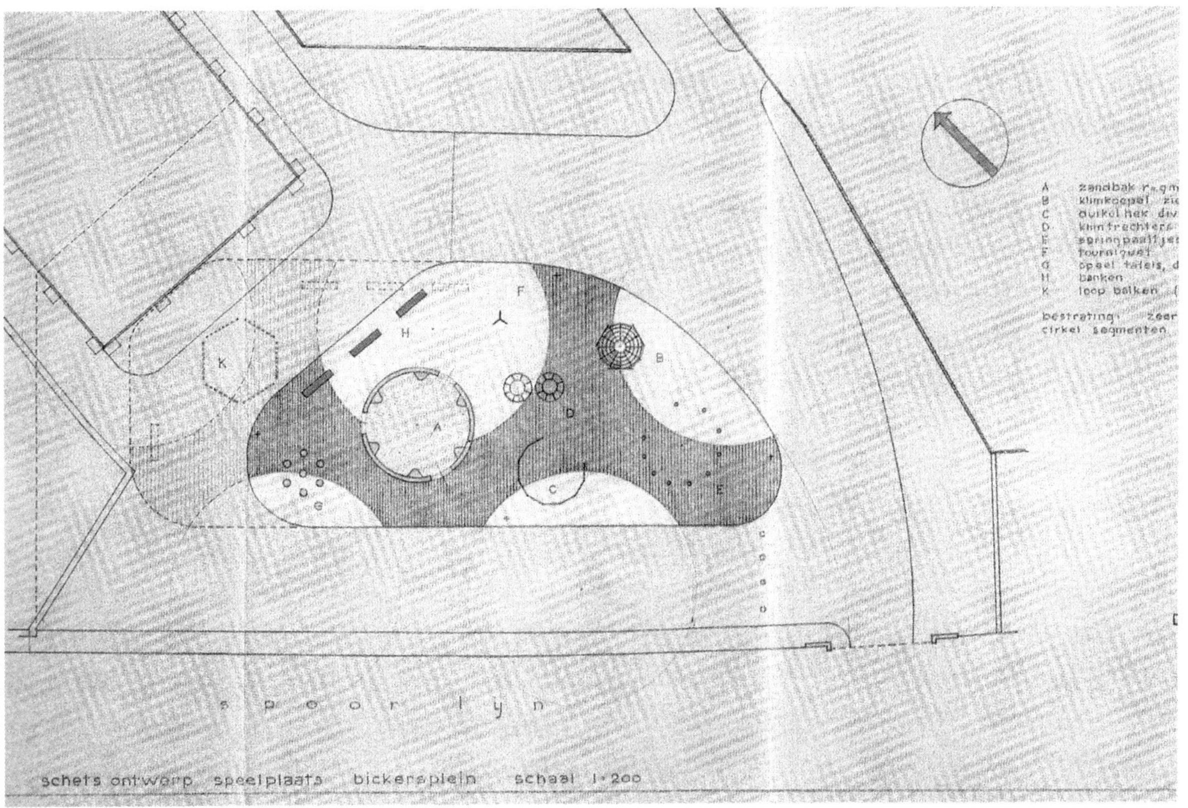

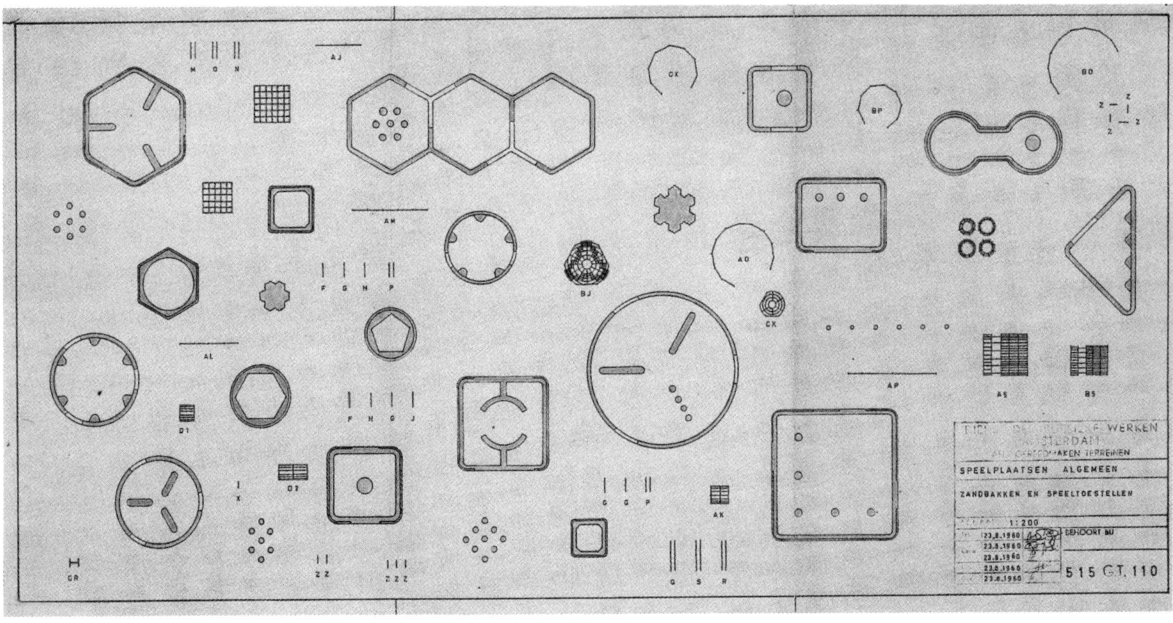

FIG. 86/ Aldo van Eyck, Crossroads plans
The Playgrounds were located in residual and ordinary spaces.

FIG. 87/ Square refurbishment division of Amsterdam City's Works Department, Street furniture catalog, Amsterdam, Holland, 1960.
The document includes climbing piles, sand areas, swings, play tables, jumping rings. An exportable catalyst catalog.

Anselmushof.

Anselmushof. Google Street View 2010.

Hasebroekstraat 1954.

Hasebroekstraat. Google Street View 2010.

FIG. 88/ LAB IN. Before, after and current state of the playgrounds, Aldo van Eyck

2_8 TRANSITORY PUBLIC SPACE

FIG. 89/ Skateboard cemetery in the pergola of the *plaça dels Països Catalans*, Barcelona, 10/08/2008. MBE.
The canopies are a broken skateboard cemetery. The carpet-pavement and the street furniture make the square a perfect spot for skating.

FIG. 90/ Plaça dels Països Catalans, Barcelona, 10/08/2008. MBE.
Iron-grid shadows dotted with the black spots of the pieces of skateboard.

Transience and the plaça dels Països Catalans

The *plaça dels Països Catalans* announced a new, more transparent, and emptier way of conceiving the public space of the city. After many years, it has contributed to the adoption of transience as a contemporary value in urban public spaces.

Today, besides being the site of an important building – Sants station – the square has become an important civic space for the city. The singular formalization by means of hard urban elements makes the square perfect for skateboarding, which in turn also makes it into a cemetery for their skateboards. The canopies at different heights of the square have turned into the most popular place for the skaters to say goodbye to their valued skateboards. Once a skateboard has grinded, caressed and hit all of the urban uneveness and errors in the city, the skaters meet in the plaça dels Països Catalans to honour the last flight of the skateboard. (fig. 89) They observe the old broken piece of plywood glide down with sadness, until it falls down on one of the metallic canopies of the square. (fig. 90)

Though this project has been criticized for its hard and sculptural nature, architects Viaplana and Piñón conceived of it as a space designed for children to play. The well-known photograph of the children riding their bicycles under the water of the fountains might as well have been taken by the van Eyck himself of Dutch children playing in one of his Playgrounds. (fig. 91) The similarity between the images is so direct that they look like two stills extracted from the scene of a same movie in which a child is filmed riding a bicycle through the pulverizing water of the squares' fountains. (fig. 92)

FIG. 91/ Aldo van Eyck, sprayed water fountain in an Amsterdam Playground and the bike kid.

FIG. 92/ Albert Viaplana, Helio Piñón, Plaça dels Països Catalans, Barcelona, 1983.
Fountain area and the bike kid.

FIG. 93/ Parets del Vallès' square.
In Miralles and Pinós' project the bike kid is riding too.

The evident relation between the projects of the Playgrounds and the *plaça de Sants* goes beyond the coincidence of thinking a recreational space for the children in the city; (fig. 93) both projects shared emplacements of similar characteristics. The places where the projects were placed were, in both cases, marginal spaces, crossings of road traffic, abandoned places, ordinary spaces in transition, residual places of the city where, both van Eyck as Viaplana, got to recognize the value of the transitory in order to project the public space.

Albert Viaplana himself, at the project report of the plaça de Sants explains it this way:

"Initially, we felt desolated. The ones who knew the place where we had to work would understand it. But we didn't complain too much; we didn't even complain; we thought that, from that moment, only the project had to keep the feelings that the place would initiate; the astuteness is indispensable in our profession, and silence is one of its forms. With an astute smile, we planned a horizontal surface in order to join all its parts, even the most difficult to deal with, as only a surface with the same width as length could do it. But, even the existing streets got lost in that desert, and the people didn't have other option that to remain standing still. On one hand, they felt the need to spread in order to find balance, as the water spilt through the floor; but I knew that quietude, as silence did before, makes distant things closer, the closed things open, puts the inanimate things into movement, faces the things, behind, above, below, inside or out; it makes silence be heard as a scream and the noise as a rumor, because, for an instant, it will be the center of all things.

The water diminished into a spot in the floor, and the floor bowed as something that spends too much time inside the oven. The most singular thing was that the more we centered in every part of the project, the emptier the city appeared, more space was open to the doubted, to the ignored and to the opposite of what was stated there. Regardless, the desolation was now bearable".[31]

31_Albert Viaplana, "Memoria del proyecto de la plaça dels paisos catalans" in *Obra. Viaplana/Piñón* (Barcelona: COAC, 1996).

FIG. 94/ Kurt Schwitters, Merzbau's wall preserved in the Hatton Gallery, Newcastle-upon-Tyne University, 1947. From John Elderfield, *Kurt Schwitters* (Paris: Centre Pompidou, 1994).
Construction of an indefinite and unfinished interior space.

Aldo van Eyck, Kurt Schwitters and the lesson of the transcience

At the end of the forties, when Van Eyck started designing the Playgrounds project, he became friends with one of the most important Dadaist artists of the European scene. Understanding the influence of Kurt Schwitters and his work *Merzbau* on Van Eyck is crucial in order to have a better understanding of the the ephemeral character of the Playgrounds project.

The Merzbau and the Playgrounds were conceived in a similar way. (fig. 94) Both projects were posed as systems with the capacity of adapting to the different emplacements where they were executed. They were projects understood as works without a physical final limit, informal projects that were defined by precise interventions realized during a long period of time, works that also shared the interest to transform the space by means of small scale elements. But Schwitters's clear influence on van Eyck is not only recognized in the way both projects were thought, but also in the seduction by the genuine force of the marginality as a catalyst of the project.

Yago Conde, in his doctoral thesis *The architecture of indetermination*, dedicates the chapter "Around Dada in Berlin" to analyze three fundamental works of art of the 20th century that, according to Conde, represented the Dadaist current of the time. In his doctoral thesis, Conde wanted to investigate the influence of Dada objects and words on modern architecture. Conde contested that Dadaism, based on the transience and indetermination, had formally contributed to the construction of the modern movement. Conde proposed the comparative analysis of three constructions: the drama Dio Dada by Johannes Baader, the tower to the Third International by Vladimir Tatlin, and the *Merzbau* by Kurt Schwitters.

Kurt Schwitters was a pioneer artist in using abandoned or unused materials, as waste and pieces of wreckage. Schwitters, by means of the manipulation of these old-new materials, wanted to construct a new type of collage. His project *Merzbau*, an unfinished collage travelling by three European cities, served Schwitters to discover a new way of relating and mixing different materials that, apparently, were impossible to associate. It was a way of composing a collage from materials full of memories, a way of working with found remains that some years later, Alison and Peter Smithson, friends and fellows in the Team 10 of van Eyck, would also try out in the assembly of the pavilion "This is Tomorrow", of 1956.

FIG. 95/ Aldo van Eyck's Playground, Gemeentearchief, Amsterdam, Holland.

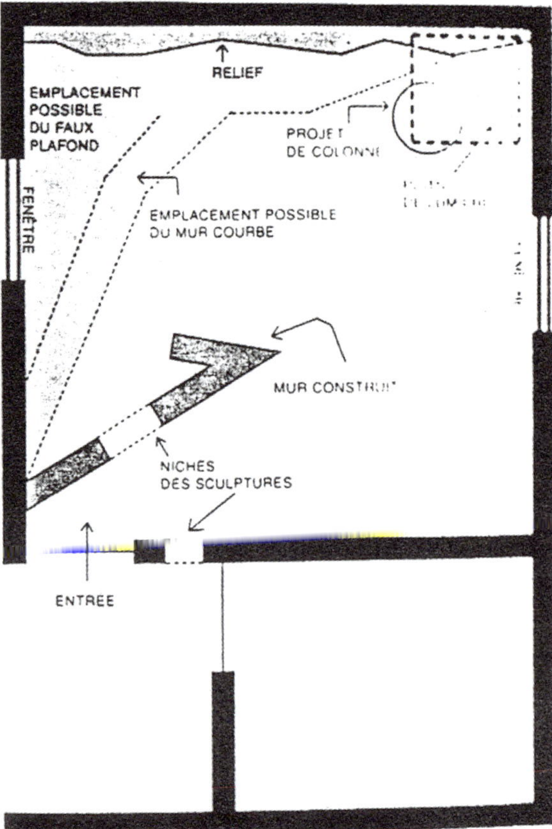

FIG. 96/ Kurt Schwitters, Merzbau. Plan from John Elderfield, *Kurt Schwitters* (Paris: Centre Pompidou, 1994).
The Merzbau's drawing looks like the extrusion of Van Eyck's Playground floor plan.

Yago Conde, in his doctoral thesis, commented about the *Merzbau*:

> It was a construction inside his house that was growing in height and dimensions day after day until it practically managed to exceed the limits of the space where it was contained in. It was a living document of Schwitters, of his art and his friends. There were caverns dedicated to each of them, for example the caverns of Arp, Gabo, Doeburg, El Lissitzky, Malevich, Mies van der Rohe and Ritcher. Every cavern contained an object that was property of every person. In a cavern there were some false teeth with some teeth still in it; in another one there was a small bottle with urine labeled with the name of the donor... At first sight, we might say that the visual appearance of the Merzbau in its beginnings was similar to Baader's model: a collection of objects placed one on another. But, as it was growing from day to day, new geometric forms surrounded the old caverns. When that happened, the work would change completely and would acquire a much more constructive appearance. It transformed into an alive example of the process from the destruction up to the construction.[32]

The spatial construction that Schwitters proposed at the Merzbau helped Van Eyck to consolidate his Playgrounds project. Though Van Eyck, by means of his furniture's catalogue, proposed a game based on the repetition and the variation, his projects established a dialectical relation and integration with their emplacements. Van Eyck achieved, as Schwitters with his three Merzbau, that each of the 794 of the Playgrounds became the construction of a new space from a precise game of relations between diverse objects and the context. The wise arrangement of each one of these objects was capable of interpreting the place and transforming it. The Playgrounds and the Merzbau shared marginal site conditions. (fig. 95)

The formal and material coincidence between both projects is so strong, that a quick and vague look at the drawing of the floor plan of the *Merzbau* can mislead us to think that we are looking at the floor plan of the Playground that occupies the empty space left in the middle of some former industrial buildings. The floor plan of the *Merzbau* is a space defined by walls that are deformed and enlarged by the superposition of a new relief. (fig. 96)

FIG. 97/ Kurt Schwitters, Merzbau's wall preserved in the Hatton Gallery, Newcastle-upon-Tyne University, 1947, from John Elderfield, *Kurt Schwitters* (Paris: Centre Pompidou, 1994).

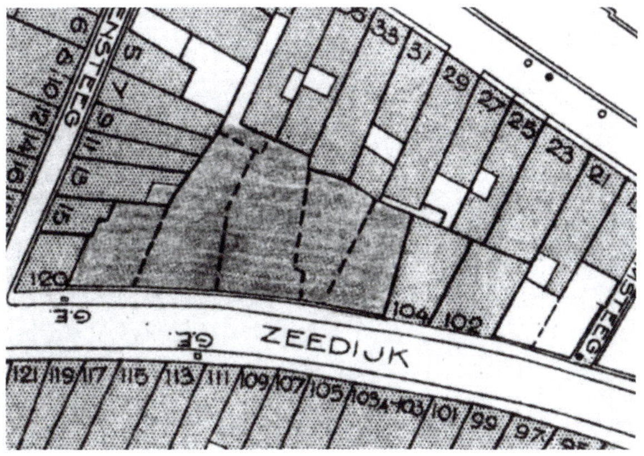

FIG. 98/ Aldo van Eyck, Playground Zeedijk, Amsterdam-Centrum, 1955-1956. Location.

The formal resemblance of the floor plan and the Schwitter's wall is surprising.

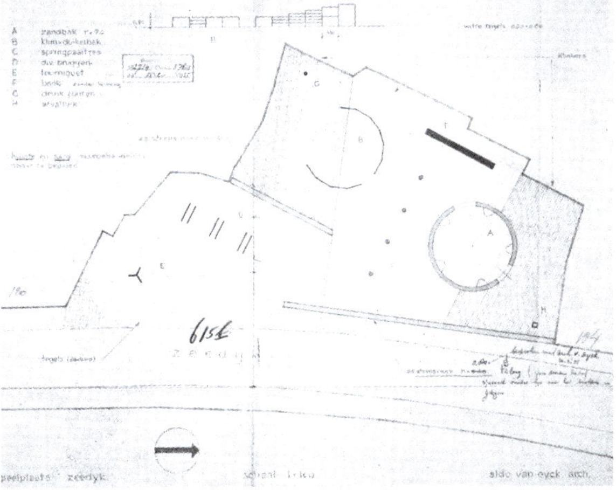

FIG. 99/ Aldo van Eyck, Playground Zeedijk, Amsterdam-Centrum, 1955-1956. Floor plan.

The Playground of van Eyck is also a place defined by a perimeter constructed by thick walls, an enclosure formed by a collage of several pieces of rough surfaces. Bricks, holes, blocked windows and drain pipes create the sensation of an enclosure closed almost in its four sides. Taking an absent look at the floor plan of the *Merzbau*, it is possible to end up thinking that you can enter the Playground passing through the adjacent ancient industrial building. Inside this semiclosed space defined by ancient walls, both projects include foreign geometries constructed by means of objects that, without a concrete final form, were capable of completely transform the original place.

Schwitters's collage on the wall of the *Merzbau* preserved in the Hatlon gallery can also look like the floor plan of the Zeedijk Playground turned 180°. (fig. 97, 98, 99) The two projects form within an almost closed enclosure delimited by existing thick walls, instead space is constructed with objects of alien geometries, which interact with the place.

Schwitters and van Eyck's projects take in an ordinary place, an enclosure, and transform them with the introduction of a few elements of diverse geometries in their interior.

William Rubin commented after a visit to the *Merzbau*:

"In 1919, the walls of Schwitters's house were already packed with collages and reliefs and the floor was full of objects that were starting to merge with the furniture. Soon there was no distinction between the collage, the independent relief and the wall that supported all the waste that Schwitters had installed".[32]

32_Yago Conde, *Architecture of the Indeterminacy* (Barcelona: Actar, 2000)

FIG. 100/ Amsterdam 1954 and 1956.
Amsterdam's Playgrounds explosion. Spotlights illuminating a new city.

Van Eyck the catalyst

At the beginning of this project we asked for a relationship between two public spaces as different as Saint Peter's Square in Vatican City and the pixades of Sao Paulo. The dissimilarity of these two places was the trigger of a personal interest lead us to try to discover how such different spaces were both successful public places in the city.

We saw the similarity between the *Piazza del Campidoglio* in Rome and the *Djemaa el Fna square* in Marrakech. Though they are formal opposites, both had become public places of urban reference and identification for the people who lived in those cities.

Though van Eyck's playgrounds were an informal project, as the *pixades* or *Djemaa el Fna square*, the Playgrounds benefitted from their careful design by an architect. The Playgrounds of van Eyck were not randomly constructed spaces but rather they were an informal design strategy to reform the whole city. In spite of their strong informal origin, the Playgrounds were intensely and intelligently designed parks; delicate public spaces defined from minor scale elements, capable of catalyzing and transforming the marginal corners they inhabited.

The Playgrounds project of van Eyck was the key – the catalyst – to discovering the public catalysts. (fig. 100)

The Playgrounds help us see the apparently slight but essential elements that are actually the engines of the formation of the public space. Van Eyck recognized their transformative power despite their apparent fragility. In the Playgrounds he gave those transient elements emmense responsibility – and they succeeded.

FIG. 101/ LAB IN.
Football field transitory project.

Transitory project

The transitory project is formulated as one more step in the evolution that the treatment of the public space of Barcelona has experienced towards the immateriality and the transience. It consists of thinking the collective space trying to incorporate the time as an instrument of project; it consists of reforming the marginal and ordinary spaces of the contemporary city by realizing temporary actions with a minimal investment, light actions executed by means of some public catalysts – minimal elements – that must be capable of activating some places that until then were inert and unoccupied. (fig. 101)

The transitory project is posed from the principle of understanding the public space as an alive process in constant transformation. It proposes a kind of unfinished intervention, which avoids freezing the space and the activity. It is an open project that constructs the minimum conditions needed to activate a place, and trusts in the action of the future users in order to define the formalization and the usage of the space.

FIG. 102/ Jordi Bernadó's image of the indifferent city.

3_ INDIFFERENCE

Richard Sennet. The indifferent city.

In his article *New Capitalism, New Isolation*, American sociologist Richard Sennet discusses the indifferent cities built by modern society out of cookie cutter work environments. Sennet writes, "Now, just as the workplace is affected by a new system of flexible working, so the city, too, risks losing its charm as businesses and architecture become standardised and impersonal." He writes of flexible work in the modern capitalist world replacing old fashioned long-term work standards. The idea of being faithful to a single enterprise during an entire career has been replaced by the execution of sporadic jobs consisting of specific and limited tasks.

Sennet argues that this new capitalism, which demands flexibility to survive, creates neutral and impersonal spaces so that they can be modified with ease. Sennet maintains that time is now consecutive, not accumulative: a project is developed and finished, and then another begins, unrelated to the first. This dynamic goes on successively. The stressful demand for flexibility requires non-linear work. The accumulative pyramid system that assured upward mobility in a company with a job well done, has disappeared. Ancient cities were accumulative, but today's cities are not. We live in consecutive cities, in indifferent cities.

The new work environment is set in indifference: in empty, impersonal, reprogrammable buildings; in a global architecture of universal values. We live in a transportable architecture that does not put down roots in the place it is built. We inhabit neutral and abstract spaces that are unenthusiastic and generic. The modern flexible work standard built indifferent cities and public spaces. (fig.102) New capitalism developed a new model of behavior and social isolation. The German philosopher Emmanuel Levinas describes this new isolation as "the good vicinity of strangers." In this cold new world diverse people of different origins coexist anonymously in a distant and polite conviviality without space or time for personal contact.

In this modern, indifferent city – a diverse, complex and rich place based on flexibility in consecutive time – how can we repair the loss of collective value and attack the consecutive? If this indifferent city is deprived of spaces of individual or collective intensity, how can new public spots of identity be constructed? How can a new model of public spaces be designed for these indifferent cities?

Against indifference. Public catalysts.

A catalyst is defined as:

"A substance that enables a chemical reaction to proceed at an unusually faster rate or under different conditions than otherwise possible.
An agent that provokes or speeds significant change or action"[33]

We demand that the city have public spaces of intensity and propose that a public catalyst is an agent capable of activating a place that was previously indifferent.

The analysis of historic and contemporary public spaces by the Laboratory of Indifference led to the following discovery: vivid public spaces of identity and reference succeeded because of the urban effect of these catalysts. In the Laboratory, we look to illustrate the existence of public catalysts, as well as to demonstrate the necessity of these agents if an indifferent place is to be activated.

33_Source: Merriam Webster Dictionary
http://www.merriam-webster.com/dictionary/catalyst

FIG. 103/ Opisso's drawing of *Canaletes'* fountain.
Puig i Cadafalch's kiosk and the Streetlamp-Fountain of *Canaletes.*

To activate a space

Like chemical catalysts, public catalysts are responsible for generating the conditions needed to accelerate the activation of a public place.

The aim of this project is not to create a catalogue of the formal qualities of urban furniture objects. The years of analysis were not spent on catalysts' formal characteristics, but on their aptitude to generate the conditions for an urban space to transform. As chemical catalysts may be solid, liquid or gas, the Laboratory of Indifference demonstrates that public catalysts may take a range of formal states from the highly constructed to the spontaneous.

Designed or spontaneous public space

The Canaletes fountain at the head of la Rambla de les Flors is one of the most vivacious public places in the city of Barcelona. (fig. 103) This traffic space located on one of the most popular streets of Barcelona is the place chosen by the blaugrana fans to celebrate the victories of Barcelona teams. Why is the fountain the most intense and representative place for a blaugrana celebration? Why precisely this place and not any other? What really moves the blaugrana supporters to celebrate their team victories in this fountain today? What definitively activated this spot? The journal *La Rambla, Esport i Ciutadania*, whose headquarters were just in front of the Canaletes fountain, used to hang a scoreboard from its balcony on the days Barça was playing out of town. The impatient *blaugrana* supporters would come from around the city to read the day's results on that blackboard. Although both the soda fountain and the journal are now gone, this blackboard made the Canaletes Fountain the chosen spot for the *blaugrana*'s celebrations. The blackboard announcing the results was the true catalyst, transforming an ordinary intersection into an excellent public space.

The analysis of many formal and informal public spaces by the Laboratory of Indifference revealed that despite very different appearances and origins, successful public spaces have one thing in common: the public catalysts.

The Laboratory of Indifference discovered and verified the existence of these urban agents that were previously unrecognized; these secret urban activators have been hiding behind their varied formal images – solid, liquid or gaseous.

FIG. 104/ Images of 2011 Champions League Barça's winning celebration at the *Canaletes'* Fountain.
Barça supporters climbing to the Streetlamp-Fountain.

The case of the Canaletes (fig. 104) fountain illustrates how a public space can be activated by random causes rather than from a formal architectural design. The work to identify the public catalysts has served not only to recognize the differences and the similarities between these constructed and spontaneous spaces, but, moreover, to discover a new kind of public space that can be a model to activate the indifferent city.

Transitory public space

If the public catalysts activate both constructed and spontaneous spaces, how can public space be designed using catalysts?

We propose to design collective space in a temporary and unfinished way, trusting in the force of the catalysts to initiate the transformation process of the public space.

We propose a way of imagining the public space where the usual order of a project is inverted. In the typical design of a public space, we try to consolidate a place through the execution of a project and then we wait for the place to be activated. We propose an inverse and open order. First the place is activated with a catalyst, and then the activity that takes place in it is consolidated. Stimulate expectant places and awaken their authentic civic and social potential, with a minimal investment.
If the proof that a public space is successful is that people use it, why is it that in the design of a public space, the first thing that is done is to formalize and to construct the space instead of thinking about the people from the beginning? We propose a way of designing the public space that is more than a half-hearted consultation of prospective users. We look to take advantage of a place's capacity for participation and transformation through a transitory design. We propose an open kind of project in which, once a space is catalyzed, the decisive capacity belongs to the people to consolidate and define it. (fig. 108)

The study of public spaces in conditions of extreme austerity –like the barber shop of Kinshasa or the urban spaces formed after catastrophe in Barcelona – reveals the essence of their construction.

The sincere and naked effect of the people on the construction of the public space is direct and essential: when a Congolese man decides to take out a mirror and a chair and to put them under the shade of an eucalyptus, the construction of a new public space in Kinshasa begins; when a Moroccan man decides to carry a water tank on his back and to hang a collar made of bronze cups around his neck, the construction of a new public space in Marrakech also begins. The immediacy between the desire and the result is evident.

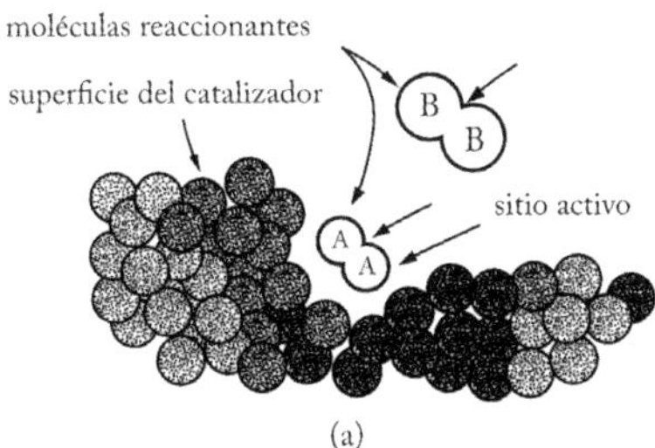

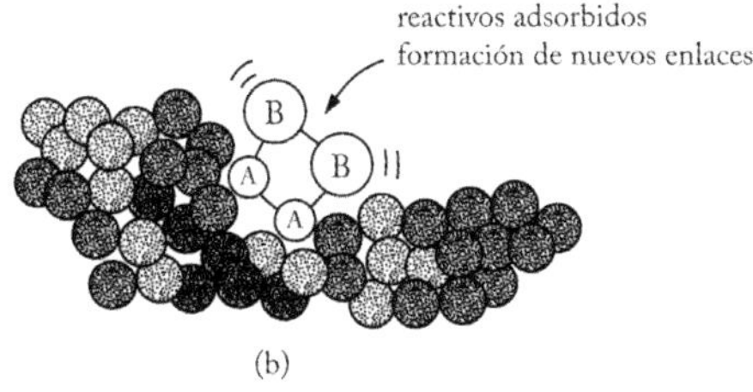

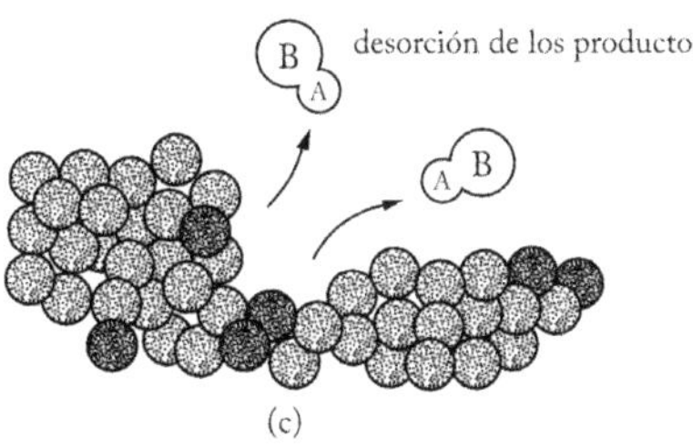

FIG. 105/ Diagram of a chemical reaction's activation process due to some catalyst effect.

The transitory project establishes a new format of work for the contemporary architect, an area of work that goes beyond the simple popular consultation, which is often political and trivial. The use of the public catalysts allows us, without falling into half-hearted consultations or into impositions of formal architectural excesses, to play the role of a mediator by projecting. It is a new vague and vivacious way of thinking today's public space.

Through this lens we look again to our city of Barcelona. If the public spaces constructed at the beginning of the eighties have been modified, restored and transformed constantly ever since they were executed; now is possibly the correct moment to assume the transitory condition of the public space and to look for a new way of conceiving it, open and indefinite. This new type of public space does not go against all the work previously done in Barcelona; rather it is meant to initiate a reimagining of each space.

Urban planner Joan Busquets proposed to study the informal city as way to imagine the city of the future in his doctoral thesis, *La urbanización marginal* (1975). Busquets discovered the secret laws behind the precarious and spontaneous barrack huts, then proposed new systems of aggregation for housing as new systems for the cities to grow.

After 35 years of witnessing the different stages of transformation of the streets, parks and squares of Barcelona; I can verify their transience personally. I feel that the moment has come to uncover the secret laws behind the temporary and sometimes spontaneous construction of public space. I innocently imagine the future of these public spaces – and I propose new instruments to design them: the public catalysts.

Belonging and opportunity

In the development of the project, we often questioned the real capacity of a catalyst. We asked ourselves – how would we know the most effective catalyst when we saw it? And why do some catalysts fail to completely activate a place? We found the answer to these questions in the science behind chemical catalysts. In the same way that a chemical catalyst is built to accelerate a certain chemical reaction, each public catalyst must fit precisely to the context it looks to activate. A public space will only activate if the right catalyst is present. As Aldo van Eyck would say, it is necessary to understand the transparent time of a place in order to find this missing piece. Every public space needs its own catalyst. This fit is not only to the space's morphologic conditions, but also to the anthropologic, geographical, geological, historical and social conditions of the place. (figs. 105, 106, 107).

FIG. 106/ LAB IN. Example of before and after the effect of Jujol's graffiti catalyst into the medieval wall of Barcelona.

1 State of the Barcelona's city wall before the effect of the catalyst.

2 Jujol's graffiti catalyst.

3 Effect of the catalyst. Recovery of the original medieval façade with public space in front of it.

FIG. 107/ LAB IN. Examples of before and after the effect of New York's Blockout catalyst

1

Original state of Brooklyn's Bridge before the catalyst's effect.

2

Blackout catalyst.

3

Catalyst's effect. The New Yorkers come out to the streets.

FIG. 108/ LAB. IN. Activation process of a space by means of a public catalyst.

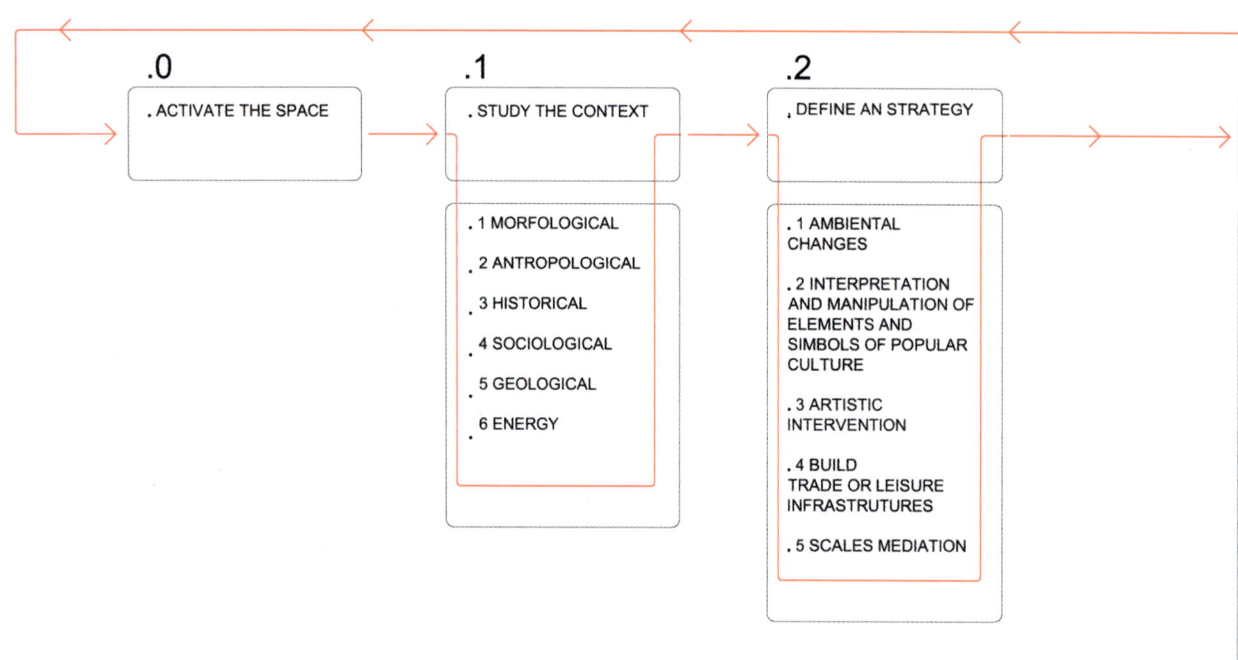

Process and classification of the public catalysts

After elaborating a summary of over one hundred different cases of public catalysts – contemporary or historic, designed or spontaneous – and analyzing in greater detail a selection of 25 different examples, we have distinguished five strategies of the successful public catalyst.

1_ Environmental Modification
Exchange of energy. A strategy based on the alteration and manipulation of the atmospheric conditions of a spot. For example, the roofs of Parets or the case of New York's blackout.

2_ Interpretation and manipulation of elements and symbols of popular culture.
The study of the habits of culture.
Robert Venturi, thanks to his capacity of fine observation, turned the ordinary into extraordinary with his pop architecture games. The Rebeca's Restaurant, by Frank Ghery, or the habit in villages on summer nights of taking out the chairs to the street for fresh air.

3_ Construction of Infrastructure for trade and leisure.
It is a strategy that activates the public space due to the execution of elements – more or less constructed, more or less permanent – that facilitate both the commercial exchange and the opportunity to enjoy moments of physical pleasure. They can be ambiguous constructions, without a well-defined use. We think of the forest of eucalyptuses in Kinshasa, Djemaa el Fna square or the infinitely long pergola of Ibirapuera's park in Sao Paulo.

4_ Artistic Intervention

Artistic actions on the public space that construct new conditions. The place is re-qualified. The placement of obelisks in Rome for Pope Sixtus V, Osario's anti-graffiti by Alex Orion in the tunnels of Sao Paulo, the monument painted for Jaume I Conquerer in Jujol, the chalk paintings made by the children playing in Bethnal Green street or the garbage pile of *Mon Oncle*, are all clear examples of this strategy.

5_ Scalar conversation

Urban scalers. Strategy of adjusting the difference between scales, sometimes uncomfortably, between the landscape, the city and the human scale. The examples of the molding of the Palazzo Farnese in Rome, the shelves in the porch of Vistabella's church or Seagram Building's step in New York are examples. (fig. 109)

FIG. 109/ LAB. IN. Cataloging diagram of the catalysts.

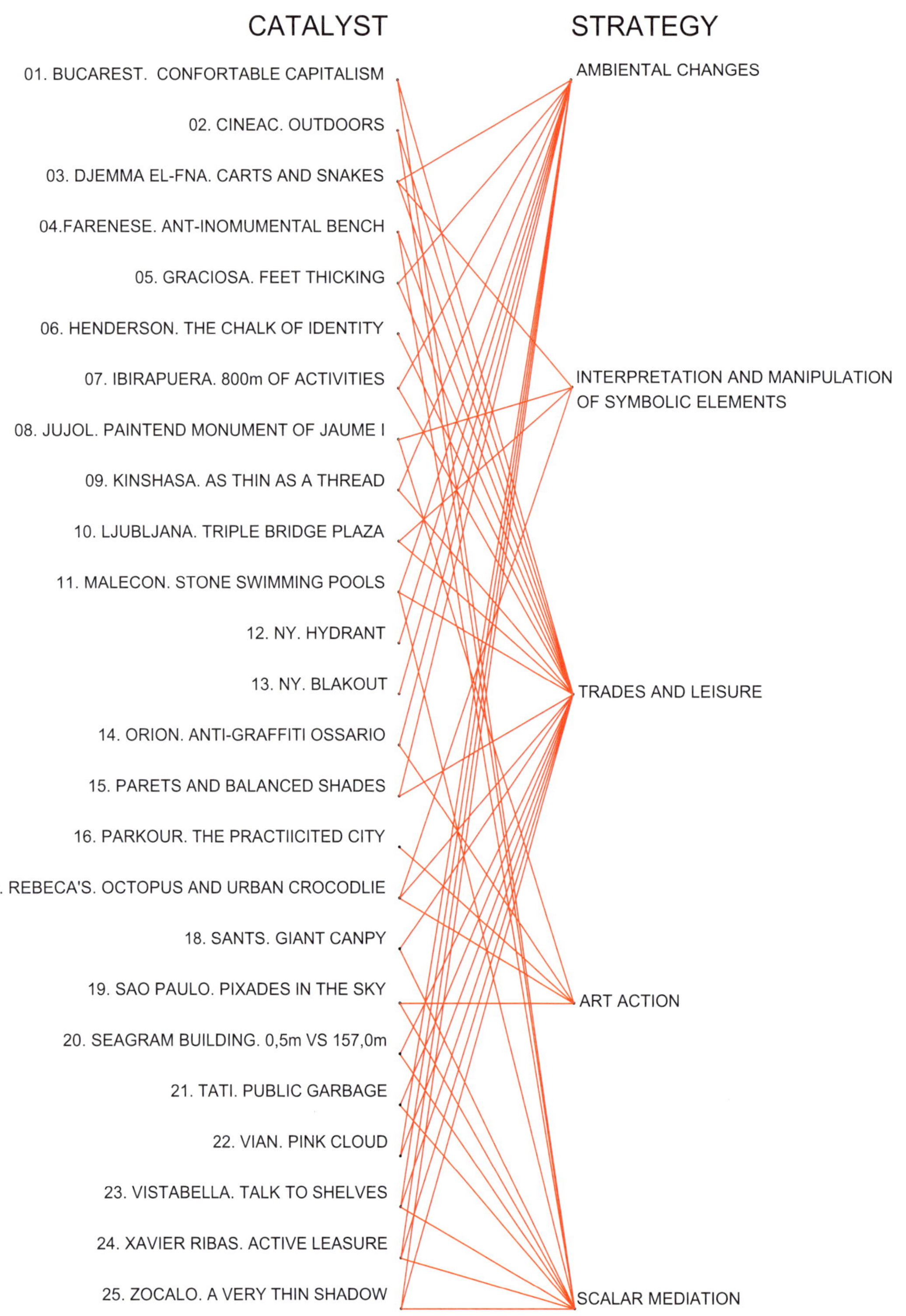

Arrangement scheme of the catalysts

The 25 examples analyzed by the Laboratory of Indifference are defined by twenty-five different catalysts with varied formal states and strategies.

The aim of this research is not only to enumerate and to classify different kinds of public spaces but also to reveal the public catalysts as a common element, hidden until now, that exists in the quality public spaces. For this reason, this project does not make the mistake of proposing a simple classification. We understand, as Quim Monzó explains in *Benzina*,[34] that despite the operative efficiency of a system of classification, it is often an excessive simplification of reality.

"In the ground floor it's placed the department of infantile books. He can't stand the books for children. He finds annoying that they are made for children. He has never understood why on earth someone decides which is the border line that makes these books the books for children, some others the books for adults, some others the erotic books, some different ones the porn books, and other ones the love novels. And also he cannot stand that quite a row of shelves shows the label poetry. What does poetry mean? What does love novels mean?

...It is not necessary to go against things. Even more: for the things to be useful to us, it is not necessary to go against them, but to accept them as they come."

34_Quim Monzó, *Benzina (Barcelona: Quaderns Crema,*1983)

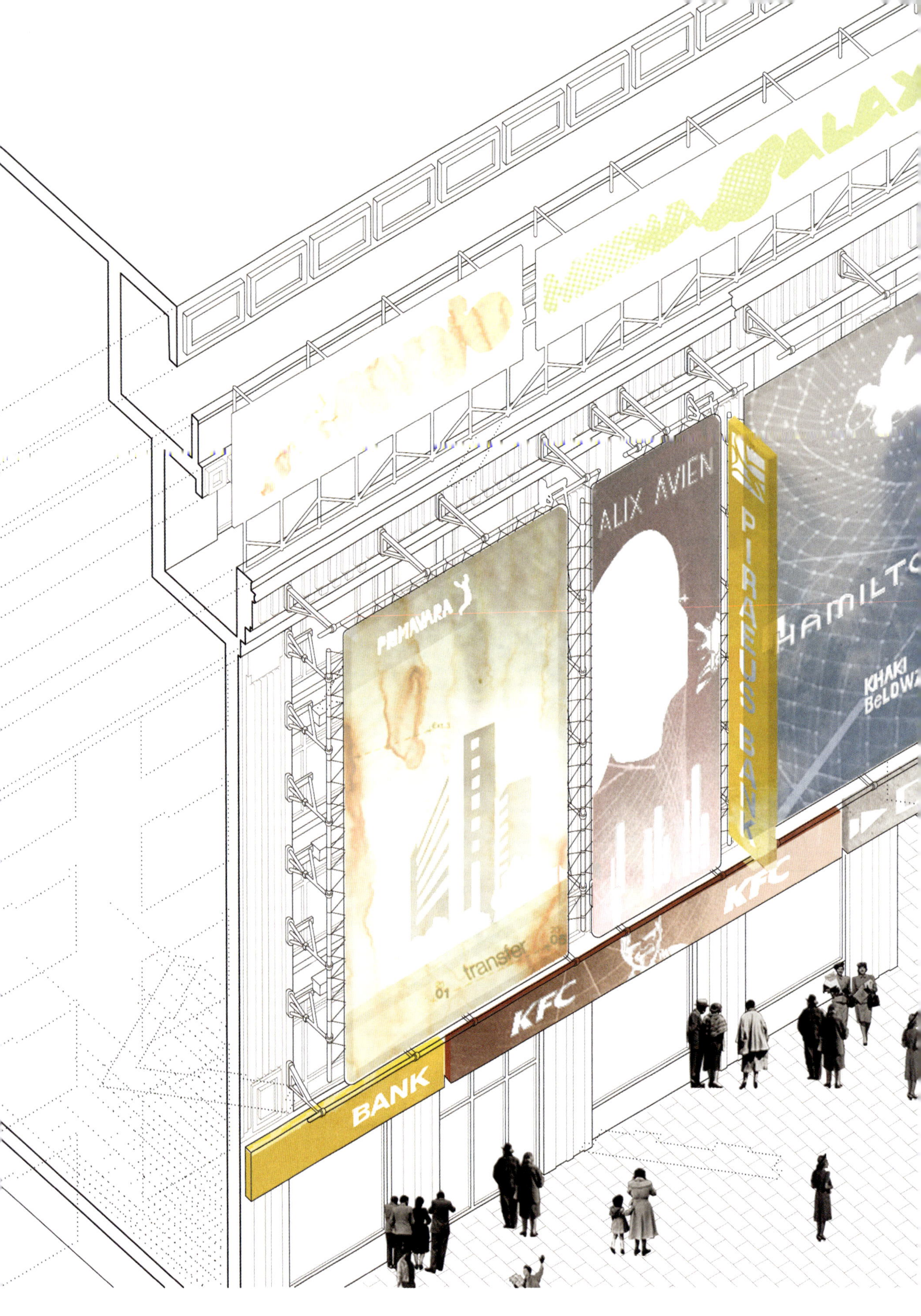
ALIX AVIEN
PIRAEUS BANK
HAMILTO
KHAKI
BeLOWZ
PRIMAVARA
transfer
KFC
KFC
BANK

LAB. IN

Ceausescu's operation of the opening of big boulevards by cutting and demolishing existing buildings had never managed to construct an actual public space. The imposed geometry consisting of concrete curtains did not catalyze any space of relation. The trade, which is added as another curtain, becomes the street's real catalyst.

Bibliography

Abalos. Iñaki

"Técnica y arquitectura en la ciudad contemporánea, 1950-2000". Amb Juan Herreros.
Ed Nerea Editorial; Edición 1992.

"Áreas de Impunidad". Amb Juan Herreros
Ed Actar 1997.

"La buena vida visita guiada a las casas de la modernidad"
Ed Gustavo Gili 2001.

"Atlas de lo pintoresco vol 1"
Ed Gustavo Gili 2005.

"Campos de batalla"
Ed Col·legi d'Arquitctes de Girona 2005.

"Atlas de lo pintoresco vol 2"
Ed Gustavo Gili 2009.

"Naturaleza y artificio.: El ideal pintoresco en la arquitectura y el paisajismo contemporáneos"
Ed Gustavo Gili 2009.

Argullol. Rafael

"Atraccion del abismo, la. un itinerario por el paisaje romantico
Ed Ediciones Destino 1991.

"Tres miradas sobre el arte
Ed Ediciones Destino 2002.

"El cazador de instantes: Cuaderno de travesía (1990-1995)"
Ed El Acantilado 2007.

Ascher. Francois

"Los nuevos principios del urbanismo: El fin de las ciudades no está a la orden del día"
Ed Alianza editorial 2008

"Diario de un Hipermoderno"
Ed Alinaza editorial 2009

Augé. Marc

"Los no lugares. Espacios de anonimato. Una antropología de la sobremodernidad"
Ed Gedisa 2000.

"El tiempo en ruinas"
Ed Gedisa 2003.

Azua. Felix

"Diccionario de la Artes"
Ed Planeta 1996.

Bachelard. Gaston
"La poética del espacio"
Ed Fondo de Cultura Economica USA 1999.

"La intuición del instante"
Ed Fondo de Cultura Economica USA 2003.

Balmond. Cecil

"Informal"
Ed. Prestel 2007.

Bedor. Guy

"La sociedad del espectáculo
Ed Pretextos 2007.

Berger. John

"Te mando este rojo cadmio: Una correspondencia entre John Berger y John Christie"
Ed Actar 2000.

"Mirar"
Ed Gustavo Gili 2009.

Brinckerhoff Jackson. John

"The necessity for ruins"
Ed Massachusetts press 1980.

"A Sense of Place, a Sense of Time
Ed Yale University Press 1996.

Bru. Eduard

"Nous paisatges nous territoris"
Ed Actar 1989.

"Tres en el lugar"
Ed Actar 1997.

"Coming from the south"
Ed Actar 2002.

Cameron. Dan

"Nick Cave: Meet Me at the Center of the Earth
Ed Yerba Buena Center for the Arts 2010.

Collins, C.C. i G.C. , LE

"Camillo Sitte y el Nacimiento del Urbanismo Moderno"
Ed Gustavo Gili 1980

Conde Yago
"Arquitectura de la indeterminación"
Ed Actar 1994.

Costa. Xavier + Andreotti Libero

"Teoría de la deriva i altres textos situcionistes sobre la ciutat"
Ed Actar1996.

"Situacionistas"
Ed Actar 2000.

Dali. Salvador.

"Diario de un genio"
Ed Tusquets editores 2004

Deleuze. Giles

"El pliegue"
Ed Paidós 1989.

Deleuze. Giles + Guatari. Felix

"Mil Mesetas: Capitalismo y Esquizofrenia"
Ed Pre-Textos 1980.

Delgado. Manuel

"El animal público. Hacia una antropología de los espacios urbanos"
Ed Anagrama 1999.

Dethier. Jean +Guiheux Alain

"Visions Urbanes Europa 1870-1993. La ciutat de l'artista. La ciutat de l'arquitcte."
Ed Electa 1994.

Edmund Bacon
"Design of Cities: Revised Edition"
Ed Penguin (Non-Classics); Revised edition (May 20, 1976)

Español Llorens. Quim

"El orden frágil de la arquitectura"
Ed Fundación Caja de Arquitectos 2001.

"Forma i consistencia"
Ed Fundación Caja de Arquitectos 2008.

"El espacio intenso"

Friedman. Yona

"Hacia una arquitectura científica"
Ed Alianza Editorial 1971.

Galí Izard. Teresa
"Los mismos paisajes. Ideas e interpretaciones"
Ed Gustavo Gili 2006.

García-Germán. Javier

"De lo mecánico a lo termodinámico. Por una definición energética de la arquitectura y del territorio"
Ed Gustavo Gili 2010.

Hegemann. Werner

"Civic Art. American Vitruvius"
Ed Princeton Architectural Press, 1988.

Iribas. José Miguel

"El efecto Albacete. Una investigación territorial"
Ed Actar 2007.

Koolhaas. Rem

"Delirious New York"
Ed Monacelli Press 1994

"Mutations"
Ed Actar 2001.

"Small, Medium, Large, Extra-Large"
Ed Monacelli Press 2002.

"La Ciudad Genérica"
Ed Gustavo Gili 2006.

"Espacio Basura"
Ed Gustavo Gili 2008.

"Grandeza o el problema de la Talla"
Ed Gustavo Gili 2011.

Le Corbusier

"Como concebir el Urbanismo"
Ed. Infinito 2002

Lefaivre. Liane

"Aldo van Eyck. Humanist rebel"
Ed 010 publishers 1999.

Lermer. Jaime

"Acupuntura Urbana"
Ed IaaC 2004.

Lynch. Kevin

"La imagen de la ciudad"
Ed Gustavo Gili 1998.

Marina. Jose Antonio

"Elogio y refutación del ingenio"
Ed Anagrama 2004.

"La inteligencia fracasada"
Ed Anagrama 2010.

"Las culturas fracasadas: El talento y la estupidez de las sociedades"
Ed Anagrama 2011.

Marti Casanovas. Miquel

"Hacia una cultura urbana del espacio público. La experiencia de Barcelona (1999-2003).
Tesi Doctoral 2004.www\upccommons.upc.edu

Merleau-Ponty. Maurice

"Fenomenologia de la percepción"
Ed Peninsula 1975.

Michael. Sorkin

"Variaciones sobre un parque temático.: La nueva ciudad americana y el fin del espacio público"
Ed Editorial Gustavo Gili 2010.

Moure. Gloria

"Dan Graham"
Ed Fundacio Antoni Tapies (1 de mayo de 1998)

"Urban configurations2
Ed Poligrafa 1994.

"Tony Oursler"
Ed Poligrafa 2001.

"Gordon Matta-Clark. Obras y escritos"
Ed Poligrafa 2006

"Vito Acconci. Escritos, obras, proyectos"
Ed Poligrafa

Munford. Lewis

"La ciudad en la historia"
Ed Infinito 1979.

Muntadas. Antoni

"Muntadas On Translation"
Ed Actar 2002.

"Muntadas. la construcción del miedo y la pérdida de lo público"
Ed Diputacion de Granada 2008.

Muñoz. Juan
"Escritos"
Ed La central 2009.

Ockman. Joan
"Out of ground zero"
Ed. Preste 2002.

Parcerisa. Pep + Rubert de Ventós. Maria

"Materilas d'Urbanisme"
Ed ETSAB UPC. 1999.

"La ciudad no es una hoja en blanco"
Ed ARQ Chile 2000.

Peran. Martí

"Post-it City"
Ed CCCB 2008.

Perejaume

"Oisme: una escriptura naturala a partir del corquis pirinenc de Jacint Verdaguer"
Ed Edicions Proa 1998.

"Deixar de fer una exposició"
Ed Actar 1999.

"Ludwing Jujol"
Ed Ediciones Originales 2005.

"L'obra i la Por"
Ed Galaxia Gutemberg 2007.

"Tres dibujos de Madrid. Un accion con Perajaume"
Ed Anibal Rama Complutense 2008.

Quetglas. Josep

"Pasado a limpio I i II"
Ed Pre-textos 2002

"Pasado a limpio"
Ed Gustavo Gili 2004.

Risselada. Max

"Alison & Peter Smithson: From a House of the Future to a House of Today"
Ed 010 publishers 2004.

"Team 10"
Ed NAi Publishers 2006.

"Alison & Peter Smithson: A Critical Anthology"
Ed Poligrafa 2011.

Rossi. Aldo

"La arquitcteura de la ciudad"
Ed Gustavo Gili 1986.

Sennet. Richard

"El respeto"
Ed Anagrama 2009.

"La cultura del nuevo capitalsimo"
Ed Anagrama 2006.

"El artesano"
Ed Anagrama 2009.

"Carne y piedra: El cuerpo y la ciudad en la civilización occidental"
Ed Alianza Editorial 2010.

"El declive del hombre público"
Ed Anagrama 2011.

Serra Riera. Enric

"Geometria i el projecte del sòl als orígens de la Barcelona Moderna. La vila de Gracia"
Ed Universitat Politècnica de Catalunya 1995.

Sitte. Camillo

"Construcción de ciudades según principios artísticos (1889)"
Ed Gustavo Gili 1980.

Sloterdijk. Peter

"Esferas I: Burbujas. Microsferología"
Ed Siruela; Edición: 2007

Smithson. Alison & Peter

"Urban Structuring"
Ed Littlehampton Book Services Ltd 1967

"Ordinariness and Light: Urban Theories, 1952-1960 and Their Application in a Building Project, 1963-1970"
Ed The MIT Press 1970

"Changing the Art of Inhabitation"
Ed Watson-Guptill 1999

"AS IN DS: An Eye on the Road: Alison Smithson"
Ed Lars Muller Verlag; 1 edition 2001.

"The Charged Void: Architecture"
The Monacelli Press 2001.

"The Charged Void: Urbanism"
The Monacelli Press 2005.

Smitshon. Robert

"Robert Smithson: el paisaje entrópico : una retrospectiva, 1960-1973"
Ed IVAM 1993.

"Un recorrido por los monumentos de Passaic, Nuevo Yersey 1967"
Ed Gustavo Gili 2006.

de Solà Morales. Manuel

"Les formes del creixement Urbà"
Ed Universitat Politècnica de Catalunya 1997.

"De cosas urbanas"
Ed Gustavo Gili 2008.

"Deu lliçons sobre Barcelona"
Ed Col·legi d'arquitectes de Catalunya 2008.

de Solà Morales. Ignasi.

"Jujol"
Ed Ediciones Poligrafa 1991.
"Present i futurs"
Ed Col·legi d'arquitectes de Catalunya 1996.

"Minimal architecture in Barcelona"
Ed Architectural Press 1996.

"Diferencias: Topografía de La Arquitectura Contemporánealsncrip"
Ed Gustavo Gili 2000.

"Inscripciones"
Ed Gustavo Gili 2003.

"Territorios"
Ed Gustavo Gili 2003.
"Intervenciones
Ed Gustavo Gili 2003.

"Diferencias"
Ed Gustavo Gili 2003.

Sontag. Susan
"Estilos radicales"
Ed Santillana 2005

Soriano. Federico
"sin_tesis"
Ed Gsutavo Gili 2004.

Tatjer. Mercè

"Barraques. La Barcelona informal del segle XX"
Ed Institut de Cultura de Barcelona 2010.

Taut. Bruno

"Escritos expresionistas"
Ed El Croquis1997.

Thompson. D'arcy

"Sobre el crecimiento y la forma"
Ed Blume 1980.

Thorn. René

"Parábolas y catástrofes"
Ed Tusquets Editores 1993.

Torres. Elias

"Luz cenital"
Ed Col·legi d'arquitectes de Catalunya 2005.

Torres. Francresc

"Belchite.South Bronx"
Ed. University Gallery. University of Massachusetts 1988.

Tsukamoto.Yoshiharu + Kaijima. Momoyo

"Made in Tokyo: Guide Book
Ed Kajima Institute Publishing Co2001.

"Pet Architecture Guide Book Vol 2"
Ed World Photo Press, Japan 2002.

"Graphic Anatomy"
Ed Toto 2007.

Venturi. Robert

"Learnig from las Vegas" amb Scott Brown. Denise
Ed The MIT Press 1977.

"Complejidad y Contradicción en la Arquitectura
Ed Gustavo Gili 1994.

Vian. Boris

"L'escuma dels dies"
Ed Catedra 2007

Virilio. Paul

"Estética de la Desaparición"
Ed Jucar 1998

"El procedimento silencio"
Ed Paidós 2000.

"Unknown Quantity"
Ed Thames & Hudson (May 2003)

Wagensberg. Jorge

"Proceso al Azar"
Ed Tusquets 1996.

"Ideas sobre la complejidad del mundo"
Ed Tusquets editor 2002.

"Ideas Para La Imaginacion Impura
Ed Tusquets editor 2002.

"El Gozo Intelectual: Teoria y Practica Sobre la Inteligibilidad y la Belleza
Ed Tusquets editor 2007.

Walker. Enrique
"Lo Ordinario"
Ed Gustavo Gili 2010.

Acknowledgments

I have with no doubt managed to finish this research thanks to Enric Serra's intense and patient monitoring. His intelligent, opportune, accurate and sometimes also different points of view have been fundamental to be able to settle it, develop it and finally finish it. Without Enric this book would never have been published.

There have been many people that have joined and supported me during all these years but among all of them I would like to be grateful to Rosa Rull and Cristina Lladó for their suport; to Paula Poveda and Kathryn Dean for their comments and final indications; to Joan Mateu for his concise and indispensable Catalan corrections. And to Olga Velasco for her final sweet crucial push.

The always brilliant comments and ideas of Jordi Sardà have also been a key element to find the path in some decisive moments and to encourage me to continue the initiated work. And also Pep Parcerisa's aptitude to arrange the tangled material, his easy and clear suggestions and his demonstration of sincere interest has been fundamental to reach the final moment.

But above all, there are two people who have realized one of the most important parts of this research work. I am referring to Lluis Alexandre Casanovas and Daniel López Doriga, who have helped me to draw the public catalysts. Especially, this thesis would have never turned out as it is without Lluis Alexandre. His patience, skill, illusion and generous obsession have been fundamental to discover and to learn how to draw things that we had until then never even imagined that they existed. Thank you Lluis!

This publication arrives also thanks to Diputació de Barcelona who helped me during the research process with his Comerç Grant. Also thanks to the final support of the University of Virginia, especially to the Dean of the School of Architecture Kim Tanzer, the Research Grant Program and to Iñaki Alday chair of the Architecture Department. This book has arrived here thanks to Margaret Rew who has edited patiently all of the English text and Marcus Brooks who has carefully reviewed the drawings. I also thank Associate Professor Sanda Iliescu for exhibiting the catalyst drawings in the Deans Gallery and William Haynes for his generous help.

And, of course, to my parents. To my dad for his constant silence and infinite support and to my mum, Isabel, who helps me gain hours every day and to make the work be always a pleasure.

Against Indifference
Urban Catalysts

_Author:
Manuel Bailo Esteve

_Research and Drawings:
Special thanks to
Lluis Alexandre Casanovas Blanco

_Research Team
Mavi Hita
Daniel Lopez Doriga
Anna Mañosa
Paula Poveda
Ursa Tork

_Exhibition:
Marcus Brooks
William Haynes
Sanda Iliescu
Matthew Pinyan

This book is the result of the research developed for the PhD dissertation presented at the Escola Tècnica Superior d'Arquitectura de Barcelona on May the 25th 2012, obtaining a cum laude grade, in front the jury composed by: Iñaki Abalos, Jaime Coll, Quim Español, Gloria Moure, Yoshiharu Tsukamoto.

English translation:
Elia Canadell and Carlos Sanchez
Copy editing: Margaret Rew and Katherine Gleysteen

Copy editing:
Ana Tetas Palau

Graphic Design:
Papersdoc

Printed and bounded in China.

_English edition
Published by
Actar Publishers, New York,
Barcelona, 2015
www.actarpublishers.com

Distributed by
Actar D Inc.
New York
355 Lexington Avenue, 8th Floor
New York, NY 10017
T +1 212 966 2207
F +1 212 966 2214
salesnewyork@actar-d.com

Barcelona
Roca i Batlle 2
08023 Barcelona
T +34 933 282 183
salesbarcelona@actar-d.com
eurosales@actar-d.com

ISBN: 9781940291208
Library of Congress Control Number:
2015934392

A CIP catalogue record for this book is available from the Library of Congress, Washington, DC, USA.

Against Indifference **PUBLIC CATALYSTS**

Manuel Bailo Esteve

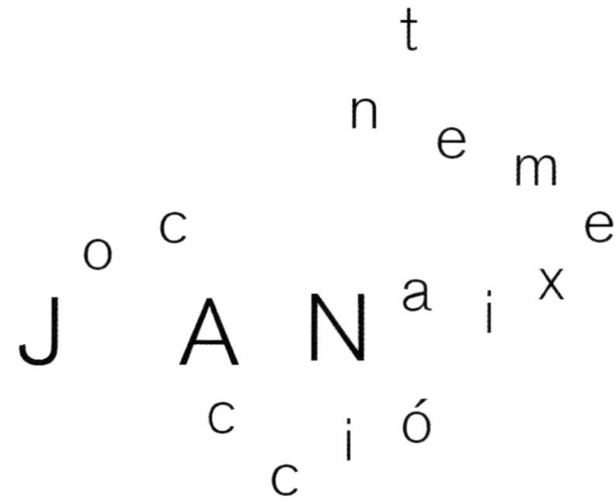
JAN
Joc
Acció
Naixement

INDEX

1. INTRODUCTION LABORATORY OF INDIFFERENCE 7

2. CASE STUDIES 11

CASE STUDY #1/ Bucharest. Comfortable capitalism 12

CASE STUDY #2/ Cineac. Outdoors 24

CASE STUDY #3/ Djemma el Fna. Carts, snakes and storytellers 32

CASE STUDY #4/ Farnese. And the anti-monumental bench 42

CASE STUDY #5/ Graciosa. Feet tickling 50

CASE STUDY #6/ Henderson and the chalk of identity 60

CASE STUDY #7/ Jujol. And the painted monument of king Jaume I 72

CASE STUDY #8/ Kinshasa. As thin as a thread 82

CASE STUDY #9/ NY. Hydrant water always writes in plural 98

CASE STUDY #10/ NY. Blackou 106

CASE STUDY #11/ Orion. Anti-graffiti Ossario 116

CASE STUDY #12/ Parets. And balanced shades 126

CASE STUDY #13/ Parkour. The practiced city 140

CASE STUDY #14/ Sao Paulo. Pixaçaos in the sky 148

CASE STUDY #15/ Seagram building. 50cm vs 15.700cm 156

CASE STUDY #16/ Tati. Public garbage 166

CASE STUDY #17/ Vian. Pink cloud 176

CASE STUDY #18/ Vistabella. And talk to shelves 186

CASE STUDY #19/ Xavier Ribas and active leisure 196

CASE STUDY #20/ Zocalo. A very thin shadow 206

3. AGAINST INDIFFERENCE NOTES ON THE DRAWINGS OF MANUEL BAILO. By Sanda Illiescu 215

1. INTRODUCTION
LABORATORY OF
INDIFFERENCE

INDIFFERENCE

The contemporary city is diffuse, it is an alive and complex organism; formed by empty spaces, thematic buildings, retails of urban unfinished textures, with an excess of construction; these are in many occasions places in contrast with the homogeneous historical centers. We live in cities that are characterized by the coexistence of spaces of homogeneous identity with informal places without meaning.

The generic city has become a reference in which most of us feel reflected. These are places of provisional identity transfer, weak and brief, the spaces of anonymity have become the values of our cities.

However, as Quim Español explains in his text "The intense space", even if we feel citizens of many places at the same time, and even if we feel that we can feel at home in many different places; in today's cities, both types of places need to coexist: the spaces of identity, and the places of the generic city. The contemporary city cannot exclude any of the two. Its beauty depends exactly on the fact of being a complex artifact, which is a consequence of both the voluntary and involuntary acts and constructions. Therefore, it is sure that reducing the city to a unique model is not recommendable. Quim Español himself says, "The places and the no-places have to build up a complex constellation of nodes in the nets of the global city."

DRAWING

In the Laboratory of Indifference, we have tried to work on the public spaces that belong to the over-modernity era. We have tried to discover what are the aspects that convert public spaces into active and vivacious places, an existential place, a place of identity, of civic expression and social representation. We have traveled through the territories of indifference, and we have been able to prove that there are moments of intensity there too.

PROCESS

We have worked with the conviction that a productive capacity of initiating processes is capable of opening research paths. We undoubtedly think that a good way of developing an investigation consists on starting by a hypothesis and following the intuition with the resources that we have.

In the Laboratory of Indifference, we have worked with the conviction that researching also means experimenting. We did not want to fall into the paralysis that is often provoked by the need of taking the right path. We preferred to somehow start and evolve. We have always worked with a reflexive intuition and with the certainty that a methodic and meticulous development would lead us to the next step in the progress of research. We have trusted and still trust in the strength of the actions to progress.

The experimentation taken place at the laboratory has lead us to prove our intuitions and also to take the most important decisions in the process of formulation of the thesis.

This thesis is constituted by two insoluble parts that have been developed simultaneously during these years of research. On one hand, in a theoretical frame, we have realized a study about the evolution of the city's places of socialization, taking the expert investigators in this matter as a key reference. On the other hand, we have realized an empirical and anatomic study of these places.

PERSONAL LABORATORY

In the laboratory, we have worked from the beginning with a tool that has helped us initiate the research more easily: drawing.

It is the architect's oldest tool that has helped us analyze and measure some situations that apparently seemed to have poor architectures. Those drawings have lead us to understand the internal structure, the situation, the geometry, and the relation between the different parts that constitute each one of the diverse public spaces that we have been working on. Therefore, if should allow this thesis to become some sort of operative instrument, like an anatomic study of the public space, that should help to think and imagine them with a new sensibility.

Somehow, this laboratory is also a personal one. It is a place where the personal experience has been the key element to start this investigation of the public space. The curious drawing and the personal glance are basic tools that must be used to understand the invisible structures of the public spaces of all times.

2. CASE STUDIES

România liberă
ASTRA
ASIGURĂRI
UNIQA
HAMILTON
KHAKI
BeLOWZERO
Piața
Unirii
LIVE
UNBUTTONED.
Levi's
501
EDOX
McDonald's
gorenje
Kentucky
Fried
Chicken
DeFacto
AXI
ratb
CITARO

Calei Victoriei. Bucharest, Romania, 2008.

Photography M.B.E

CASE STUDY # 1

BUCHAREST. COMFORTABLE CAPITALISM

cataloging

.03 *Construction of trading and leisure infrastructures*

.05 *Scale mediation*

catalyst

ADVERTISEMENTS

example

Savage Cap talism at the Civic Center of Bucarest.

date

1989-Present.

author

Commercial companies on the urban plan designed by Nicolau Ceaucescu.

address

Calea Victoriei. Bucarest, Romania.

description

VENTURIAN EXPERIENCIES ON DICIATORSHIP URBANISM

Ceaucescu's urban plan destroyed the center of Bucharest, known as the " Eastern Paris". Decades later, the uncontrolled capitalism has returned the place into the human scale: the ads cover with colors, figures and messages the monumental socialist buildings flanking the streets.

CASE STUDY #1

BUCHAREST

Bibliography

"Palau del Poble". *Ioana Marinescu.*
Quaderns d' Arquitectura i Urbanisme, n. 238 (Barcelona: COAC)

"El trencaclosques". *Ioana Marinescu.*
Quaderns d' Arquitectura i Urbanisme, n. 238 (Barcelona: COAC)

"El nou Capitalisme, el nou Aillament". *Richard Sennett.*
Quaderns d' Arquitectura i Urbanisme, n. 238 (Barcelona: COAC)

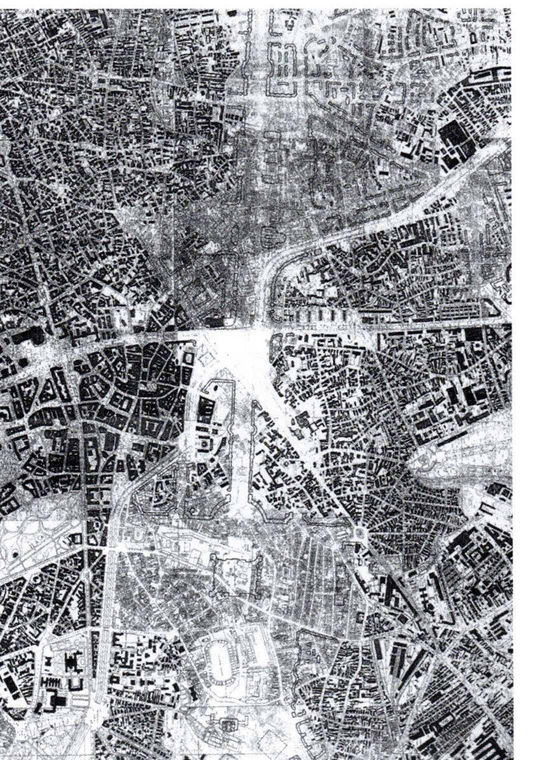

Urbanist Ceaucescu

It's impressive "to have a walk" using Goggle Earth over the city of Bucharest. It's actually quite worrying to discover Ceaucescu's concrete-curtain buildings, extended indifferently over the city, trying to construct a fake scenery that conceals the reality of its people without freedom. It is possible to imagine the atrocities that this dictator was capable of realizing, just by observing the photomap of the city.

Ceaucescu, a delirious despot, seized power of Romania in March, 1974. His political idea of constructing a "socialist society with a multilateral development". In order to achieve that, he organized a program of homogenization of the population, consistent, in many occasions, of devastating villages and relocating its inhabitants in new "modern" housing estates.

The construction of the Civic Center

His political program also included the reform of the country's capital, Bucharest. In 1977, after a strong earthquake that destroyed the city, Ceaucescu decided to place his new residence and the new center of the country's power in the old part of Bucharest, supposedly replacing only the harmed ones. However, influenced by the monumental North Korean aesthetics and with the idea of placing these new buildings in the least seismic zone, or in other words, in the least affected neighborhood; he knocked down more than 40.000 houses, removed hundreds of thousands of inhabitants of the historical neighborhoods and leveled the hill of the central area of Bucharest. The architect Ioana Marinescu, gathers diverse interviews of survivors of that barbarism, in her report on the memory and the identity of Romania. With sadness, the damaged families remember how, in a few days, they were removed to allow that the president Ceaucescu could locate his house, the new Palace of the People, and the avenue of Victory, with three kilometers of length, over their houses.

CONCRETE CURTAINS

Richard Sennett, in his article "The new capitalism, the new isolation", comments that modern society, based on flexible work, has ended up building indifferent cities. According to Sennett, the flexible work has finished substituting the model of long-term work. The idea of being faithful to a single enterprise during an entire work career has been replaced by the execution of sporadic jobs consisting of specific and limited tasks. Sennet puts forward how this new capitalism, that demands flexibility to survive, ended up creating neutral and impersonal areas; areas with the capacity of being modified with ease. Sennet maintains that flexible time is consecutive, instead of accumulative: a project is developed in the first place, then, when finished, another one takes place, even if it's not related to the first one, and so on.

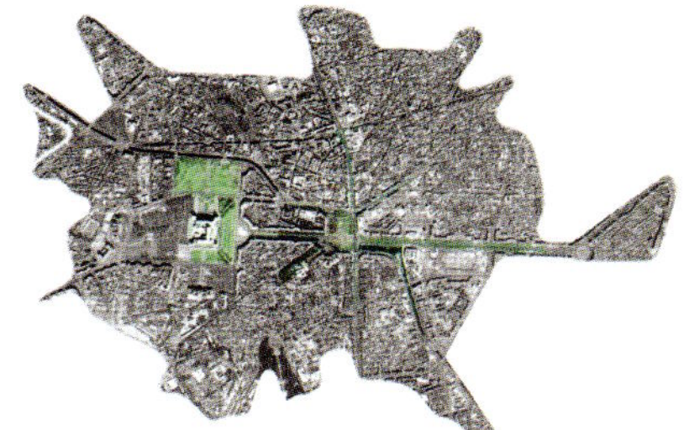

Site plan / Calea Victoriei. Bucarest,

The arrival of capitalism

In the Avenue of Victory of Bucharest, Ceaucescu tried to erase any track of the accumulative time of the history of Romania. He thought that he could suppress the identity of a whole nation by destroying the architecture of the capital's historical center. Ceaucescu was trying to raise a new "communist" space of relation, by devastating the history and constructing a few new heavy concrete buildings above it. Although his monumental urban project tried to become consolidated by repeating and extending the model of concrete curtains to other neighborhoods of the city, it was always, from the beginning, a failed urban project. The Avenue of Victory and the rest of the streets that Ceaucescu executed were empty, dead spaces and without any type of activity.

It wasn't until the arrival of capitalism and trade that a new, light and flexible curtain, support of commercial propaganda, was superposed to the concrete fronts of the streets planned by Ceaucescu; and these have turned those dead spaces into real spaces indeed.

The appearance of commerce has suddenly gathered the presence of the accumulative time, the weight of the history, and the consecutive time of this new capitalism in the same place; magically constructing the most important spaces of relation of the city.

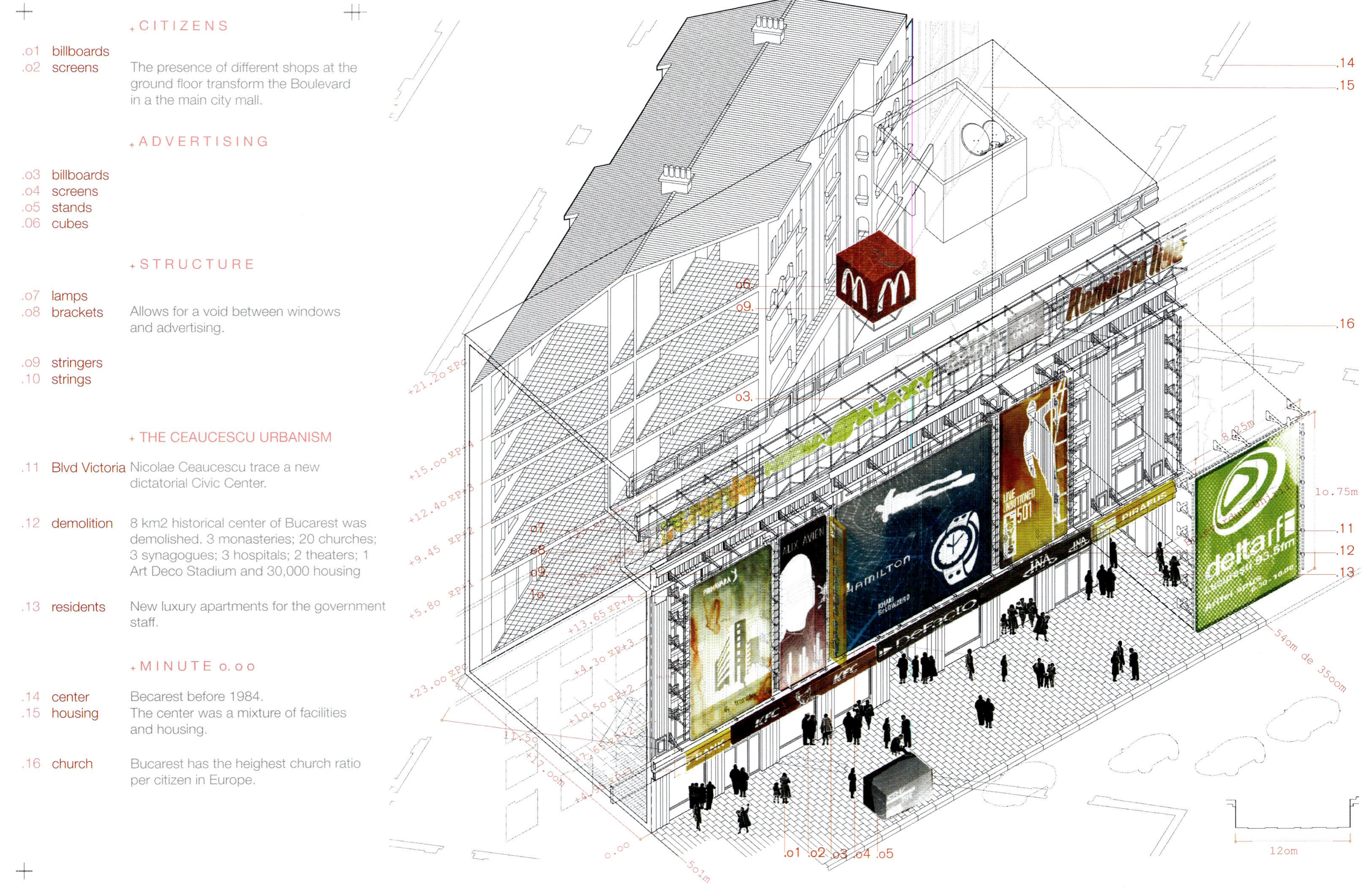
+CITIZENS
.o1 billboards
.o2 screens
The presence of different shops at the ground floor transform the Boulevard in a the main city mall.
+ADVERTISING
.o3 billboards
.o4 screens
.o5 stands
.06 cubes
+STRUCTURE
.o7 lamps
.o8 brackets
Allows for a void between windows and advertising.
.o9 stringers
.10 strings
+ THE CEAUCESCU URBANISM
.11 Blvd Victoria
Nicolae Ceaucescu trace a new dictatorial Civic Center.
.12 demolition
8 km2 historical center of Bucarest was demolished. 3 monasteries; 20 churches; 3 synagogues; 3 hospitals; 2 theaters; 1 Art Deco Stadium and 30,000 housing
.13 residents
New luxury apartments for the government staff.
+MINUTE o.oo
.14 center
.15 housing
Becarest before 1984.
The center was a mixture of facilities and housing.
.16 church
Bucarest has the heighest church ratio per citizen in Europe.
+21.2o
+15.oo
+12.4o
+9.45
+5.8o
+23.oo
+13.65
+4.3o
+1o.5o
+7.65
+17.oom
11.5o
o.oo
5o1m
54om de 35oom
8.25m
1o.75m
12om
o6.
o9.
o3.
o7
o8
o9
1o
.14
.15
.16
.11
.12
.13
.o1 .o2 .o3 .o4 .o5
GALAXY
HAMILTON
KFC
INA
PIRAEUS
deltarfi
România liberă

+CITIZENS

.o1 billboards
.o2 screens

The presence of different shops at the ground floor transform the Boulevard in a the main city mall.

+ADVERTISING

.o3 billboards
.o4 screens
.o5 stands
.06 cubes

+ STRUCTURE

.o7 lamps
.o8 brackets

.o9 stringers
.10 strings

Allows for a void between windows and advertising.

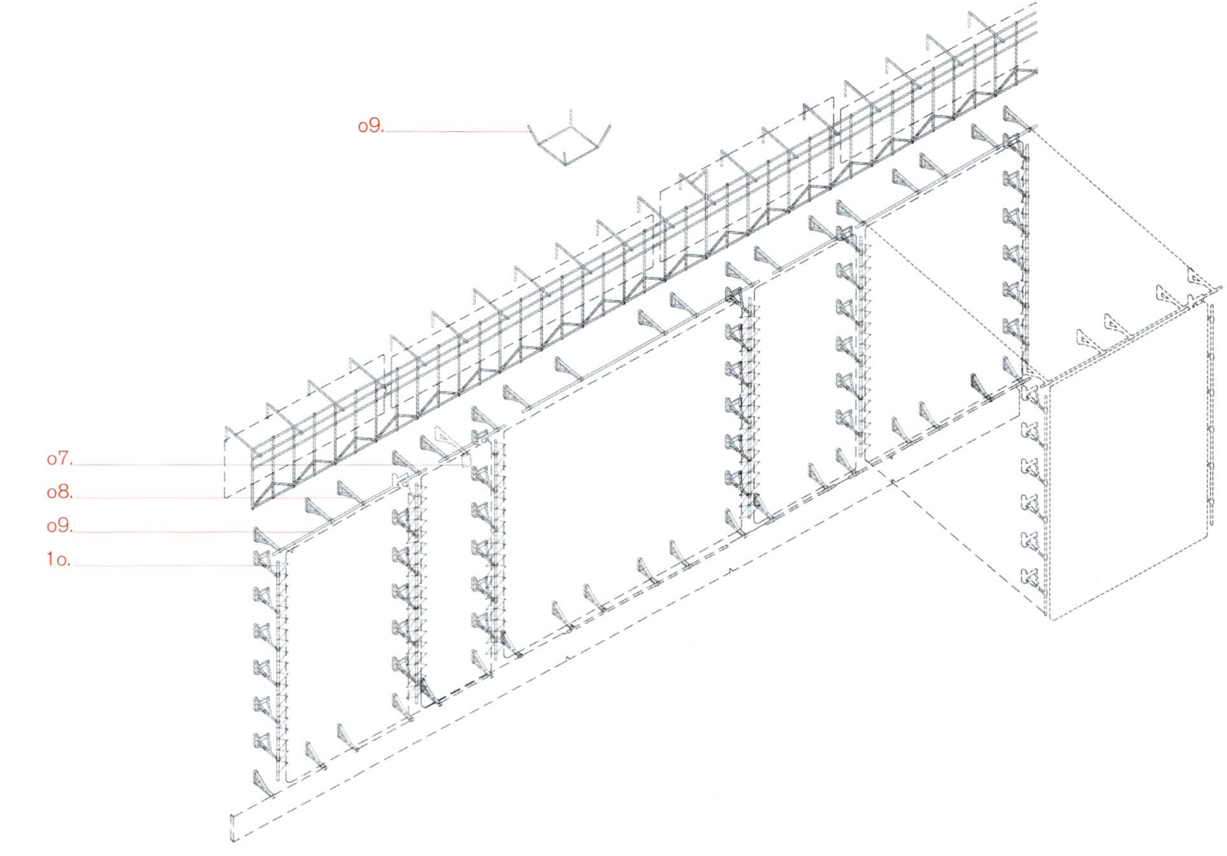

+ THE CEAUCESCU URBANISM

.11 **Blvd Victoria** Nicolae Ceaucescu trace a new dictatorial Civic Center.

.12 **demolition** 8 km2 historical center of Bucarest was demolished. 3 monasteries; 20 churches; 3 synagogues; 3 hospitals; 2 theaters; 1 Art Deco Stadium and 30,000 housing

.13 **residents** New luxury apartments for the government staff.

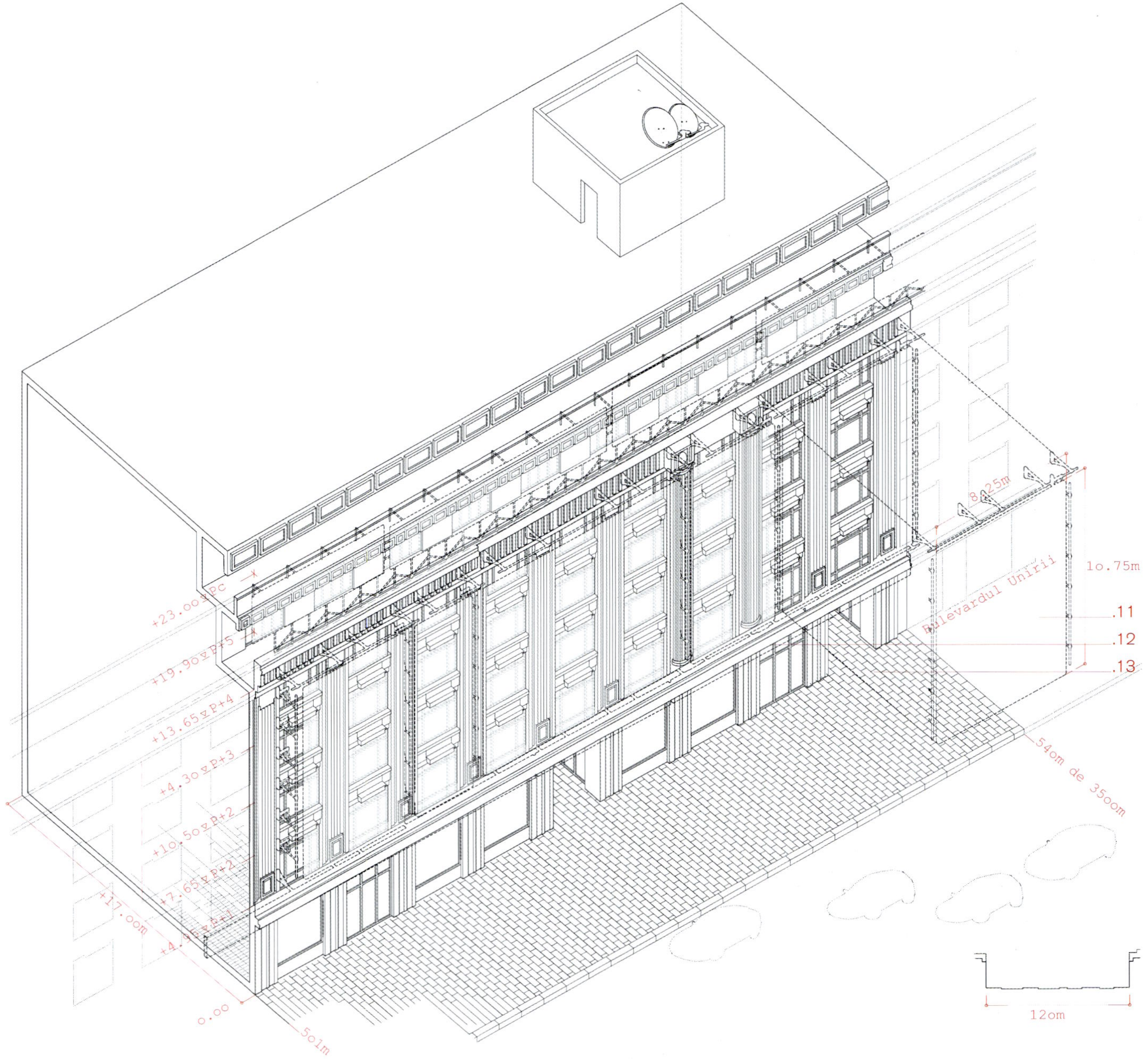

+MINUTE 0.00

.14	center	Becarest before 1984.
.15	housing	The center was a mixture of facilities and housing.
.16	church	Bucarest has the heighest church ratio per citizen in Europe.

CINEAC
CINEAC

CASE STUDY #2

CINEAC OUTDOORS

CINEAC
J Duiker, J Handelsblad. Amsterdam 1934

Photography M.B.E

cataloging	
.05	*Scale mediation*
.03	Construction of trading and leisure infrastructures
catalyst	ILLUMINATED SIGN
example	Urban Scaler Hendelsblad Cineac Amsterdam
date	1933-34
author	Jan Duiker
address	Reguliersbreetstraat, 31-33 CM, Amsterdam The Netherlands / CP: 1017

description

SKYLINES
MARQUEES

Found in Amsterdam's skyline, the experimental outdoor cinema Cineac is placed using the foundations of a pre-existing construction. Its illuminated sign stands out from the neighbor buildings and places the project in its site, catalyzing public space beside it.

CASE STUDY #2

CINEAC

Bibliography

Jan Duiker Works and projects. Jan Molema. Barcelona: Gustavo Gili.

Duiker: interior del Cineac de Amsterdam 1934. Mariano Bayon. Madrid: Rueda.

Duiker. Architect of a new era. Jan Molema. (Delft: TU Delft)

Modern architecture in the city

If you walk at night along the narrow streets of downtown Amsterdam, it is surprising to discover the luminous sign of the CINEAC. The challenging scale of the sign, placed strangely at 45 ° on the corner of the building, insinuates a mysterious force that comes from the interior. This project realized by the provocative Jan Duiker in 1934 is a sample of the interest of this architect, always relating his architecture with the city. Duiker, known fundamentally because he introduced the new technological systems discovered at the beginning of the century to the construction world; was able to formalize a new architecture without adornments and historicisms, thanks to the intelligent and sensitive use of these materials. It's an architect who designs his projects not as isolated objects but as pieces that form a part of a complex urban system.

The CINEAC is a clear example of how modern architecture is projected from the city, the same way as the Nirwana Flats in The Hague or the Outdoors school in Amsterdam.

The Nirwana Flats (1927) are not only a few houses constructed with an innovative structure of concrete, they were thought with a new type of housing program that concentrated all the facilities to provide more free time to their users. Apart from that, they also represent the proposal of a new hybrid typology between the tower and the block.

Architecture and healthy air

The project of the School in Amsterdam (1929) is part of the program of outdoors schools initiated in The United States for sick or weak children. These schools, constituted by associations of teachers, parents and doctors, were following a new school program in which the classes were brief and had place fundamentally outdoors.
It was a new educational system in which the contact with nature was a key value of these new buildings. Spacious porches that protected the pupils from the rain and wind, wide courts with thick gardens and classrooms with big windows would be some of the elements that would define the image of these new equipments.
For Duiker, the Outdoors School of Amsterdam represents not only the opportunity to test the application of the new constructive systems, but also a magnificent exercise of how to place a building in the city. After six different proposals, the school ends up inside the interior yard of a housing block, constitutes an important example of how a project is capable of relating the interior patio of a block with the street. Duiker proposed to let the air enter inside the patio, by opening a hole in one of the sides of the perimeter of the housing block by means of a "door-building" and to place the Outdoors school in the interior yard of the block, orientating the windows towards the "door-building", as if they were expecting to receive the exterior air from the street.

Site plan / Reguliersbreetstraat. Amsterdam.

CINEAC OUTDOORS

The project of the CINEAC (1934) is a project that interacts with the city, but it also represents an exercise of development of a new program by means of the application of new constructive systems.

As Duiker himself said, "the CINEAC was thought as a machine". It is a building projected with enough technical criteria to return the credibility that the architects had lost by then. Duiker thought that modern architecture was capable of giving technical and not decorative solutions to the problems that the clients and the projects were raising. The CINEAC was thought from the beginning as a project that had to be constructed with a very tight budget. For this reason, Duiker proposed to construct the building with a light metallic structure that, with few points of support, would be capable of using the foundations that already existed in the site. The building, which was constructed with some very ingenious constructive solutions, was proposing a natural air circulation system that was assuring a tight cost of maintenance of the equipment.

The CINEAC is a project that is formalized by the constant circulation of air conditioning and the permanent movement of people going in and out of the building. Duiker uses the street as a foyer of access and organizes the spectators queue under a small porch that distributes them to the different levels of the cinema.
According to Duiker, the theater is projected attending to acoustic issues, with a paraboloid that restrains itself on the metallic structure.
The screen is at the end of the paraboloid, on a black frame that makes it "float in the space".
The movement of people, the air circuit and the sound of the loudspeakers translates the sign CINEAC outdoors in a way that makes it turn into a catalyst of the streets of downtown Amsterdam.

"The deck was holding an immense metal framework with a luminous sign that could be seen from any point of downtown. It is like a little man in a crowd of people that wants to call attention and has to raise a sign with a stick in order to be seen by the people around him. This way of doing it is a bit pretentious.

Jan Duiker

+ CITIZENS

.o1 **viewers** the billboard organizes the line

.o2 **canopy** redraws and collects the people to the box office

+ CLAIM

.o1 **billboard** the structure of the cinema pops up and hangs outside the billboard. Las Vegas before Las Vegas

.o2 **structure**

+ MINUTE o.oo

.o5 **skyline** domes, chimneys and roofs define the context at the height of the CINEAC billboard

.o6 **street** Reguliersbreestraat

.o7 **foundations** Duiker designed the Cineac over an existing foundation

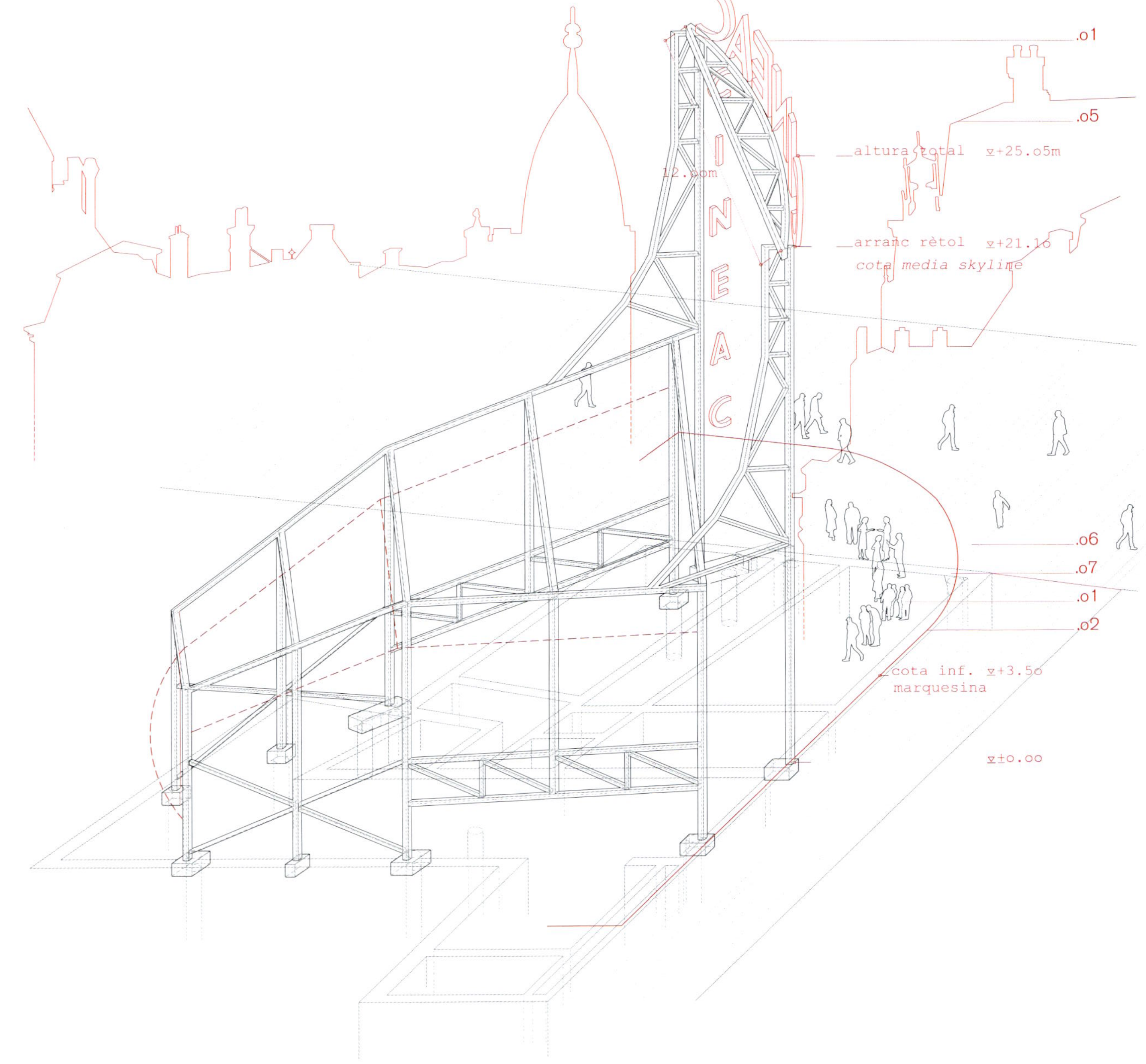

+ CITIZENS

.o1 **viewers** the billboard organizes the line

.o2 **canopy** redraws and collects the people to the box office

+ CLAIM

.o1 **billboard** the structure of the cinema pops up and hangs outside the billboard. Las Vegas before Las Vegas

.o2 **structure**

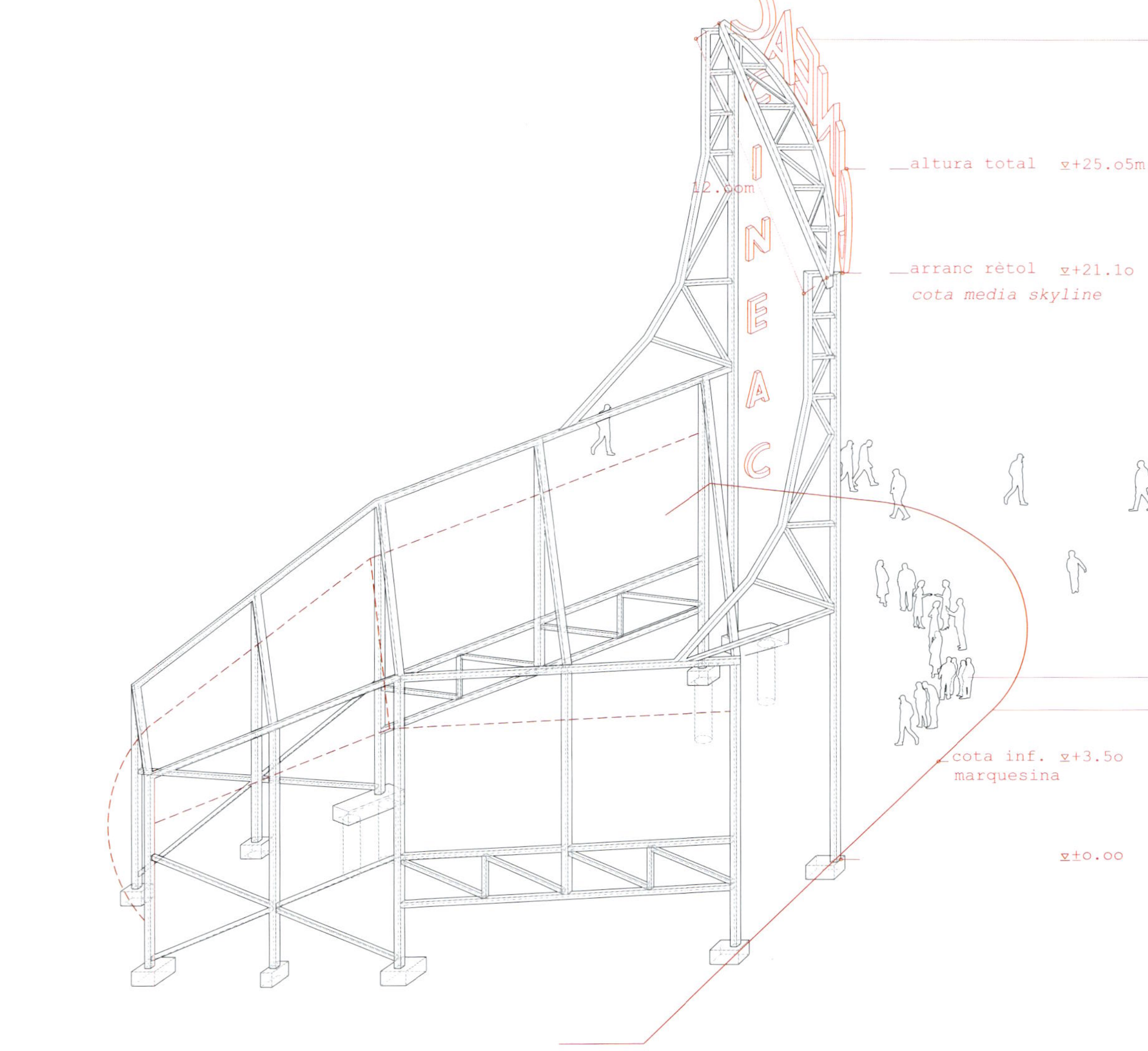

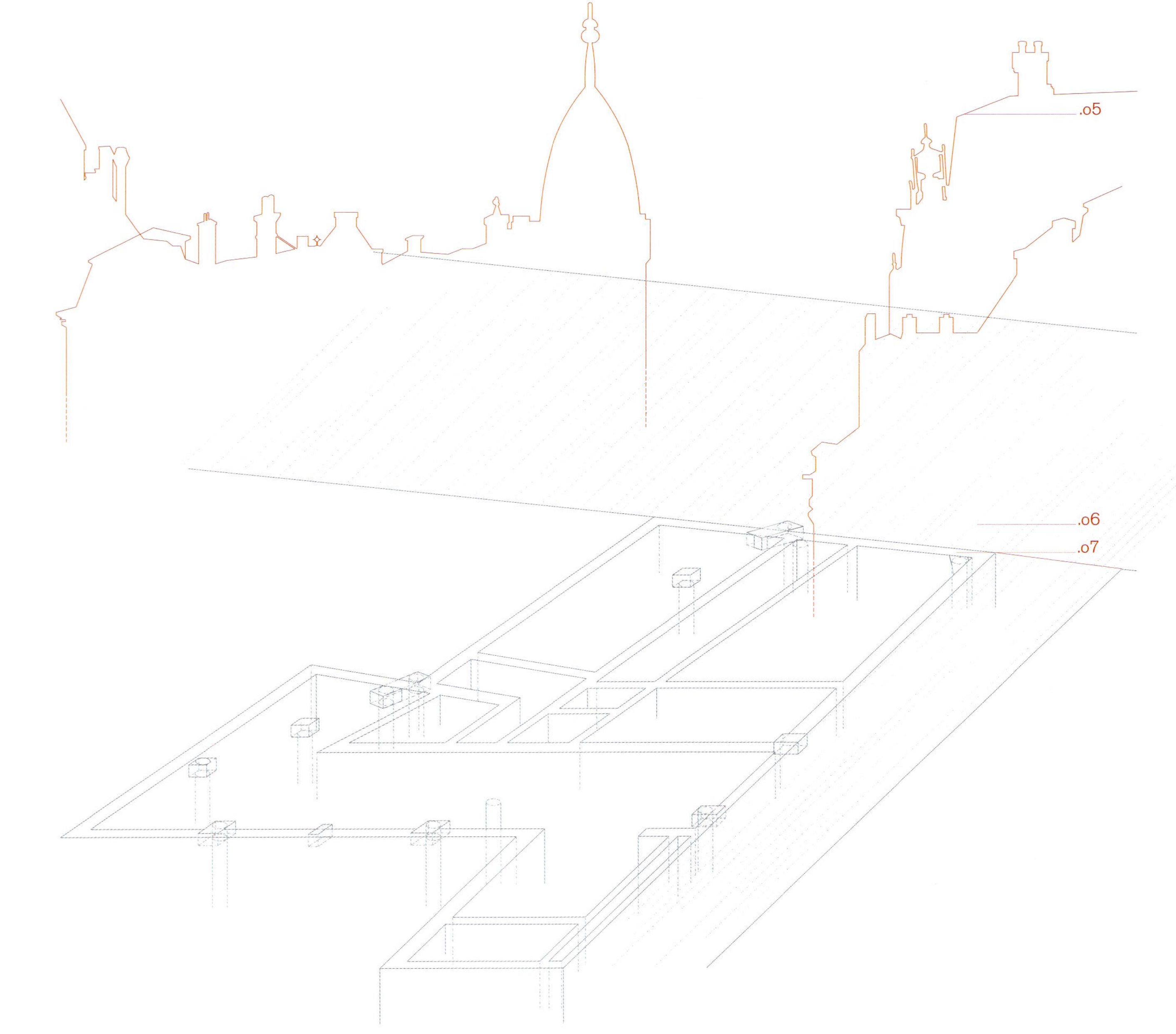

+ MINUTE o.oo

.o5	skyline	domes, chimneys and roofs define the context at the height of the CINEAC billboard
.o6	street	Reguliersbreestraat
.o7	foundations	Duiker designed the Cineac over an existing foundation

CASE STUDY #3

DJEMMA EL-FNA. CARTS, SNAKES AND STORYTELLERS

Xai's party day. Marrakech 2006.

Photography M.B.E

Cataloging	
.03	*Construction of trading and leisure infrastructures*
.01	*Environmental modification*
.02	*Interpretation and manipulation of pop culture elements*
catalyst	ORAL TRADE
example	Spaces of Oral and Intangible Heritage of Humanity Djemma El Fna Marrakech
date	1070 -Today
author	Traders and spectators
address	Jemma El Fna Square

description

INTANGIBLE
ORAL
MIXTURE
DIFFERENCE

It is a place that has always wanted to preserve the mixture and difference as urban conditions; as its essential vocation. The strength of the Jemma El Fna Square does not rely on its shape or on its architectural project, but on the oral and immaterial aspects of the place.

CASE STUDY #3

DJEMMA EL-FNA

Bibliography

"El partimonio de la plaza Jemma el Fna de Marrakech: entre lo material i lo inmaterial". Ouidad Tebbaa.

"Las mil i una noches de Xemáa el Fna". Juan Goytisolo.

"Discours d'ouverture de la réunion du jury por la proclamation des chefs d'oeuvre du Patrimoine Oral e Immatériel de l'Humanité". Juan Goytisolo.

A rich and austere space

The Jemma el Fna Square has been a fundamental example for the development of this work on public catalysts. Its singularity and difference with regard to the classic European squares has served us to find out which are the necessary conditions for a public space to be vivacious. To study an urban place constructed from austerity, without material or architectural resources, has all lead us to discover the essence of the public space.

The experience of visiting the Jemma el Fna Square has been essential to understand a public space that is characterized by its spatial informality.

During the first visits, you get shocked by the frenetic movements of the people, the noise, the yelling, the intense smells, the smoke and heat; you discover a disordered and spontaneous public space, one that has been built freely and stimulating imagination. It is a place that has always wanted to preserve the mixture and difference as urban conditions; as its essential vocation. It is a fascinating public space, formed by the mixture of different cultures, ethnic groups, generations and social classes.

A dissonant environment, confined by the chaos of images, rich and poor together, both country and cosmopolitan people, active and idle, old and young; all this mixture without minding about their origin, social condition, age, political color, either religion or social condition.

Once you are able to leave behind Jemma el Fna's atmospheric charm, you start to realize that there's a total absence of architecture in the space of the square.

The fortune of having met with Marrakech's city exactly on the day of the sacred holiday of the slaughter of the Lamb was crucial. It was a key moment, because it is the only day of the year that you are able to visit the square totally empty, without people or activity, and to discover the importance of the minor scale to construct the public space. The absence of cars, stops, stalls, storytellers, snake charmers, etc; It was suddenly exhibiting a totally naked public space. A raw, ordinary and marginal place.

Goytisolo proposes the oral patrimony

The writer Juan Goytisolo moved to Marrakech in the 70's seduced by the poetic charm of this

peculiar square; and became the promoter of its new heritage category.

His long walks around the square helped him understand the oral and intangible value of the space, while he observed the jugglers, the snake charmers, the musicians, the singers and dancers, etc.

In 1997, Goytisolo convinced the UNESCC to create a new program that would define the Spaces of Oral and Intangible Heritage of Humanity. The aim of this new category consisted of protecting some activities that were ancestral traditions, in continuous renovation, and very tied to the city. On the 18th of May of 2001, the

Site plan / Jemma El Fna Square

UNESCO declared the Jemma el Fna Square the Oral and Intangible Heritage of Humanity.

CARTS, SNAKES AND STORYTELLERS

The fortuitous visit to the square on the day of the Lamb let us recognize the value that Goytisolo was announcing and demanding.

The strength of this public space does not rely on its shape or on its architectural project, but on the oral and immaterial aspects of the place.

Through the drawing of the transitory spaces of these catalysts, we have been able to distinguish between two types of activities. Some catalysts are of reduced mobility and are placed with precision on the paving that is traced following the "Zoco el Bahja" façade. And some others, more nomadic, circulate around the square without a precise or fixed position.

CONSTRUCTED CATALYSTS
.o1 cars
.o2 stall
MOBILE CATALYSTS
.o3 snake charmer
.o4 water man
MINUTE o.oo
.o6 Djemaa El-Fna
Public space precedent. An active placewithout an architectural design.
.o7 pavement
Continuous carpet that allows any activity.
.o8 facade
The porch becomes a geometrical reference. The pavement is sited as a grid taking the facade corner.
X Y
X
X
Y
Y
o1.
o2.
o3.
o4.
o5.
o6.
o7.
o8.
textos fitxa?

+ CONSTRUCTED CATALYSTS

.o1 cars
.o2 stall

o1.

o2.

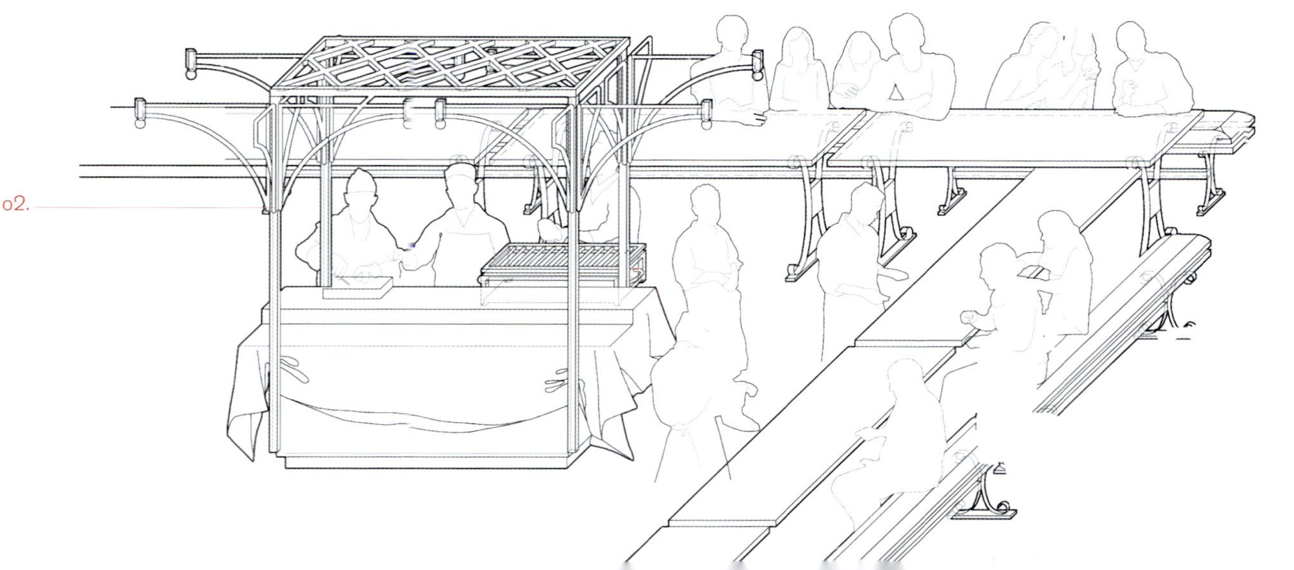

+ MOBILE CATALYSTS
.03 snake charmer
.04 water man
03.
05.
04.

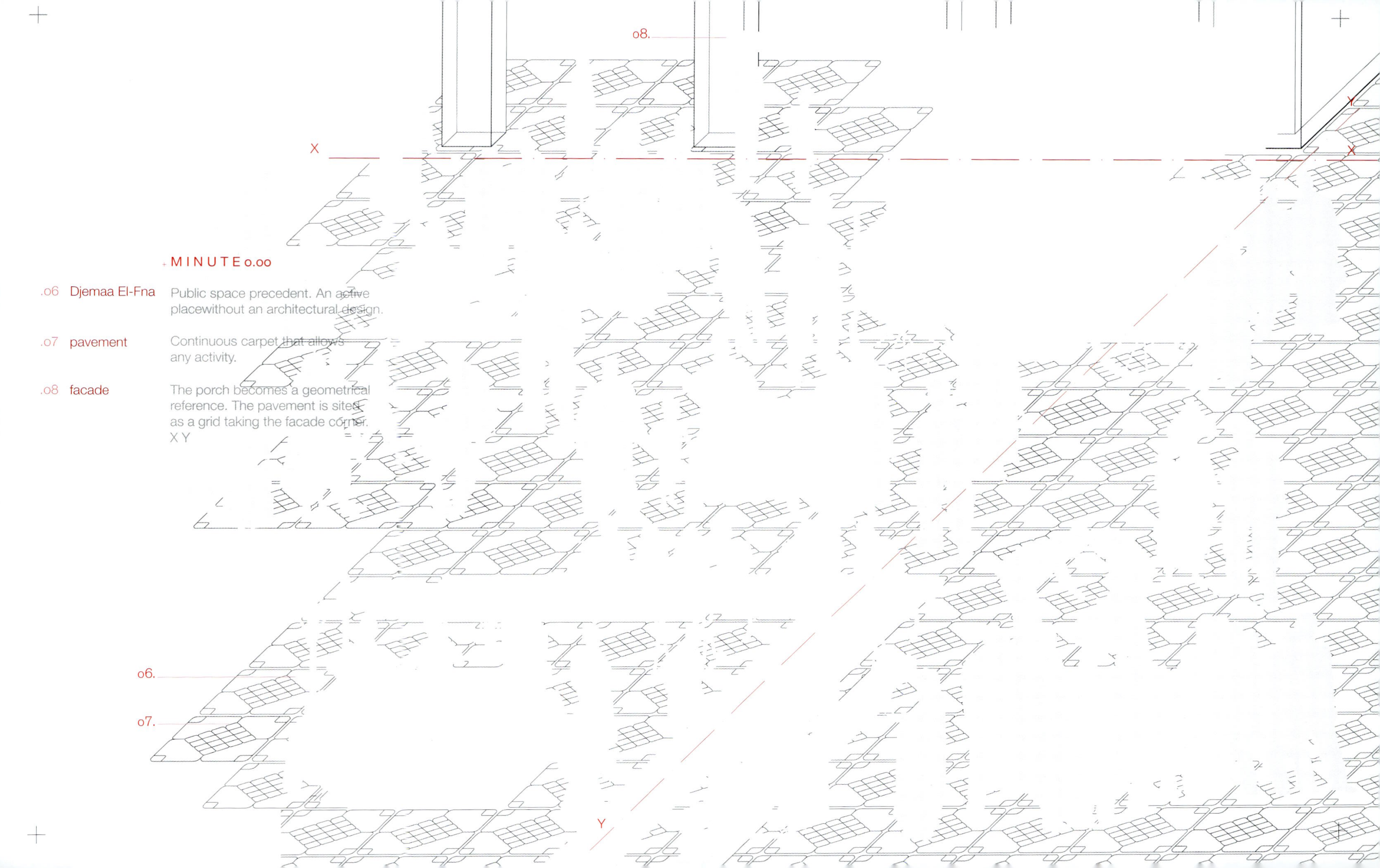

MINUTE o.oo

.o6	Djemaa El-Fna	Public space precedent. An active placewithout an architectural design.
.o7	pavement	Continuous carpet that allows any activity.
.o8	facade	The porch becomes a geometrical reference. The pavement is sited as a grid taking the facade corner. X Y

Palazzo Farnese
Rome 2005

Photography MBE

CASE STUDY #4

FARNESE AND THE ANTI-MONUMENTAL BENCH

cataloging	
.05	*Scale mediation*
.03	*Construction of trading and leisure infrastructures*
catalyst	BENCH
example	Minor element balances the scales of the place Palazzo Farnese Rome
date	1495 - Nowadays
author	A. Sangallo; Miquel Àngel; Vignola; G della Porta.
address	Farnese Square

description

MONUMENTAL
DISPROPORTION
ACCOMMODATE
OVERLAP

In the anonymous engraving from 1541, we can see the overlapping of Sangallo's work over the preexisting building of the former Ferriz Palace, already showing the bench in the basement of the façade. It was a catalyst responsible for accommodating the giant proportions of the Palazzo with the persons and the city.

CASE STUDY #4

FARNESE

Bibliography

La arquitectura de Miguel Angel. James S. Ackerman. (Madrid: Celeste)

Miguel Angel arquitecto. Giulio Carlo Argan – Bruno Contardi. (Milan: Electa)

Jumping over uniformity

In 1495 the Cardinal Alejandro Farnesio began the purchase of the Ferriz Palace to the agustinos of the Popolo Plazza in Rome. Later, little by little, he continued to acquire the free adjacent areas. The cardinal's idea was to construct a new great Renaissance palace with the merchants' and political Florentines' style. Farnesio wanted to raise a monumental building that would follow the new urban residential architectural fashion that would be capable of expressing and symbolizing the power and the progress of a new social class. The Renaissance architects designed their projects with relation to the city, in a different way that was based in skipping one of the basic principles of the medieval ordinances of building: the uniformity.

The newly rich Florentine merchants were at that time constructing palaces that transgressed the uniform order of the city. They wanted singular buildings of extreme individuality; palaces of gigantic proportions thought more for being observed rather than for being inhabited.

In 1913 Alejandro Farnesio entrusted the construction of the Palazzo Farnese to the young architect Antonio Sangallo. The project, which lasted more than fifty years, is a good example of hybrid architecture, capable of having fused different architectures from two rival architects with different styles. How many times the Palazzo Farnese is claimed only to Michelangelo, when in fact, the façade, which is the most known and studied part of the project, was projected much more by Sangallo than by Michelangelo.

Add project

The palazzo is a dense project, formed by the overlapping of

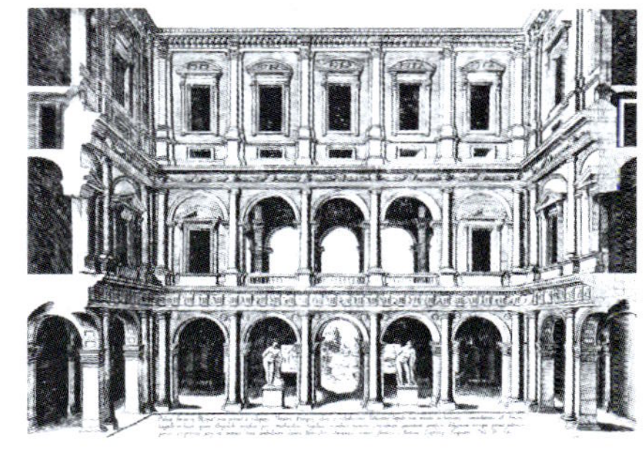

different interventions. It exemplifies a complex type of architecture for its rich and fragile hybrid integrity.

The works of the palace began in 1915 and had a difficult continuity, due to the limited financial capacity of the cardinal up to 1927. This fact obliged the works to stop. In 1934, when Alejandro Farnesio was chosen as the new Pope Paul III, Sangallo decided to modify the project of the palace for it to best express the new social status of its owner. When the works restarted in 1941, the façade was only at the height of the first floor. In 1946, after Sangallo's death, the unfinished project ends up in Michelangelo's hands (Vasari).

ANTI-MONUMENTAL BENCH

Michelangelo received the unfinished works of the palace with and un-finished second floor windows in the main façade. However, it is surprising how, in spite of his little interest for Sangallo's work, he managed to continue the project discovering and promoting the values that Sangallo had already initiated.

Michelangelo, who understood the singularity of the Palazzo's stairs, proposed a series of interventions that would improve the dialog of the immense proportions of the building with the city.

Proportions, scale and city

Michelangelo only proposed three variations to Sangallo's initial project for the main façade: to extend the dimensions of the new cornice, to increase the height of the second floor and to modify the scale and the form of the shield and of the central window. But the interesting part of Michelangelo's intervention is not only the projects that he proposed, but also the verification of how the giant proportions of the Palazzo served him as an excuse to raise a new way of relating the building with the city and the landscape.

An integral exercise of stairs with projects that go from small interventions up to proposing a new interior court that relates to the posterior garden of the palace and that jumps, with a hypothetical bridge, to the other coast of the Tiber River. A system of proposals places the giant proportions of the façade between the

landscape and the city. Lafréry's engraving demonstrates how the presence of the landscape is an important element from the interior of the court. And Beatritzet's engraving shows how Michelangelo needed to project the public space of the Popolo's Square in front of the palace. In this last engraving we can observe how these axes that continue the width of each one of the façade modules spreads over the ground. forming its pavement. This is a clear way of giving the façade a third dimension that is not only projected on the public space of the square but that also slips past through the lateral streets.

The Bench

But in this fascinating system of relations of scales that Michelangelo established, it is curious to discover how there is an element in the main façade that, in spite of all the series of interventions that he proposed, was kept intact from the first engraving that exists from the works of the palace. In the anonymous engraving from 1541, we can see the overlapping of Sangallo's work with the preexisting building of the former Ferriz Palace, already showing the bench in the basement of the façade. The bench was the catalyst responsible for accommodating the giant proportions of the Palazzo with the persons and the city. A minor element, but at the same time indispensable, capable of constructing a place for the "popolo" and activating the square.

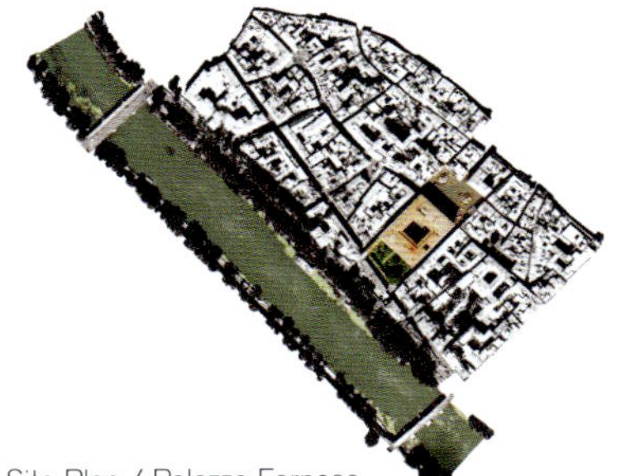

Site Plan / Palazzo Farnese

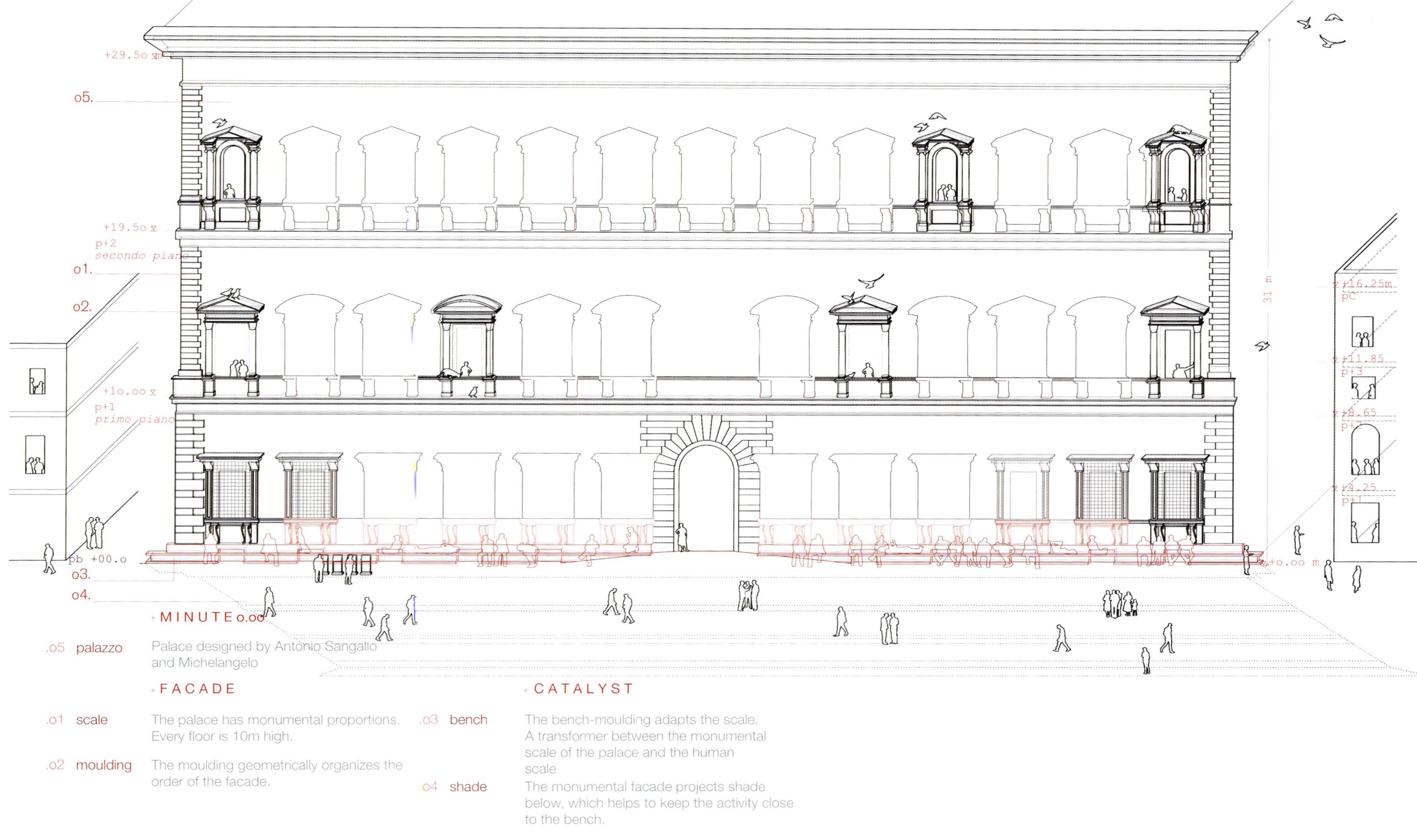

+ **MINUTE 0.00**

.05 **palazzo** Palace designed by Antonio Sangallo and Michelangelo

+ **FACADE**

.01 **scale** The palace has monumental proportions. Every floor is 10m high.

.02 **moulding** The moulding geometrically organizes the order of the facade.

+ **CATALYST**

.03 **bench** The bench-moulding adapts the scale. A transformer between the monumental scale of the palace and the human scale

.04 **shade** The monumental facade projects shade below, which helps to keep the activity close to the bench.

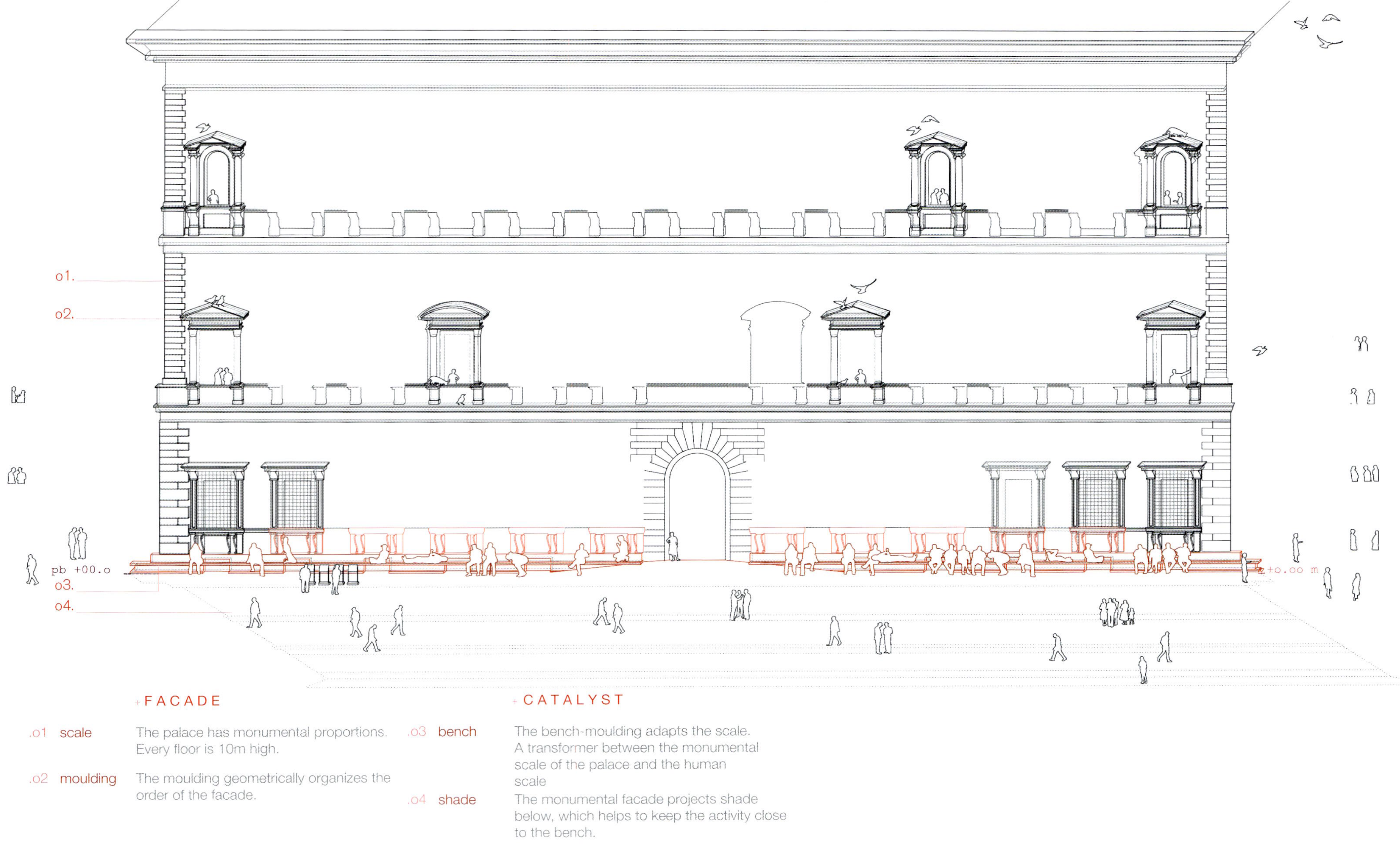

+ FACADE

.o1 **scale** — The palace has monumental proportions. Every floor is 10m high.

.o2 **moulding** — The moulding geometrically organizes the order of the facade.

+ CATALYST

.o3 **bench** — The bench-moulding adapts the scale. A transformer between the monumental scale of the palace and the human scale

.o4 **shade** — The monumental facade projects shade below, which helps to keep the activity close to the bench.

+29.50 m

o5.

+19.50

p+2

secondo piano

+10.00

p+1

primo piano

31 m

+16.25m

pC

+11.85

p+3

+8.65

p+2

+4.25

p+1

+ MINUTE 0.00

.05 palazzo · Palace designed by Antonio Sangallo and Michelangelo

Rest. ENRIQUETA
GC-3969-C

Graciosa Island 2008.

Photography MBE

CASE STUDY #5

GRACIOSA. FEET TICKLING

cataloging	
.03	*Construction of trading and leisure infrastructures*
.01	*Environmental modification*
catalyst	SAND
example	The lack of paving transforms the street into a recreational space for holidays. The streets of the Caleta del Sebo in La Graciosa.
date	S. XIX - Nowadays
author	No author
address	Chinijo Archipelago. Lanzarote

description

ASPHALT
UN-URBANIZATION
PLEASURE
RECREATION
LEISURE

The indiscriminate use of asphalt as the easiest and global economic pavement has ended erasing the particular character of each public space, annulling the original sensorial experience.

CASE STUDY #5

GRACIOSA

Bibliography

"Toward a Sensorial Urbanism". Mirko Zardini.

"The ground of modern city and the preponderance of asphalt". Mirko Zardini.

De cosas urbanas. Manuel de Solà-Morales. (Barcelona: Gustavo Gili)

Flesh and Stone. Richard Sennett. (New York: W.W.Norton, 1996)

Feet and the city

The Graciosa, a small island of 29 square kilometers at the Chinijo archipelago of the Canary Islands in the northwest of the Lanzarote Island, is now a hypnotic place where you can experiment and see how the strength of a landscape is capable of building the atmosphere of a public space. Walking through the streets of the island's only town, Caleta del Sebo, one experiences the unique character of the place through ones feet. You enjoy these public spaces by observing their honest architecture, their overwhelming volcanic landscape, and most of all by their sensuality.

William H. Whyte could nominate some of the island's streets as "sensorial streets", and Iñaki Ábalos would surely label them as picturesque public spaces, places defined not by visual perception, but by sensorial perception.

Once you approach the Graciosa Island with Google Earth, passing over Lanzarote's island, the rough landscape deformed by the sudden volcanic topography is very impressing, and the total absence of the green color in both islands is also very astonishing. The geological origin of this dry landscape of beige sand and black lava was defined 20 million years ago. The high temperatures of the subsoil, the arid extreme climate, the trade winds that permanently transport sand from the Sahara Desert and the lava of the volcanoes have consolidated an intense landscape without trees. But if we keep approaching the village of Caleta del Sebo of La Graciosa with Google Earth, the white rectangular spots at the shore of the beach seem like desalination plants at first sight, but they are actually a few houses floating on the sand of the beach.

THE TICKLING OF THE FEET

Mirko Zardini, in his article "Toward a Sensorial Urbanism", explains that the process of reparation of the city initiated in the Renaissance with the will to improve the hygienic conditions of the villages actually transformed through the years, the original character of the public space. Zardini explains that this process was born with the intention of looking for a response to reduce the powder, the mud and the noise of the horse carriages in the streets. However, it was solved by one unique solution: the paving of the public spaces. The first streets were paved with stones, that stabilized the soil; but it was not until the 19th century, with the discovery of asphalt, that they found the ideal material, capable of providing a uniform, impermeable surface, easy to clean and repair.

Loss of identity

Zardini's article helps to revalue the importance of asphalt as one of the materials that has been used most in the two last centuries. He also discovers how easy it is to associate asphalt with the problem of the pollution from the cars, and how it has ended forming a non-attractive image for this material.

The asphalt

The indiscriminate use of asphalt like the easiest and global solution for economic pavement has ended erasing the character of each particular public space, annulling the original

sensorial experience.

In the Caleta del Sebo the streets are not paved. The sand, from the beach and the mountains, slips past and occupies the space in the middle of the blocks. If you walk along the streets barefoot, you feel the sand of the beach under your feet.

While poking the sand with your fingers and putting them inside, looking for humidity; playing with the sand and doing little mountains or drawings with your feet; is when you feel the public space of the Graciosa.

Site Site plan / Caleta del Sebo. La Graciosa.

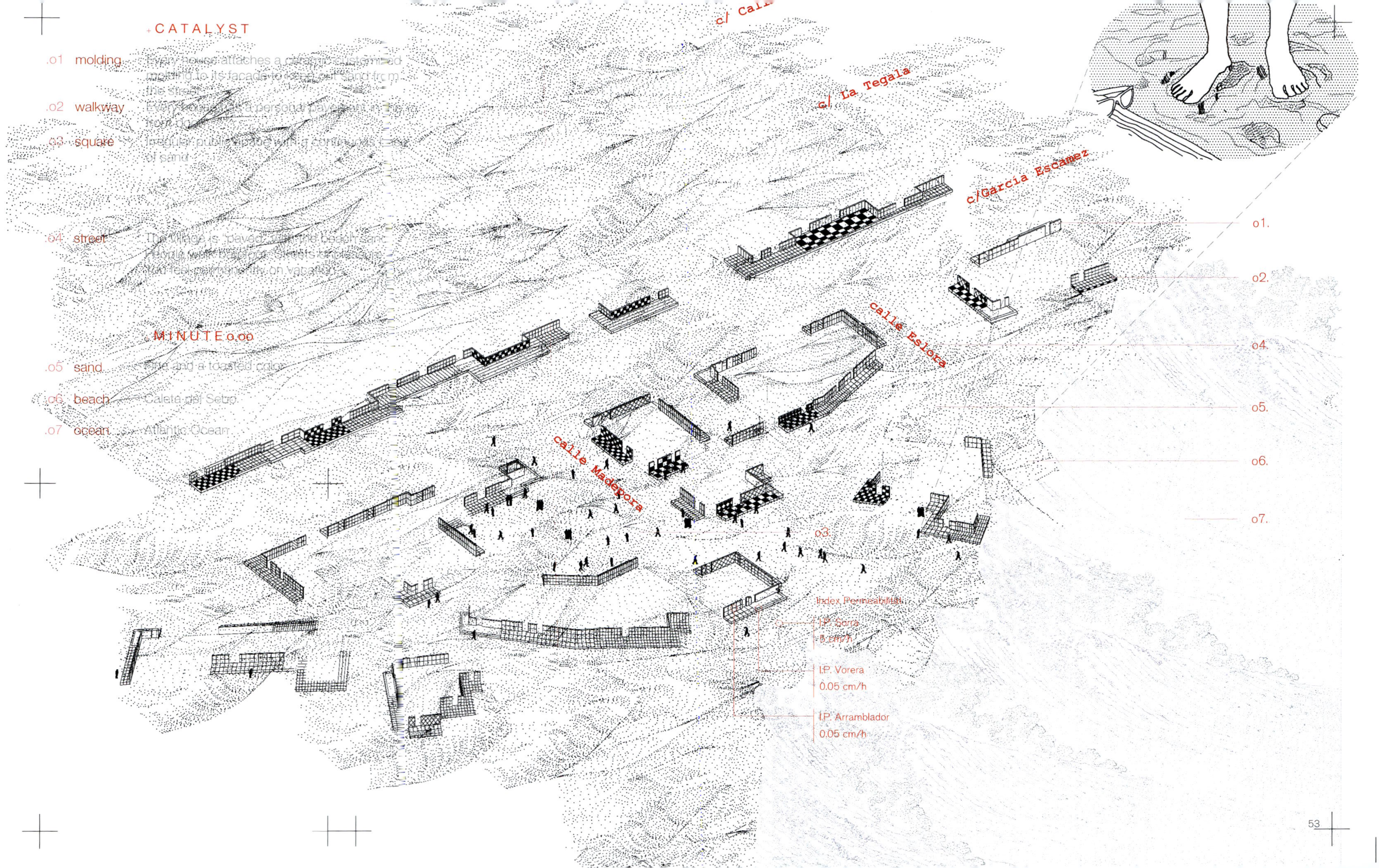
+CATALYST
.o1 molding Every house attaches a ceramic customized molding to its facade to keep out sand from the street
.o2 walkway Every house has a personal pavement in the front door
.o3 square Irregular public space with a continuous base of sand
.o4 street The village is "paved" with the beach sand. People walk barefoot. Streets of pleasure. You feel permanently on vacation
+MINUTE o.oo
.o5 sand Fine and a toasted color
.o6 beach Caleta del Sebo
.o7 ocean Atlantic Ocean
c/ La Tegala
c/Garcia Escamez
calle Eslora
calle Madepora
o1.
o2.
o3.
o4.
o5.
o6.
o7.
Index Permeabilitat
I.P. Sorra
5 cm/h
I.P. Vorera
0.05 cm/h
I.P. Arramblador
0.05 cm/h

+ CATALYST

.o1	molding	Every house attaches a ceramic customized molding to its facade to keep out sand from the street
.o2	walkway	Every house has a personal pavement in the front door
.o3	square	Irregular public space with a continuous base of sand

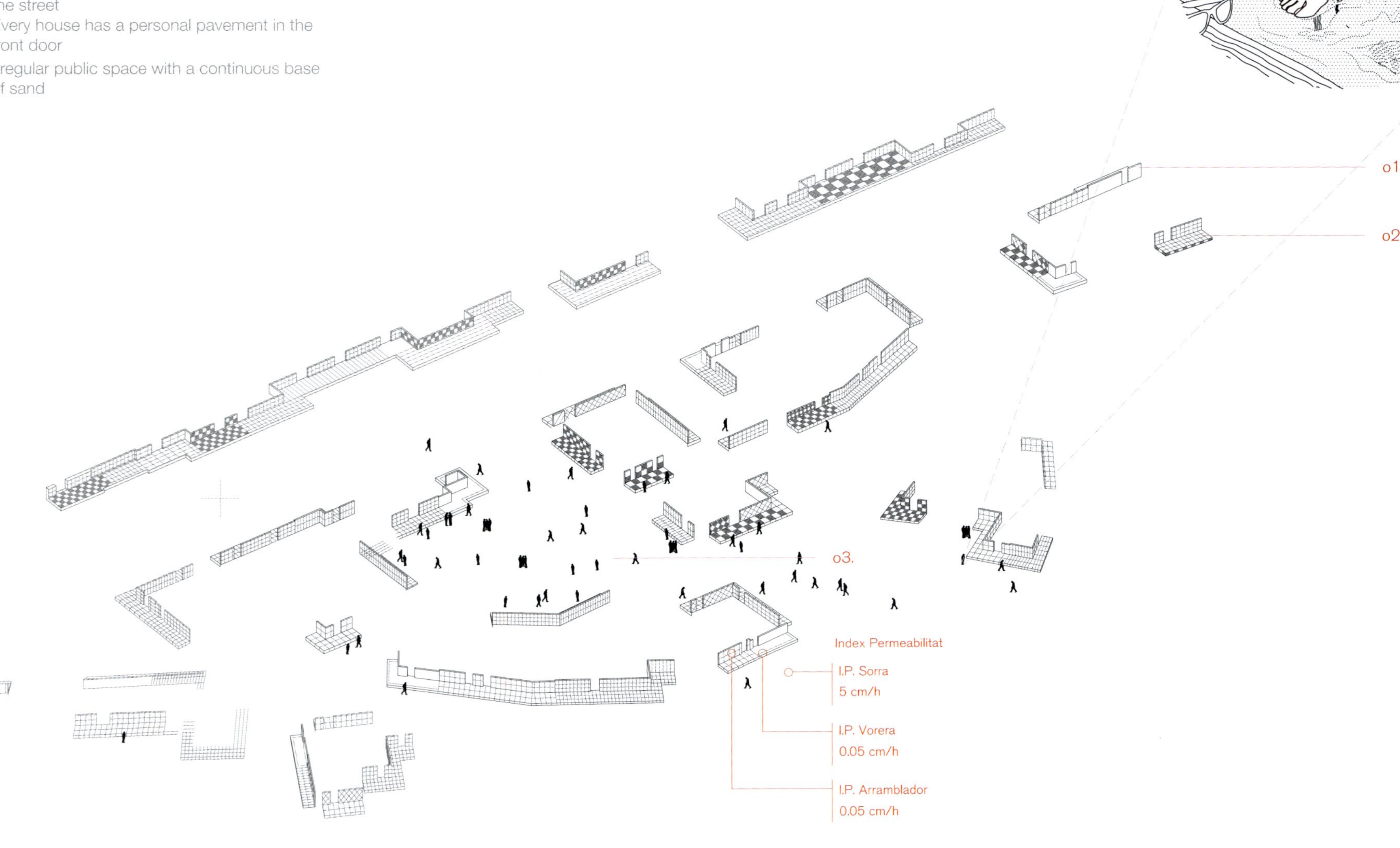

.04 street

The village is "paved" with the beach sand.
People walk barefoot. Streets of pleasure.
You feel permanently on vacation.

M I N U T E o.oo
.o5 sand Fine and a toasted color
.o6 beach Caleta del Sebo
.o7 ocean Atlantic Ocean
o5.
o6.
o7.

Henderson, N., **Crisenhale Road**. Bethnal Green, 1951.

Photography Nigel Henderson.

CASE STUDY #6

HENDERSON AND THE CHALK OF IDENTITY

cataloging .03	*Construction of trading and leisure infrastructures*
catalyst	CHALK
example	Transformation of the street into a playground for children. Crisenhale Road
date	1951
author	Nigel Henderson (1917-1985).
address	Bethnal Green, Poplar. East London, United Kingdom. E14..

description

TEAM X CHILDREN PLAY

As the Smithson made popular, a bar of chalk allows the children to transform any place into a playground. It is also necessary to emphasize the importance of the asphalt, capable of supporting all the imaginable manipulations. In conclusion, a universal and timeless resource.

CASE STUDY #6

HENDERSON

Bibliography

Urban structuring: studies of Alison & Peter Smithson. Alison Smithson. (New York: Reinhold Publishing Corporation, 1967)

AS in DS: An Eye on the Road. Alison Smithson. (Zürich: Lars Müller Publishers, 2001)

The Charged Void: Urbanism. Alison & Peter Smithson. (New York: Monacelli Press, 2004)

Smithsons' formation

In 1949, the photographer and artist Nigel Henderson realized a series of pictures of Bethnal Green's neighborhood in London. Henderson, ex-soldier from the Second World War, had had a heterogeneous formation. While he studied biology, he was in touch with the avant-garde intellectual culture of the city, thanks to the exhibitions that his mother organized as the director of the Peggy Guggheim art gallery in London. When in 1943 he married the anthropologist Judith Hendersom, they moved to Bethnal Green's neighborhood.

The series of pictures of the neighborhood gathers the social and anthropologic interests that the Henderson had in that moment.

The optimistic hardness of Herdenson's photography's of Bethnal Green was fundamental in the formation of the professional beginnings of Alison and Peter Smithson.

Henderson's realistic look, which exposed life during the postwar period in London's streets, constituted an essential modal in the way of re-formulating architecture that the Smithsons were chasing during the 50's.

The friendship and admiration that existed between the Smithsons and Henderson began in 1952 with the formation of the Independent Group (IG) with the artist Eduardo Paolozzi and the theoretical Reyner Banham, among others. The intense relation and mutual influence between the Smithsons, Henderson and Paoalozzi becomes clear in the exhibition This is Tomorrow in 1956, in which the group careates a pavilion in ruins to think about the future.

In this pavilion, the footprints, the memories, the time, the process, the tact, the identity and the place will become indispensable modals in all the future projects of the Smithsons' career.

Urban Structuring

In 1967, when the Smithsons wrote Urban Structuring, one of the most important treaties on urbanism after the Letter of Athens, a new sensitive and intelligent way of projecting the modern city was explained. Nigel Henderson's photos of Bethnal Green headed and illustrated the introduction of the book. Henderson's images helped Smithsons explain all those things that the abstract modern urbanism had forgotten.

CHALK

Henderson's spontaneous photos of Bethnal Green, in which the children played in the streets, occupying all the asphalt, emphasize that modern city projects cannot forget the spaces of relation and game.

But how can a simple asphalt street without any specific project of public space turn into a real playful space and of relation? Henderson's

images are an evident proof of how the fragile transitory chalk drawing realized on the ground, can manage to totally transform the street.

The chalk turns into the real catalyst of the public space, capable not only of turning the street into a playground, but also of filling the sad working neighborhoods of London with happiness, life and identity.

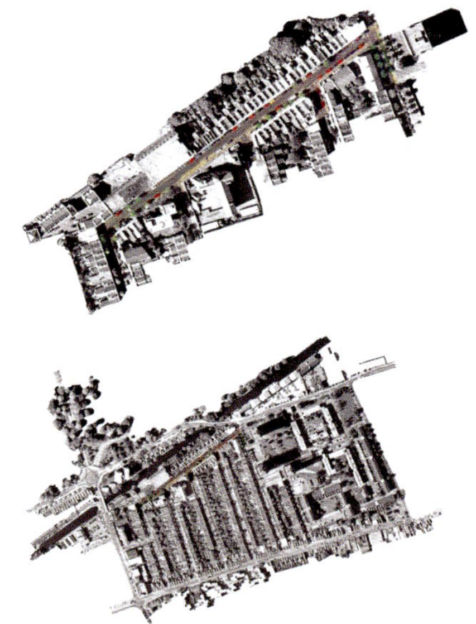

Site plan / Bethnal Green, London.

+ BOYS

.o2 kids — All kids are playing in the street.

.o3 games — Skates, bike and chalk

+ SELF REFERENCE

.o4 chalk — Has the capacity to transform space transiently.

.o5 asphalt — Continuous and homogeneous support.

.o6 reference — The chalk singularizes the place and changes the scale of the site.

MINUTE o.oo

.o7 proportion — To paint with chalk, you can change the scale of a dead street.

.o8 street — Bethnal Green, London. Working neighborhood defined by the repetition of the same housing unit. Equal streets, similar houses create a kind of continuous urban flavor.

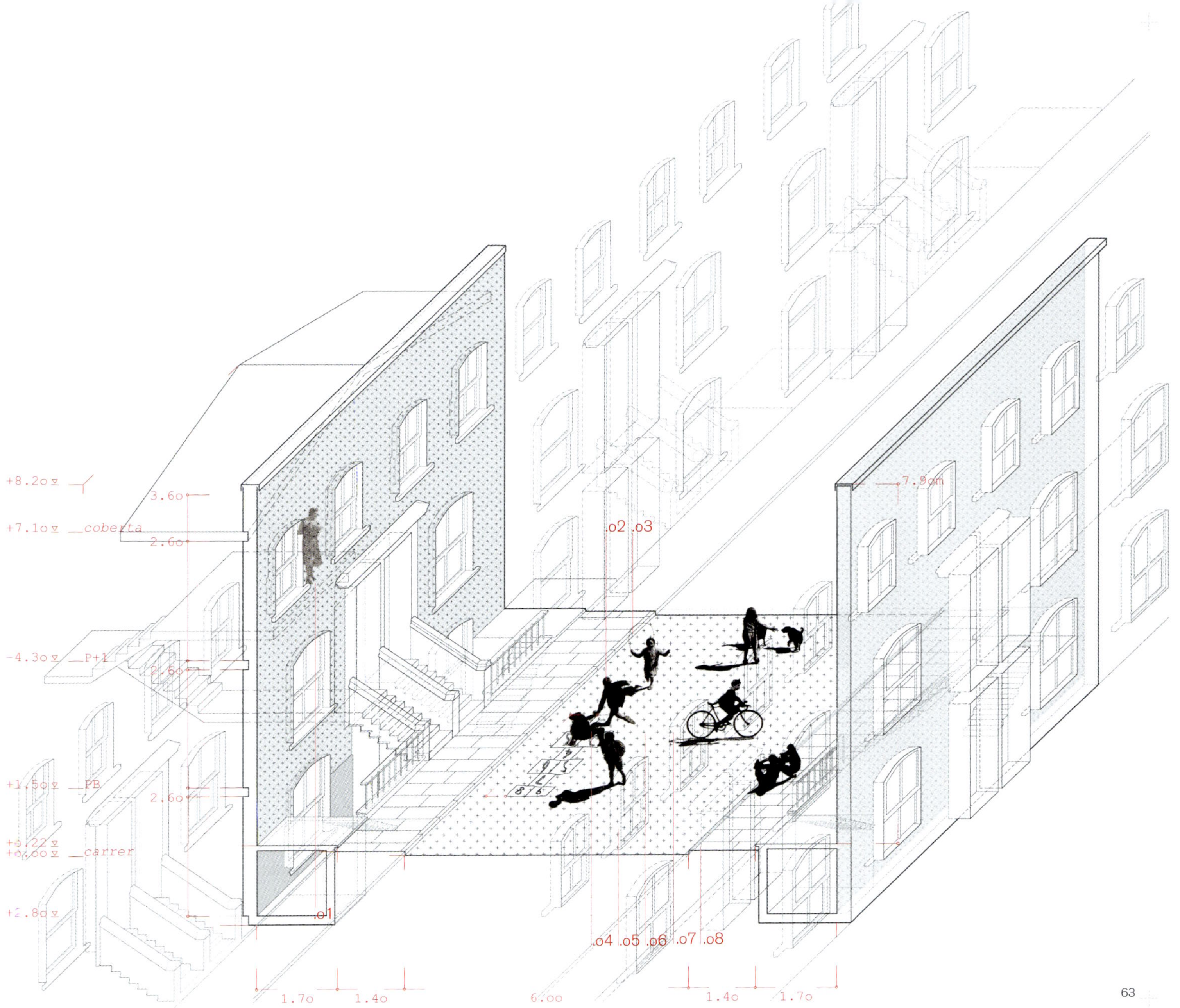

+ DOMESTIC

.o1 view

The street as a domestic room.
a place controlled from the home.

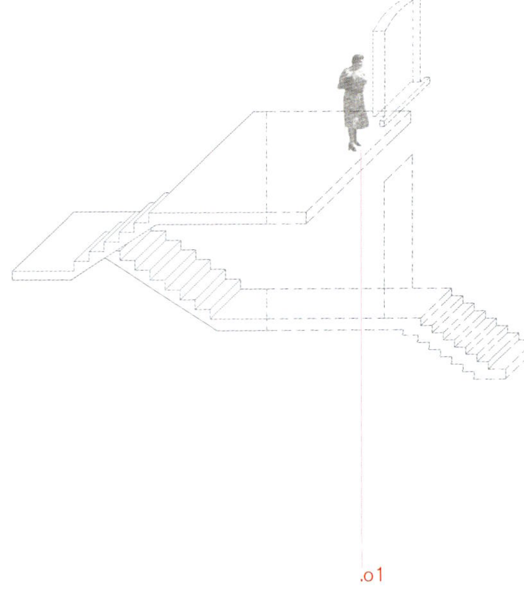

+ BOYS

.o2	kids	All kids are playing in the street.
.o3	games	Skates, bike and chalk

+ SELF REFERENCE

.o4	chalk	Has the capacity to transform space transiently.
.o5	asphalt	Continuous and homogeneous support.
.o6	reference	The chalk singularizes the place and changes the scale of the site.

.o4 .o5 .o6

MINUTE o.oo

.o7 **proportion** To paint with chalk, you can change the scale of a dead street.

.o8 **street** Bethnal Green, London.
Working neighborhood defined by the repetition of the same housing unit. Equal streets, similar houses create a kind of continuous urban flavor.

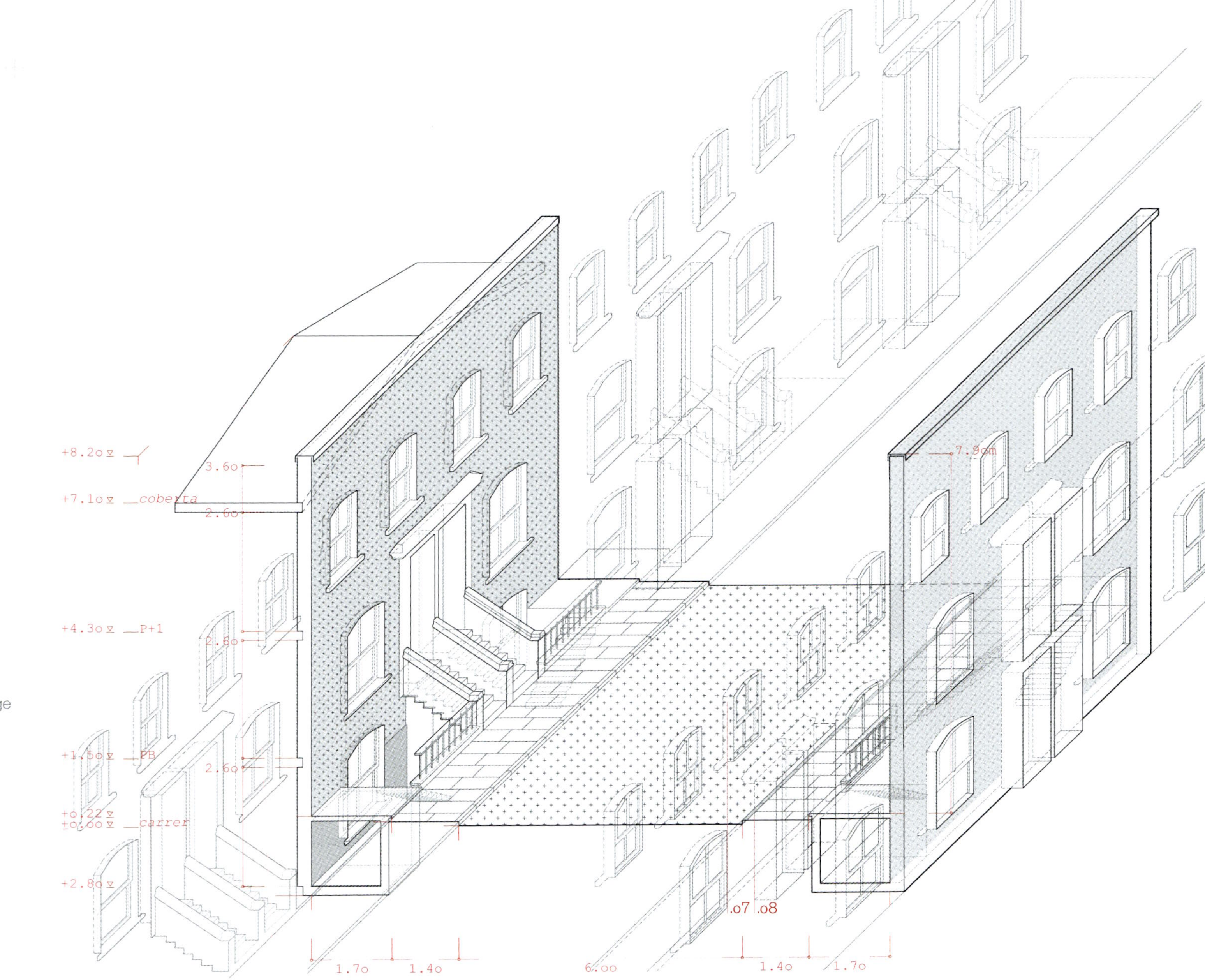

CASE STUDY #7

JUJOL AND THE PAINTED MONUMENT OF KING JAUME I

The paintings at Tapineria Street, under Santa Águeda's chapel, suggested by Gaudí and executed by Jujol

Blassi's photography was published in the newspaper *La Vanguardia*. August the 1st, 1968 and Lluis. A. Casanovas.

cataloging
.04 *Artistic intervention*

.02 *Interpretation and manipulation of pop culture elements*

catalyst
MURALS

example
Capacity of transformation of an ephemeral catalyst.
Seventh centennial of the birth of the king Jaume I the Conquerer.

date
1908

author
Josep Maria Jujol (1879-1949).

address
Antic Portal de Santa Àgueda.
Plaça Ramon Berenguer El Gran.
Barcelona / CP: 08010.

description
GOTHIC GRAFFITI EPHEMERAL

Gaudí poses a big downtown intervention to return the city of Barcelona to the way it was on Jaume the First's time. Facing the impossibility of doing that, Gaudí asked Jujol to paint a graffiti in order to commemorate him.

JUJOL

Bibliography

Josep Maria Jujol. Josep Llinàs.
(Koln: Taschen, 2007).

Jujol: Jujol's Universe. Dennis Dollens, Juan José Lahuerta.
(Barcelona: Actar and COAC, 1999).

Ludwig Jujol: Què és el collage, sinó acostar soledats?: Lluis II de Baviera, Josep Maria Jujol. Perejaume.
(Barcelona: La Magrana, 1989).

Jujol. Ignasi de Solà Morales.
(New York: Rizzoli, 1991).

Gaudí's Project

In 1908 the architect Puig I Cadafalch asked Antoni Gaudí to realize a monument to commemorate the celebration of the seventh centennial of the birth of the king Jaume I the Conquerer.

The offer presented by Gaudí did not want to construct a monument that petrified the figure of the king, but it consisted of recovering the spaces that the king had known when he lived in the city of Barcelona.

Gaudí's project was an intervention in the former entry gates to the medieval city. For that purpose, Gaudí proposed to restore the buildings that surrounded the former accesses and to knock down the houses that had been constructed in the middle of the Roman wall that fortified the city.

Looking for a substitute for Gaudí's project

Gaudí's ambitious project, which initially wanted to intervene in all the gates of the ancient city, gradually evolved until they decided to recover only the door of entry that would be behind the houses constructed on the wall of the Tapineria street. Gaudí supposed that the houses constructed inside the arch that was under the chapel of Saint Agate were hiding a former medieval door of the city; but he was wrong. Gaudí had the idea of knocking down the houses and constructing a new stairway that would connect the new Laietana street, (which was under construction at that time), with the Plaça del Rei (King's Square). But the resources to realize the eviction and demolition of the housings constructed in the wall were few and ended up by making the accomplishment of Gaudí's ambitious project impossible.

Finally, Gaudí, discouraged, because he could not execute his project, asked his brilliant collaborator Josep Maria Jujol to go to the Tapineria street to think something out; that's when the intervention started to concrete.

MURAL

The interventions made by Gaudí and Jujol on 1902 on the Cathedral of Palma are known thanks to Bishop Campins' writings. Campins explains how Gaudí sat on a bench in the church and gave orders to Jujol, helping him execute his painting full of stains inside the cathedral, throwing paint buckets at the walls.

Jujol collaborated in many of Gaudí's last projects, realizing the most compromising and delicate pieces of work; and he was the responsible of realizing the first neo-Gothic graffiti's in Barcelona.

Jujol knew Gaudí's difficulties in realizing his work on Saint Agata's chapel, so he decided, next to his master, to make Gothic style paintings around the chapel of Saint Agata's arch to commemorate the birth of King Jaume I.

Jujol's paintings were made without demolishing those houses that had been built on the Roman wall, hiding the original appearance of the fortification. And these paintings provoked these houses to gradually disappear until the wall that we nowadays see showed.

Curiously, nowadays, there is almost no sign of those houses that used to be on the wall, but, in exchange, those ephemeral graffiti's that Jujol made are still present.

Site plan / Carrer Tapineria. Barcelona.

MONUMENT

.01 **symbol** — The mural is sited in a singular place of the gothic fort. It is a space of celebration and memory. Simple thin paint can transform a historical place. A new, transient layer.

JUJOLS MURALS

.02 **stair** — Gaudí wanted to recover the atmosphere of the Gothic city while king Jaume the 1st was alive. He proposed to reveal the gothic fence and connect the King Square with Tapineria street seven meters bellow.

.03 **Jaume I**

.04 **Jesus** — The name Jesus with a crown of thorns.

.05 **shield** — Jujol paint Jaume's shield burnt.

.06 **inscription** — National inscription.

.07 **year**

OCCUPATION

.08 **housing** — The old gothic fence was occupied by housing. Gaudí's proposal to take off the precarious housing inserted inside and reveal the gates of the city.

MURAL INTERIOR

.09 **empty** — The arches define a space to be occupied.

MINUTE 0.00

.10 **gate** — Santa Agueda gate.

.11 **fence**

.12 **Tapineria St.**

+ MONUMENT

.o1 **symbol** The mural is sited in a singular place of the gothic fort. It is a space of celebration and memory. Simple thin paint can transform a historical place.
A new, transient layer.

+ JUJOLS MURALS

.o2 **stair** Gaudí wanted to recover the atmosphere of the Gothic city while king Jaume the 1st was alive. He proposed to reveal the gothic fence and connect the King Square with Tapineria street seven meters bellow.

.o3 **Jaume I**

.o4 **Jesus** The name Jesus with a crown of thorns.

.o5 **shield** Jujol paint Jaume's shield burnt.

.o6 **inscription** National inscription.

.o7 **year**

OCCUPATION

.08 **housing** — The old gothic fence was occupied by housing. Gaudí's proposal to take off the precarious housing inserted inside and reveal the gates of the city.

MURAL INTERIOR

.09 **empty** — The arches define a space to be occupied.

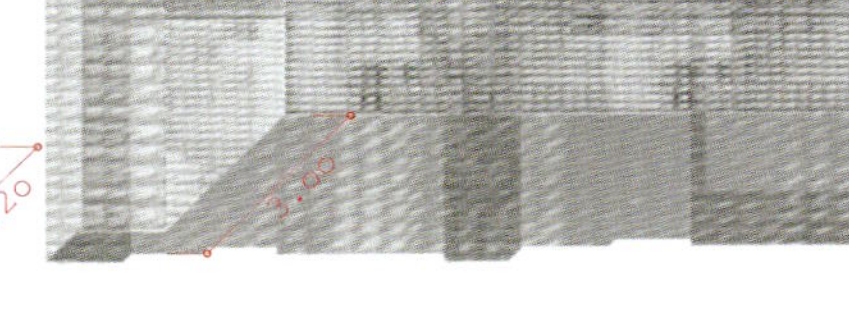

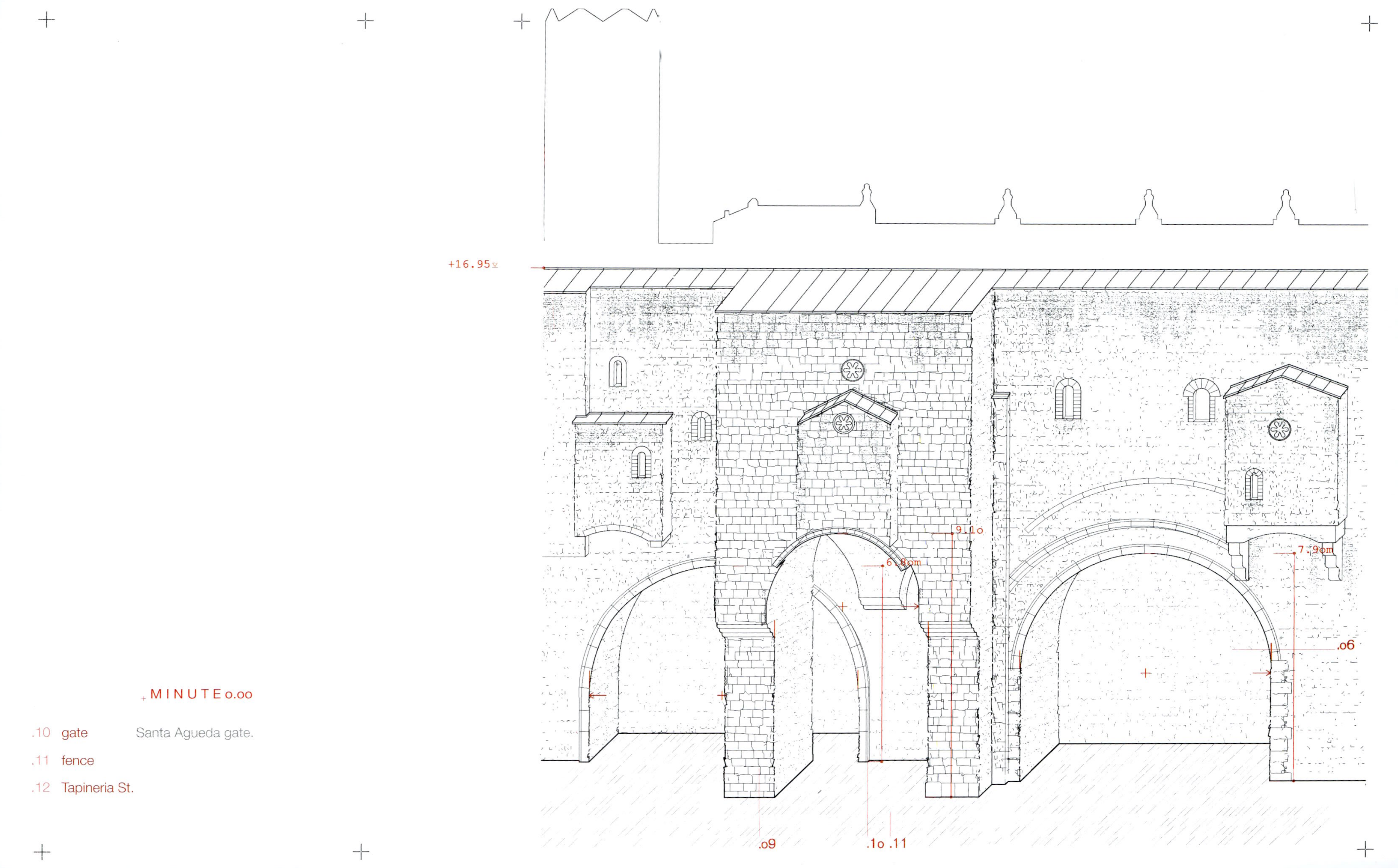

MINUTE o.oo

.10 gate Santa Agueda gate.
.11 fence
.12 Tapineria St.

SHARP
SHARP

Parlamentaires-debóut at Eucalyptus Park, Kinshasa, RDCongo, 2006.

Published in de Boeck, F., Plissart, M. *Kinshasa Tales from the Invisible City.* (Antwerp: Ludion, 2006)

CASE STUDY #8

KINSHASA. AS THIN AS A THREAD

cataloging .03	*Construction of trading and leisure infrastructures*
.01	*Environmental modification*
catalyst	PAPERS, BARBER'S SHOPS, SCRIBES
example	Minimal infrastructure Eucalyptuses Park in Kinshasa.
date	Nowadays.
author	Kinshasa's citizens.
address	Ngafula's Mount. Lumumba, Comuna de N'djili. Kinshasa, RDCongo.

descriptio

POLITICS
SPONTANEOUS
AUSTERE
ASTUTE
EFFICIENT

Spontaneous discussion, called "Parlamentaires-débout", appear in Kinshasa's parks during Mobutu's dictatorship. They started around newspapers hanging on threads. This public space constitutes the quarry where the democracy's politics emerged. Besides, the Congolese urban parks work as outdoors malls, arranged by the trees plot.

CAS E STUDY #8

KINSHASA

Bibliography

Kinsahsa tales from the invisible City.
Filip de Boeck, Marie-Franqouise Plissart.
(Antwerp: Ludion, 2006).

City and Forest

The Eucalyptuses Park in Kinshasa is one of the catalysts to which we paid particular attention in this Thesis. During the past years, the new African metropolis have turned into one of the new areas of interest for the contemporary culture.

Eucalyptus Park

They are the final destination of the European and American cities, according to some theorists. Current urbanism has understood these cities as laboratories of art and essay of the contemporaneousness (Koolhaas, R. et al., *Lagos. How It Works*, (Zürich: Lars Müller Publishers, 2006).

Placed in Lumumba's district, crossed by the road that leads from the airport to the center, the Eucalyptuses Park is one of the examples of how trade is one of the fundamental assets at the moment of articulating the public contemporary space.

It is placed over the preexisting clearings of jungle caught inside the city. The irregular grid of eucalyptuses of the Congolese jungle forms a kind of invisible infrastructure that the merchants (who until then had been ambulant) started occupying.

The mechanism is simple: each of them occupies a tree and its surroundings, as if the shade that this one generates determined the plot of land.

Many of these merchants reserve their positions in a more 'official' way, tying tapes around the trunks of trees with the name of the supposed establishment or owner. This kind of park - market has the peculiarity of containing all types of products of the most diverse manufacture (from food up to car tires), we can also find services like barber's shops, writers, and kiosks... and all of this happens outdoors.

AS THIN AS A THREAD

The trade is produced in a transitory, spontaneous way, without needing big previous infrastructures... And it is precisely this formless and changeable character what awards the park with this public dimension.

It is not only a question of selling, the place acquires a function of a contemporary "agora" of instantaneous character, in a place where no type of urban planning exists: the citizens of Kinshasa debate the political solutions to the economical situation of the country in a place close to the kiosks, the barber's shops turn into small spaces of conversation, the trees where the shops have not opened yet are occupied by citizens who read... Before the lack of resources, the public space is formed with the spontaneity, the improvisation and the activity that this not planned and transitory way of understanding the trade supposes.

In our country we can find similarities with the traditional markets. However, in Catalonia, the markets are put on the squares or public spaces in which the commercial offer is already completed by other infrastructures, such as covered markets, shops, or others. There is not enough confidence on trade as a unique activator of the public space, as it happens in Kinshasa.

Eucalyptus Park

Trade is added over an existing structure; it is not an element that is counted on from the beginning of the design.

In this Thesis, we have tried to translate to drawings the same way in which this interaction between green places- public spaces – trade in produced.

Site plan / Ngafula's Mount. Kinshasa.

WRITER

.o1 ribbon — Fix the position of the activities.

.o2 writer — Governmental officers.

PARLIMENTARY

.o3 clip

.o4 thread

.o5 cardboard

.o6 mast — Structural support for hanging the thread and the newspaper.

.o7 debate

NIGHT LIFE

.o8 prostitutes — During the day, the park is in an active public space. During the night, it becomes a place for prostitution.

HAIR DRESSER

.o9 billboards — Portrait of the JB Mpiana billboard.

.10 hairdresser

.11 mirror

.12 make up

.13 umbrella

SHOP

.14 car

.15 fit men

.16 tires — All of the elements in this public space are recycled.

MINUTE o.oo

.17 eucalyptus — Planted by the council with the idea to create a chain of public spaces along Lumumba Road.

.18 shade — Kinshasa tropical climate. Average min 18°C, max 35°C

.19 glade

.20 extension

.21 power

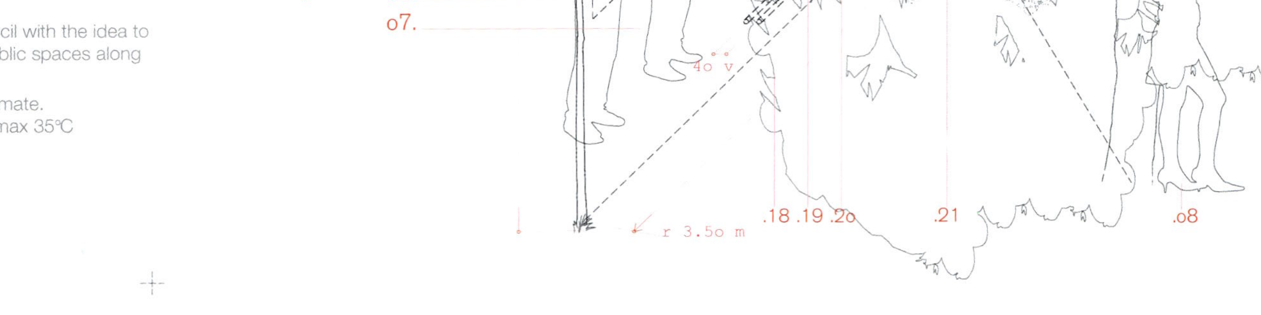

+ WRITER

.o1	ribbon	Fix the position of the activities.
.o2	writer	Governmental officers.

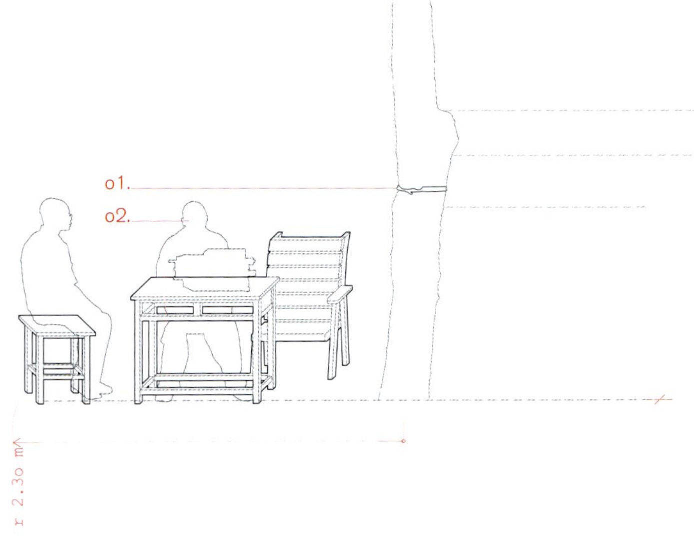

+ PARLIMENTARY

.o3 clip

.o4 thread

.o5 cardboard

.o6 mast — Structural support for hanging the thread and the newspaper.

.o7 debate

o3.
o4.
+1.8o m
o5.
o6.
o7.
r 3.5o m

+ NIGHT LIFE

.08 **prostitutes** During the day, the park is in an active public space. During the night, it becomes a place for prostitution.

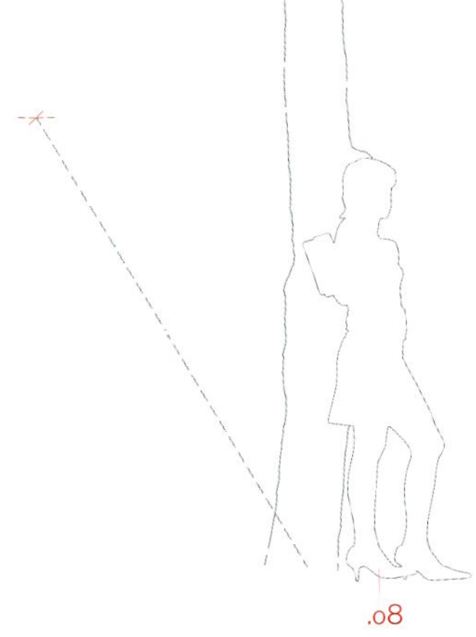

HAIR DRESSER

.09 billboards Portrait of the JB Mpiana billboard.

.10 hairdresser

.11 mirror

.12 make up

.13 umbrella

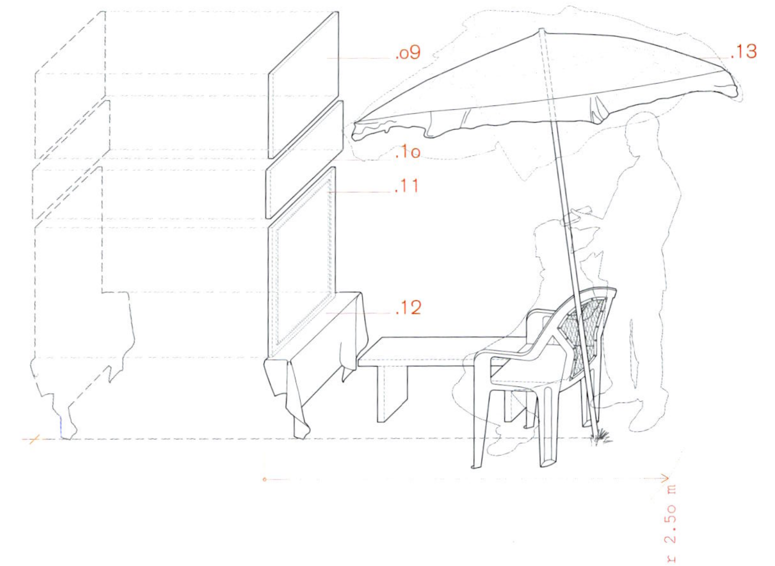

+ SHOP

.14 car

.15 fit men

.16 tires

All of the elements in this public space are recycled.

.14 .15

.16

r 4.5o m

r 2.5o m

.17

3ocm apro

4o v

ombra 4.oo pm

.18 .19 .2o

.21

MINUTE o.oo

.17	eucalyptus	Planted by the council with the idea to create a chain of public spaces along Lumumba Road.
.18	shade	Kinshasa tropical climate. Average min 18ºC, max 35ºC
.19	glade	
.20	extension	
.21	power	

Children in NY playing with the water from a fire pump

F. Getty Images. Avax news

CASE STUDY #9

NY. HYDRANT, WATER ALWAYS WRITES IN PLURAL

cataloging	
.01	*Environmental modifications*
.03	*Construction of Infrastructures of Trade and Leisure*
catalyst	WATER
example	Spontaneous alteration of the urban normality. Street in NY during the summer.
date	Until today.
author	New Yorkers.
address	NY

description

ACCIDENT
MINIMAL
GAME

Some children from a big dense American city like NY use the accidental water escape of a firemen hose to convert the streets into a place for games. It is an example of how a hazardous situation of minimal resources can transform the city.

CASE STUDY #9

HYDRANT, WATER ALWAYS WRITES IN PLURAL

Bibliography

"Complexity and contradicion in architecture". Robert Venturi. (1996)

"La arquitectura de la indeterminación". Yago Conde. (Barcelona, ACTAR, 2000)

| Published in AvaxNews.com

Monumental fountains

The monumental fountains are objects to be thoughtfully observed. They are urban elements that furnish the public space and that in many occasions symbolize the moments in which the city has suffered subsequent transformations or important events. Water spouts, sometimes of great height, turn into urban modals that splash and scare away the pedestrians who look at them from far away, avoiding to get wet.

Ornamental fountains

Bernini's fountains in Rome that remind us of the floods that the city suffered, or Salvi's Fontana di Trevi that represents the image of the celebration of the arrival of the water to the city, due to the torn down aqueduct of the Aqua Virgo; are both cases of fountains that are at the same time monumental and ornamental.

These are fountains that propose another scale of relation between water and the people.

In the case of the Barcaza fountain in Rome, Bernini decided to place the water level slightly below the pavement of the street, resolving a technical problem of low water pressure, and at the same time using the different levels of the square to situate a bench around the fountain that gave it a new urban dimension that made the people approach the fountain to have a look at it and to chat around it.

The Fontana di Trevi is not only placed in a public square but it is also a place of public activity in which people toss coins in the water, imagining a better future.

Scales and water

Nowadays, it is not very common to project an urban fountain.

Probably, Robert Venturi's projects in Philadelphia and Yago Conde's project in Barcelona must have been the last ones to think about this strange and complex condition that the fountains contain: they are distant objects that can feel close at the same time.

In the case of Venturi's project, it responded to a large scale, placing the dark gray aluminum fountain right on the visual axis of the Parkway Avenue that diagonally crosses the regular streets of the city. This Site plan helped the fountain act like a stretching element that could introduce the Fairmount Park until the Town Hall building. The fountain's shape is like the one of the Town Hall building in Philadelphia, with metallic finishing, similar to a car; and it was not only projected as an element to be observed from the big buildings surrounding it, but it was also thought in relation to its interior space, where you could hear the sound of the water.

Conde's fountain is an alternative to the monumental fountains that contained a single element and unique aesthetics.

It was proposed as a disperse fountain, capable of creating disseminated places. It is a fountain treated as a "geological score" coming from the "marriage de contours of the shapes of the city of Barcelona and the graphical score of John Cage's Fontana Mix. Therefore, this would provoke different situations, some monumental ones in the central part, and some others at the surface tied to little surprises and games for children".

WATER ALWAYS WRITES IN PLURAL

New York, it's summer, it's hot, the children don't go to school because they have holidays, and suddenly an unpredicted phenomenon is about to transform an ordinary street of the city. The spontaneous explosion of a firemen water hose coincidentally becomes the urban catalyst that is capable of changing this place that was ordinary until then. The children, without prejudices, got naked and knew how to take profit of such a surprising situation. The water escaped out of control and offered the possibility to identify the body with the city. The children played and got wet. Suddenly, the city had become a place for leisure and games.

A spontaneous water hose is not only a clear example of how the ephemeral strength of a catalyst is capable of modifying a city, but it also offers a modal that is able to easily prove the contextual value of the catalysts in the urbanity.

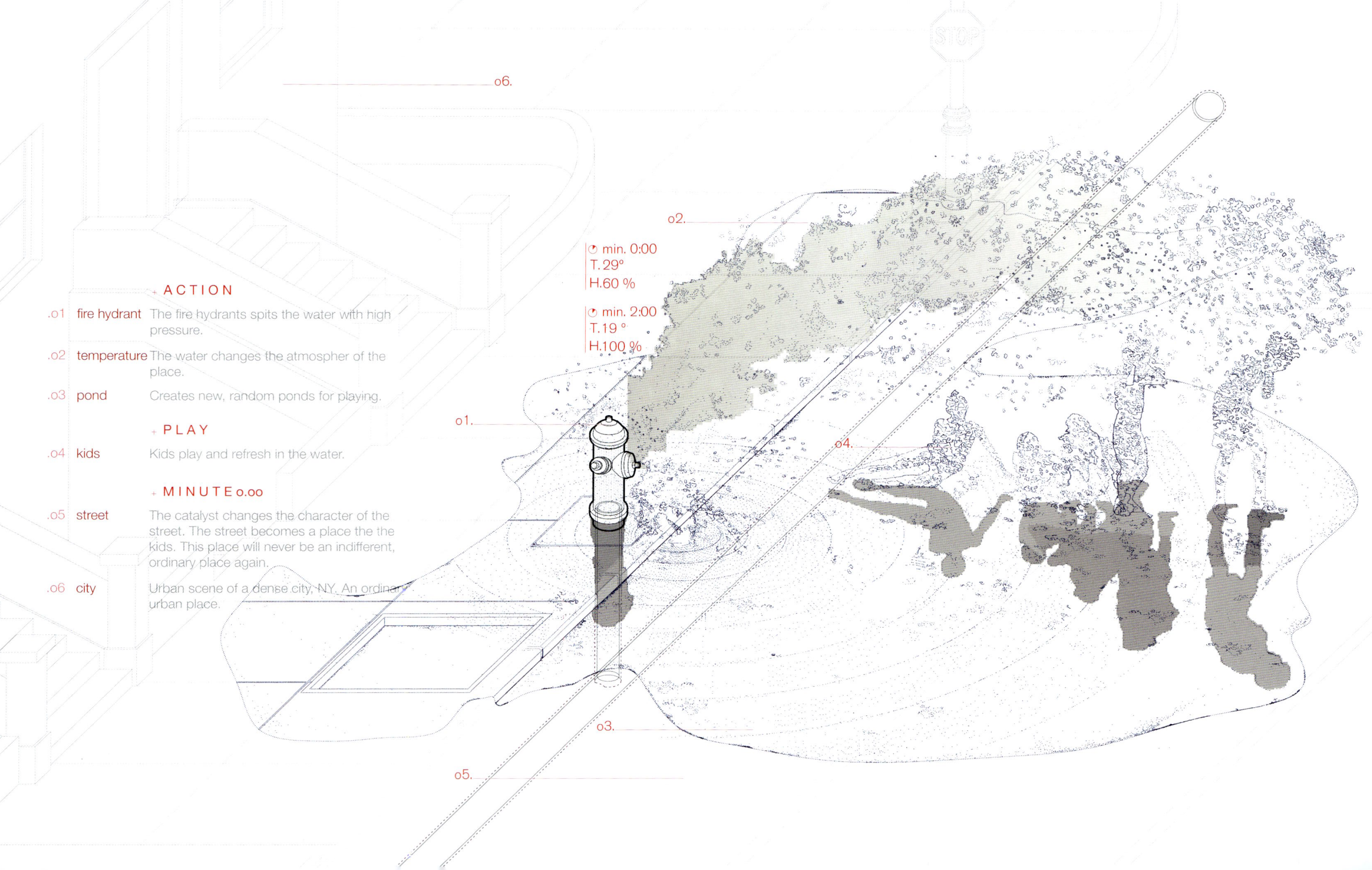
o6.
o2.
min. 0:00
T. 29°
H.60 %
min. 2:00
T. 19 °
H.100 %
o1.
o4.
o3.
o5.
STOP
+ ACTION
.o1 fire hydrant The fire hydrants spits the water with high pressure.
.o2 temperature The water changes the atmospher of the place.
.o3 pond Creates new, random ponds for playing.
+ PLAY
.o4 kids Kids play and refresh in the water.
+ MINUTE o.oo
.o5 street The catalyst changes the character of the street. The street becomes a place the the kids. This place will never be an indifferent, ordinary place again.
.o6 city Urban scene of a dense city, NY. An ordinary urban place.

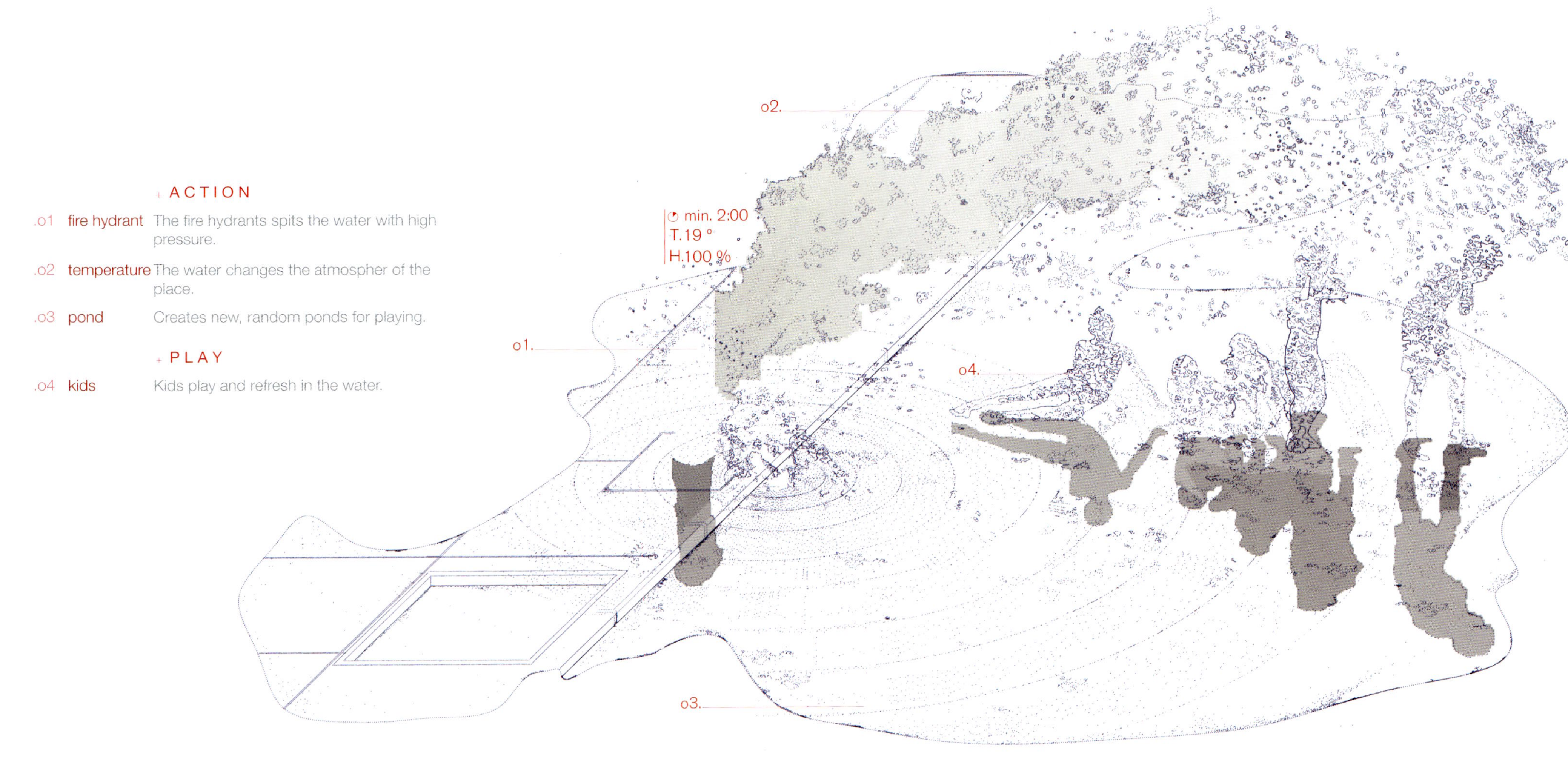
+ ACTION
.o1 fire hydrant The fire hydrants spits the water with high pressure.
.o2 temperature The water changes the atmospher of the place.
.o3 pond Creates new, random ponds for playing.
+ PLAY
.o4 kids Kids play and refresh in the water.
min. 2:00
T.19 °
H.100 %
o1.
o2.
o3.
o4.

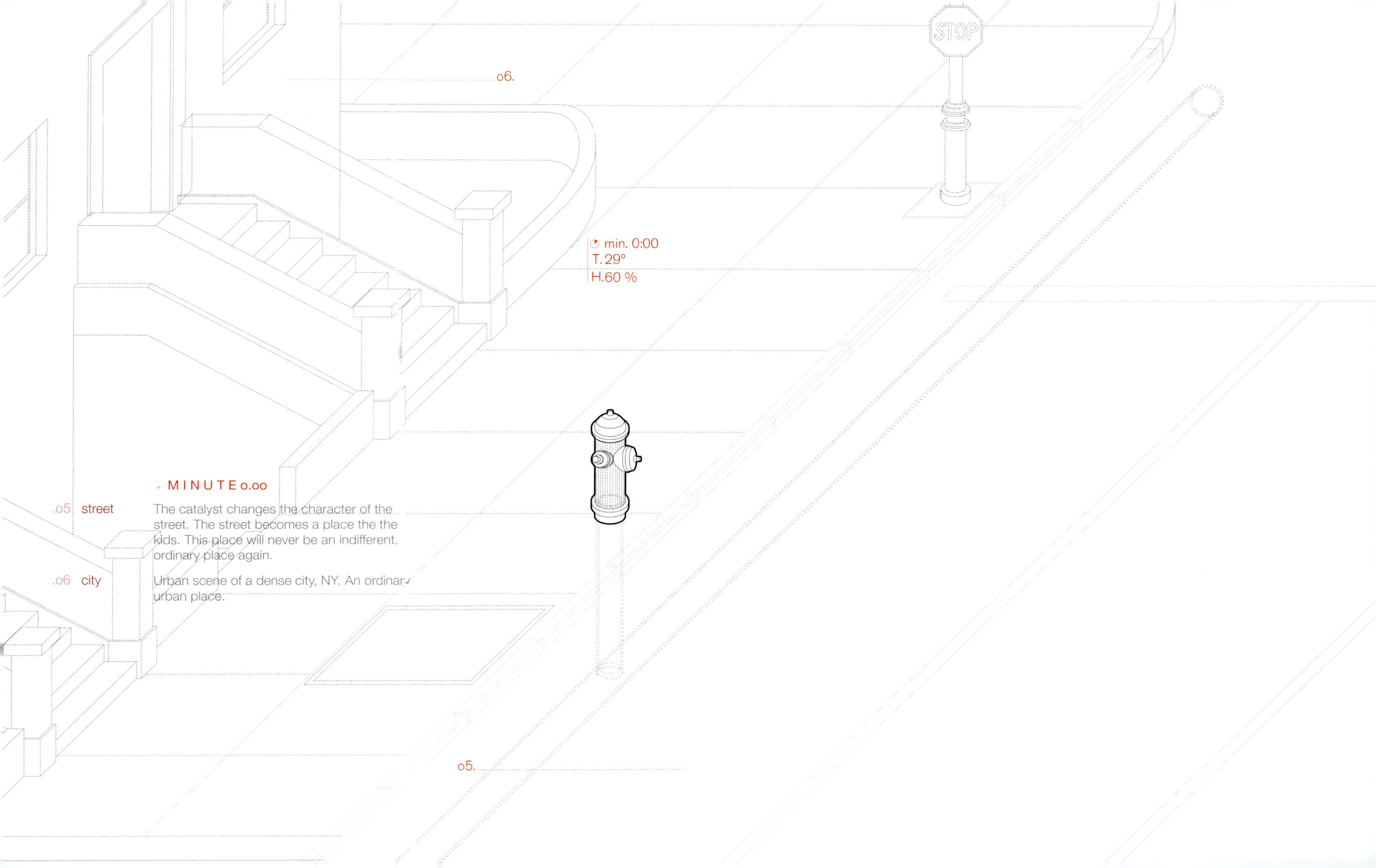
o6.
STOP
min. 0:00
T. 29°
H.60 %
+ MINUTE o.oo
.o5 street
The catalyst changes the character of the street. The street becomes a place the the kids. This place will never be an indifferent, ordinary place again.
.o6 city
Urban scene of a dense city, NY. An ordinary urban place.
o5.

New Yorkers and commuters leaving Manhattan Island through **Brooklyn's Bridge**. New York, 2003.

© Jonathan Fickies.

CASE STUDY #10

NY. BLACKOUT

cataloging .01	*Environmental modification*
catalyst	SHUTTED DOWN
example	Catastrophies as the origin of public spaces. Blackout in North-East USA.
date	August the 14th, 2003.
author	Accident in the First Energy Corp.
address	North-east and Mid-west (USA) Ontario (Canada)

description

ACCIDENT TO OCCUPY ENTROPY

The effect of the blackout ended up turning the city into a space of freedom, without pre-established programs or rules; a city suddenly turned into periphery.

CASE STUDY #10

BLACKOUT

Bibliography

De lo mecánico a lo termodinamico. Javier Garcia-German. (Barcelona: Gustavo Gili)

"Un recorrido por lo monumentos de Passaic". Robert Smithson. (Barcelona: Gustavo Gili)

"La entropia se hace visible". Robert Smithson. (Barcelona: Gustavo Gili)

Art. "Ciudad Indiferente". Jacques Herzog. (Madrid: *El País*)

November, 9, 1965; 5.30 P.M.

An excess of electrical demand in the interconnected network that joined Canada with the East cost of the United States makes the automatic protection systems blow. The comings and goings of the overage end up provoking that the Ontario hydroelectric plant collapses and stays out of service. Thirty million persons from eight different states of the east coast of the United States remain without light during more than 14 hours.

August, 15, 2003; 4:00 P.M.

After the great blackout of 1965 and the long losses of electrical supply of July, 13, 1977 and of August 11, 1996; on August 15, 2003, New York goes back to dark. A coin-

cidental ray on an electric power station in the Niagara causes the loss of service, provoking that nine different states of the USA and a province of Canada stay without electricity during 24 hours.

At the beginning of the 20th century, the biologist Patrick Geddes proposed a different point of view, that brought the use of energy closer to city planning. For this visionary scientist, there was a clear relation between the degree of development of a society and the level of availability and consumption of their energetic base. For Geddes, the future and progress of the cities were tied to a rational use of energy.

BLACKOUT

On August, 15, 2003, when New York was left without light, the city suddenly transformed. The scared people went out to the streets or public spaces, to see what was going on. The streets were occupied in an indiscriminate, free way, without any rules. The bridges that surround the island of Manhattan were filled with people that escaped from an unplugged city.

The article "A tour of the monuments of Passaic, New Jersey" written by the artist Robert Smithson in 1967, discovers a new landscape of opportunities at the edge of the city of New

York. Smithson was born in Passaic, a population next to the great city symbol of progress and modernity. He proposes to reveal how New York maintains its low levels of degradation, thanks to the increase of entropy of these new left landscapes; by walking along the industrial and abandoned neighborhoods of his natal city. According to Smithson, a clear existing correlation between the transitory landscapes of Passaic's periphery and the finished city of New York. Smithson himself says: "Passaic seems to be full of holes in comparison with the city of New York, which looks strictly stiff and solid. But

in some way, these holes are monumental hollows that define the vestiges of a memory of a game about abandoned futures ".

If according to Geddes, New York represents the progress of the modern society, probably because of that, pleasure and freedom appear when the city goes out. How many times people have talked about the correspondence of the blackout of November 1965 with the increase of birthrate nine months later! In 2003, once they confirmed that the blackout did not have any terrorist link, the streets of the city turned into a space of equality and of democracy; like in the anterior occasion.

Possibly, the effect of the blackout ended up turning the city into a space of freedom, without pre-established programs and without rules; a city suddenly turned into a periphery. New York was transformed,

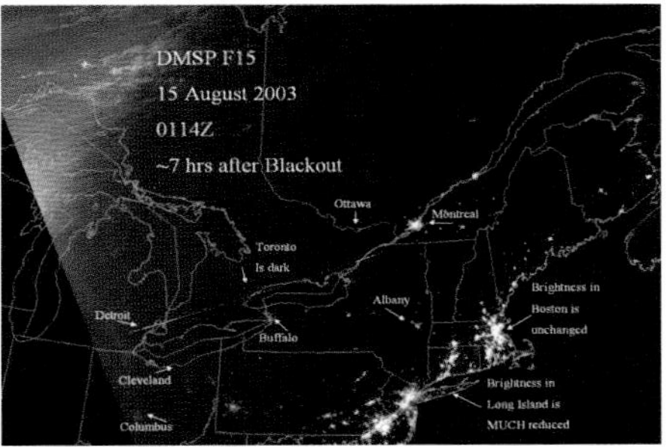

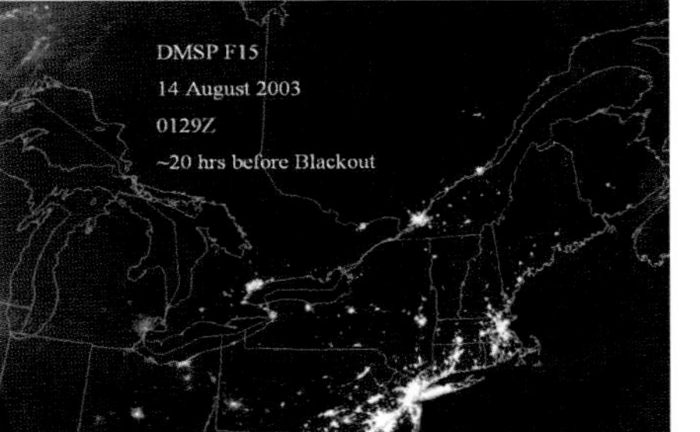

Site plan / American North - East.

+ACTION

.o1 Citizens — The citizens go outside of their homes. It is summer and the city has no power and their air conditioning does not work.

.o2 Coummuters — Commuters leave the city by walking, occupying the bridges.

BLACKOUT

.o3 Power — At 4:11pm the city of NY has a blackout because the Ohio net is not working.

+MINUTE o.oo

.o4 NY
.o5 Citizens
.o6 Underground
.o7 Cars

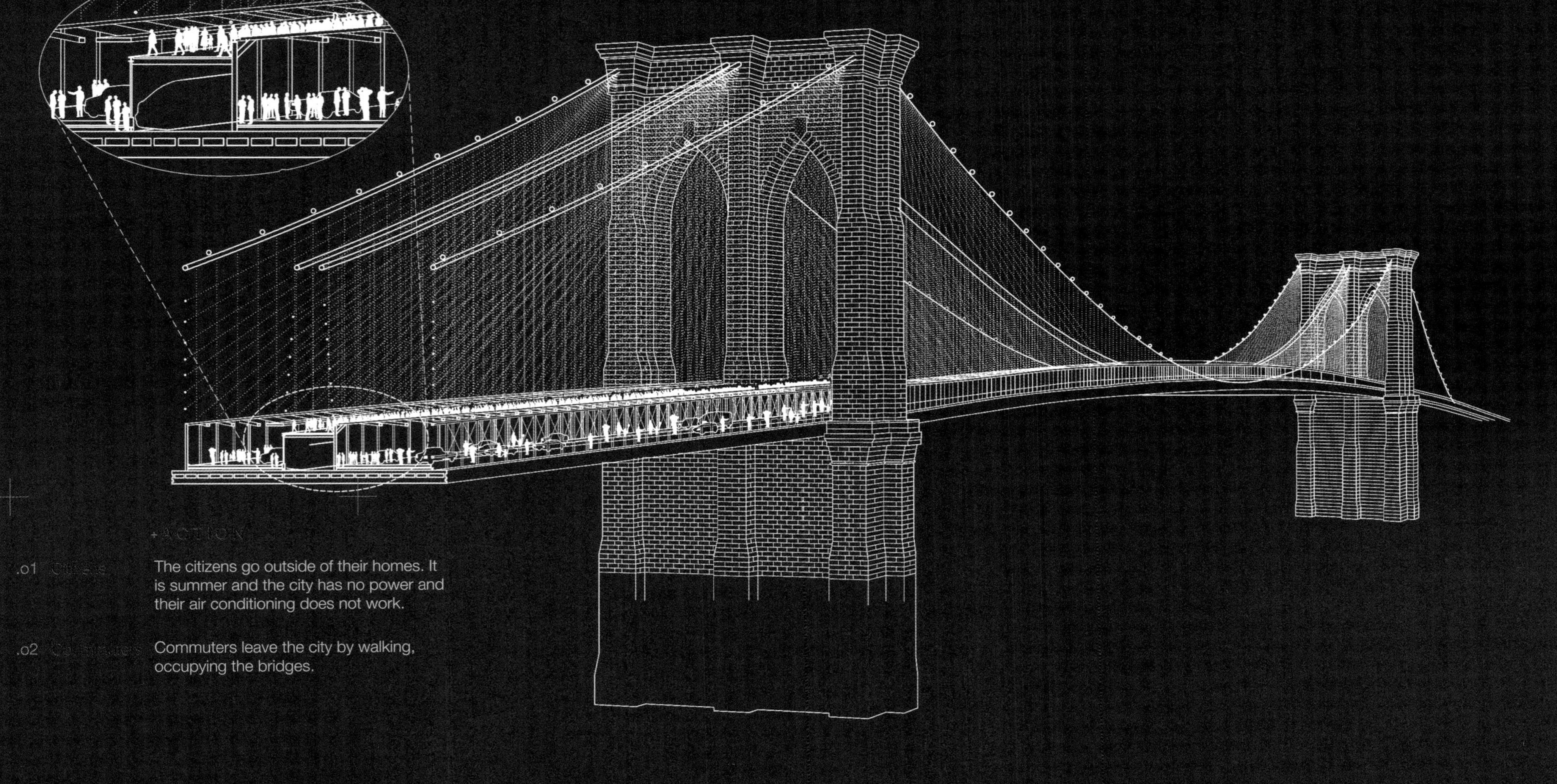

+ACTION

.o1 Citizens — The citizens go outside of their homes. It is summer and the city has no power and their air conditioning does not work.

.o2 Commuters — Commuters leave the city by walking, occupying the bridges.

.o3 Power

+BLACKOUT

At 4:11pm the city of NY has a blackout because the Ohio net is not working.

zoom 2x

+MINUTE 0.00

.04 NY
.05 Citizens
.06 Underground
.07 Cars

CASE STUDY #11

ORION. ANTI-GRAFFITI OSSARIO

Orion, A., Ossário. **Sao Paulo,** Brasil, 2006.

©Alexandre Orion.

cataloging	
.04	*Environmental modification*
.01	*Artistic intervention*
catalyst	ANTI-GRAFFITI
example	Art less polution. Ossario Sao Paulo.
date	2006
author	Alexandre Orion.
address	Tunnel Max Feffer between Cidade Jardim and Europe Avenue. Sao Paulo, Brasil. / CP: 01028-000

description

TO PAINT BY ERASING SMOKE

Orion paints a reverse-graffiti to condemn the car useand the polution that generates in Sao Paulo. The response of the authorities consisted in cleaning the smoke-stains of all the tunnels in order to avoid the proliferation of more graffities.

CASE STUDY #11

ORION

Bibliography

Ossario. www.osario.net

http://www.alexandreorion.com/ossario/ossario_eng.html

Sao Paulo's tunnels

In July, 2006, the drivers who were routinely crossing the Max Feffer tunnel that joins Cidade Jardim with the Avenue of Europe of the city of Sao Paulo, were suddenly discovering a change of aspect in that space: the light, the color of the tunnel were different.

In the densest second city of the world, with 12 million inhabitants, the boring drivers, who were always suffering this city's traffic, were realizing that in a few days all the tunnels of Sao Paulo were changing. Those inhospitable, abandoned, contaminated dirty pipes that all the drivers wanted to cross as fast as possible, were suddenly turning into different places.

Smoke as raw material

The night of July 13, 2006, the artist Alejandro Orion decided to start an intervention in the Max Feffer tunnel, which would last one month. Orion wanted to take part in an urban action, which would question the quality of life of the great city, an action that would use the material that the city itself had produced with its activity. Orion decided to use the smoke from the cars as base material to dye the tunnels' walls.

ANTI-GRAFFITI

The video recorded by Big Bonsai that explains how Orion realizes his intervention in the Feffer tunnel, clearly describes the process of intervention. Orion loaded a bag with white paper and provided himself with solvent and a gas mask, decided to enter the darkness of the tunnel in the middle of the night. Once inside the tunnel, Orion did an "inverse graffiti" that nobody had ever done before.

Orion's working method consists of drawing by erasing the smoke that existed on the walls of the tunnel. The graffiti that he realizes is the opposite of all the graffitis that had been done until then. His graffiti was not dirtying the walls with paintings, but it was actually cleaning them from the smoke stains of the cars.

The video of Orion's action explains how the police were surprised when they went into the tunnel and discovered that they could not denounce Orion because what he was doing was not a graffiti, but a cleaning of the tunnel walls. Before the confusion provoked by Orion's civic action, the final decision taken by police was to warn a cleaning team to come with a water hose and to finish erasing the skulls of Orion's anti-graffiti.

Orion's first intervention ended when the cleaning team erased the 160 meters of skulls that Orion had drawn. One month later, Orion decided to return to the Max Feffer tunnel and to continue his action. In that occasion, when Orion had drawn 120 meters of skulls, the police decided that the cleaning team should clean the 120 meters of Orion's skulls, and that they should also clean all the dirty tunnels of the whole city.

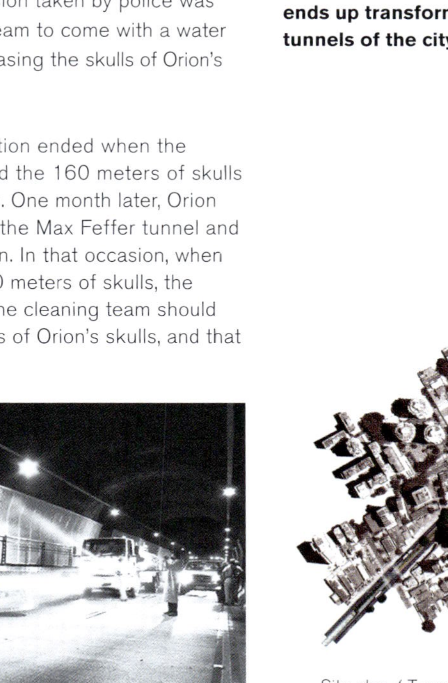

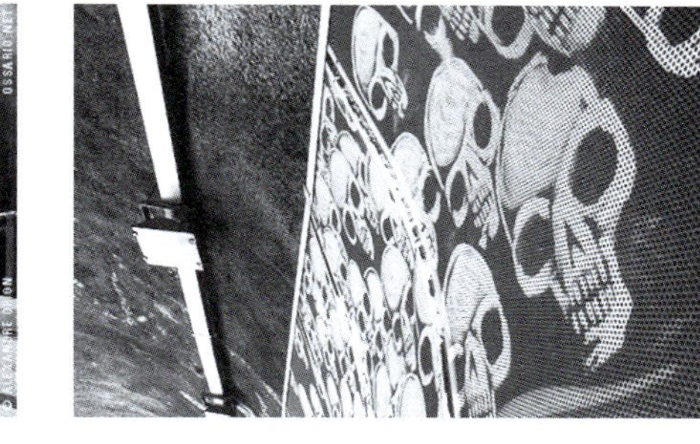

Magically, Orion's anti-graffiti makes that a minimal action, to "erase" the walls with paper roles, by cleaning all the smoke; and ends up transforming the aspect of all the tunnels of the city.

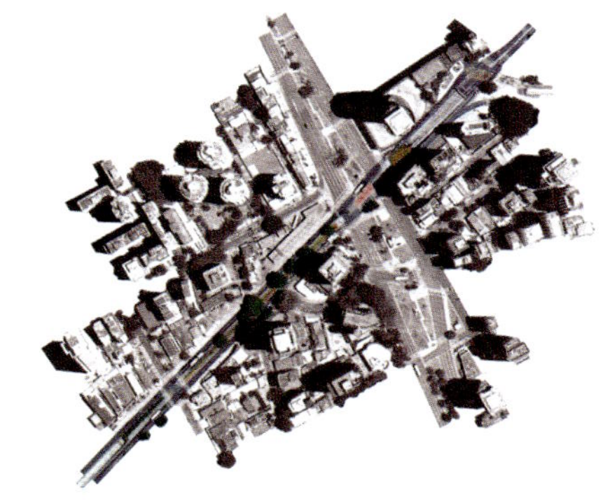

Site plan / Tunnel Max Feffer. Sao Paulo.

CLEAN. FIREFIGHTER

.01	fire truck	
.02	water and chalk	
.03	pipe	Pressurized water paints drawings of skulls through erasing.
.04	firefighter	Pressurized water cleans the smoke of the tunnels.
.05	section	The section of the tunnel includes a pedestrian path.
.06	pedestrian	The new, clean tunnels are used by pedestrians again.

ZOOM IN

.07	gas mask	The mask allows Orion to work in a contaminated environment.
.08	soap	
.09	towel	

ANTI-GRAFFITI

.10	smoke	
.11	skulls	
.12	graffiti-er	Alexandre Orion

MINUTE 0.00

.13	Cidade jardim	The city of Sao Paulo is huge, crowded extended city. Citizens use the private car for moving. The city has amazing traffic jams. It is a noisy and contaminated city.
.14	Max Feffer	Tunnel built by the Sao Paulo municipality to cross the Faria Lima avenue. The tunnel is used by 6,000 cars every day.
.15	Trees	The Faria Lima avenue has a green zone that is not occupiable in the center of his section.
.16	Boards	Wall cladding.
.17	Homeless	The tunnel is a perfect home for the homeless of Sao Paulo.

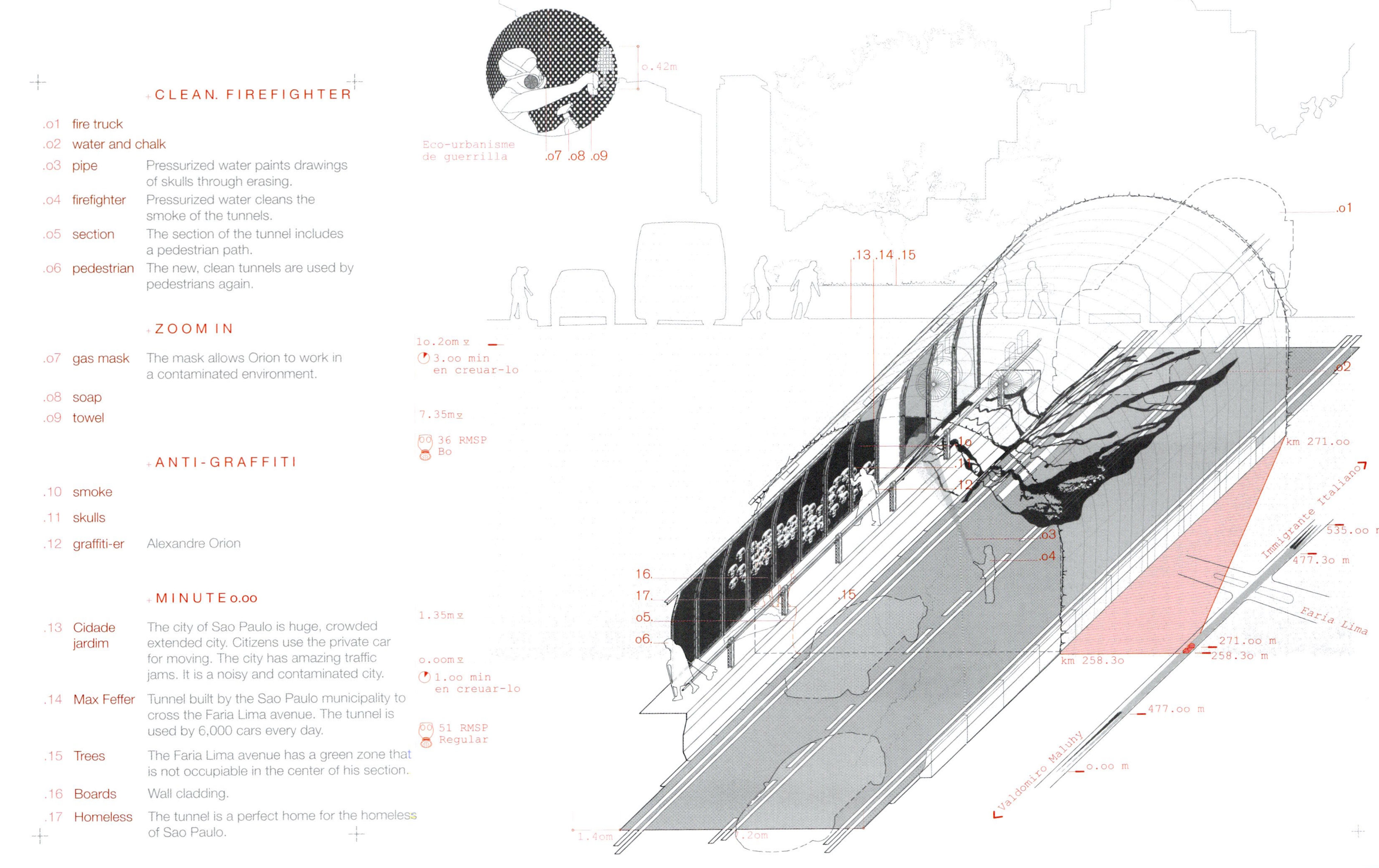

CLEAN. FIREFIGHTER

.o1	fire truck	
.o2	water and chalk	
.o3	pipe	Pressurized water paints drawings of skulls through erasing.
.o4	firefighter	Pressurized water cleans the smoke of the tunnels.
.o5	section	The section of the tunnel includes a pedestrian path.
.o6	pedestrian	The new, clean tunnels are used by pedestrians again.

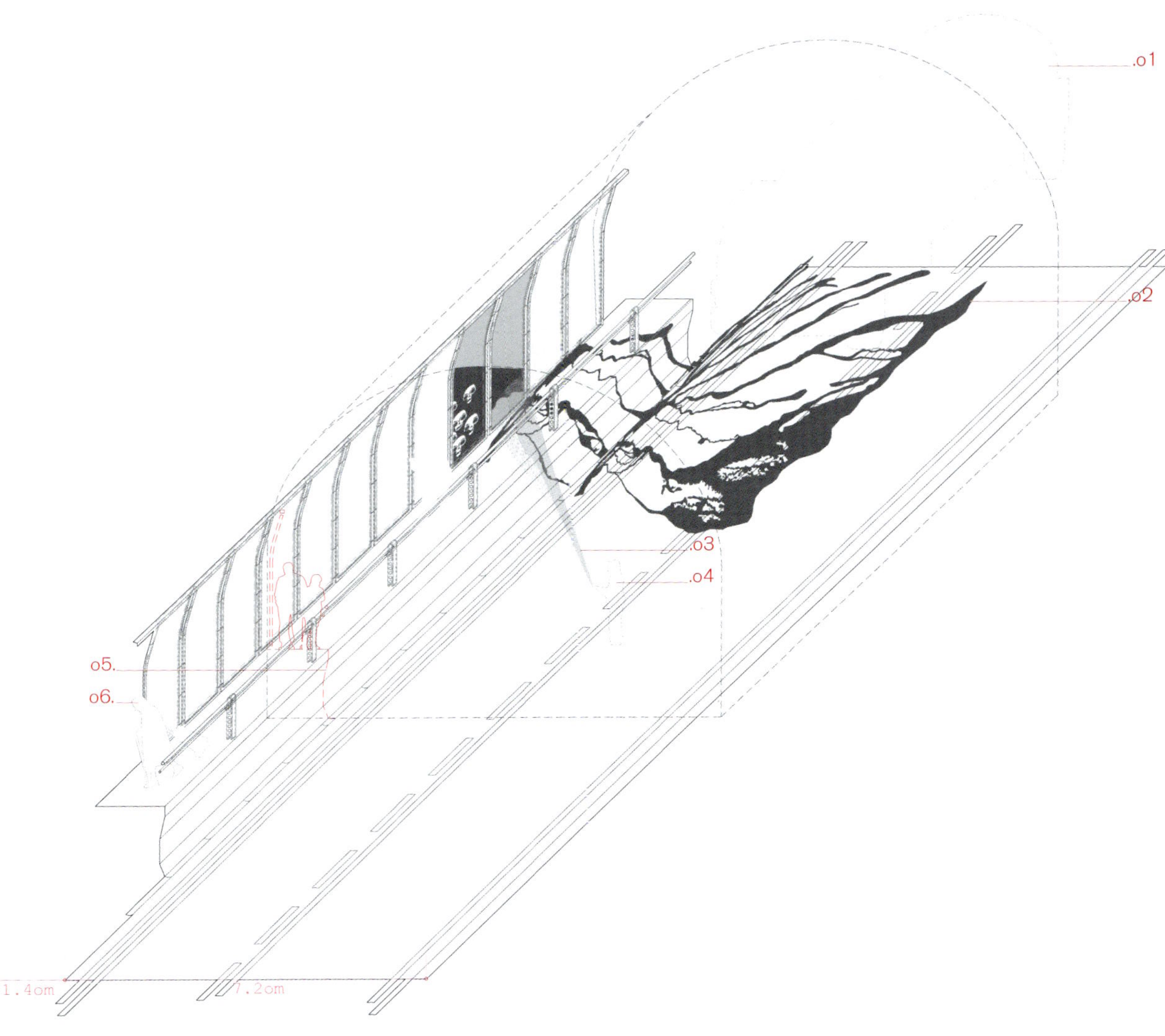

Eco-urbanisme de guerrilla

.o7 .o8 .o9

o.42m

+ZOOM IN

.o7 gas mask — The mask allows Orion to work in a contaminated environment.

.o8 soap

.o9 towel

+ANTI-GRAFFITI

.10 smoke

.11 skulls

.12 graffiti-er — Alexandre Orion

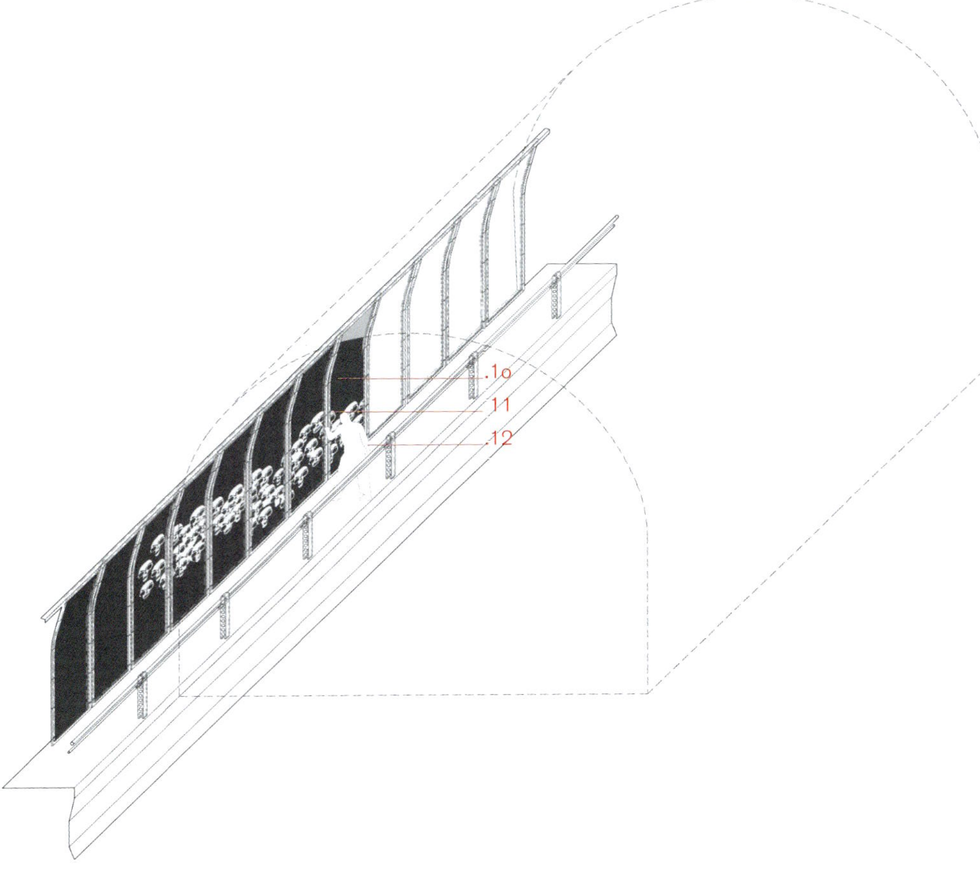

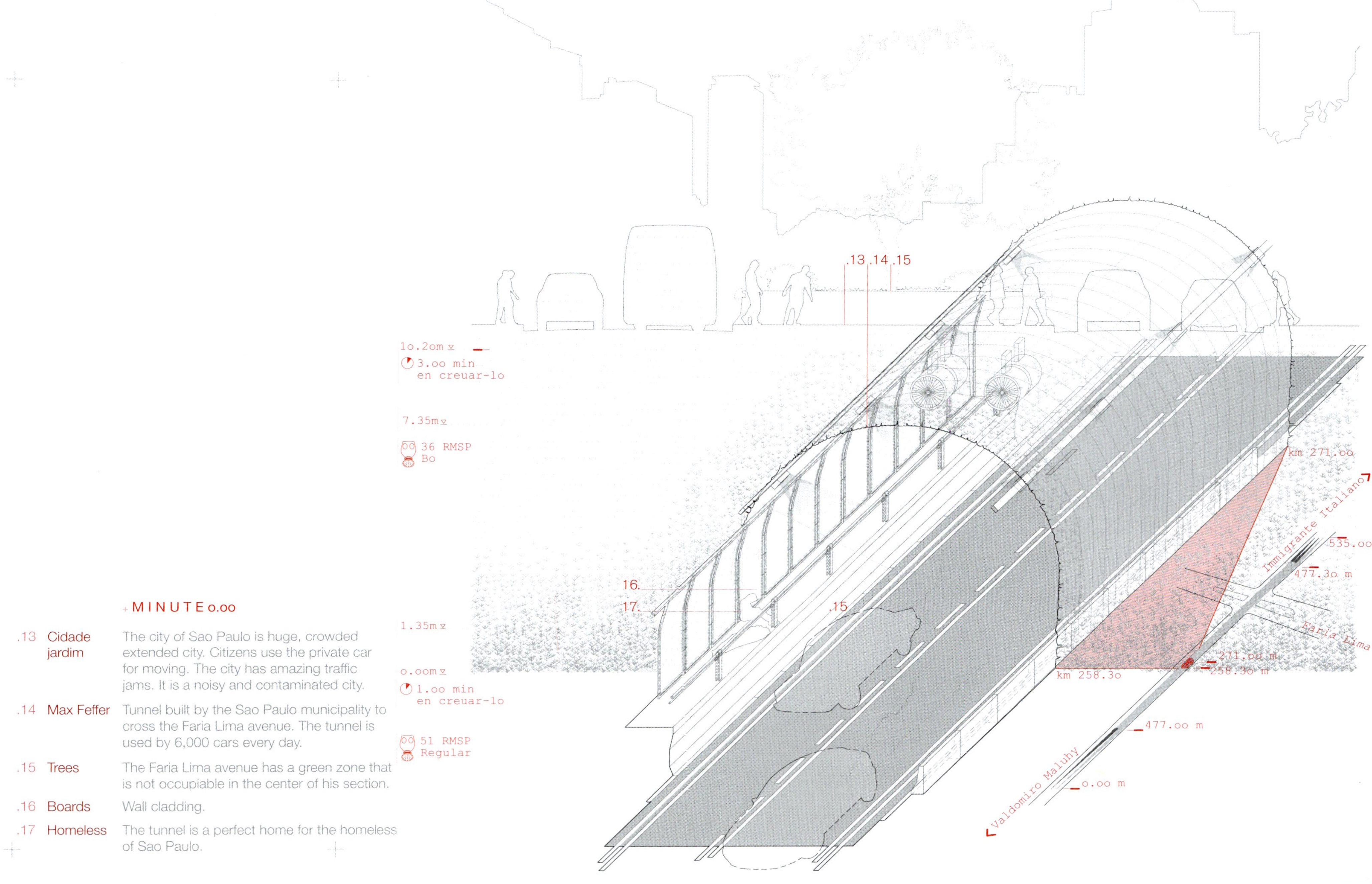

MINUTE o.oo

.13	Cidade jardim	The city of Sao Paulo is huge, crowded extended city. Citizens use the private car for moving. The city has amazing traffic jams. It is a noisy and contaminated city.
.14	Max Feffer	Tunnel built by the Sao Paulo municipality to cross the Faria Lima avenue. The tunnel is used by 6,000 cars every day.
.15	Trees	The Faria Lima avenue has a green zone that is not occupiable in the center of his section.
.16	Boards	Wall cladding.
.17	Homeless	The tunnel is a perfect home for the homeless of Sao Paulo.

Pergola Parets' Square. 1986.

Photography Ferran Freixa and M.B.E.

CASE STUDY #12

PARETS AND BALANCED SHADES

cataloging	.01	*Environmental modification*
	.03	*Construction of trading and leisure infrastructures*
catalyst		A BALANCED SHADE
example		The shades construct a public space Pèrgoles a Parets
date		1986
author		Enric Miralles and Carme Pinós.
address		Plaça de la Vila. Parets del Vallès, Barcelona. CP: 08150

description

COMFORT
ATMOSPHERE
TREES

When E and C arrived, the place had no type of attraction: it looked like the periphery, and not like the city center. They suddenly glanced towards the trees and the slopes of the square, seeing possibilities. How could they convert that ordinary place into an urban place?

CASE STUDY #12

PARETS AND BALANCED SHADES

Bibliography

Enric Miralles 1955-2000. Enrique Granell, Josep M. Rovira. (Barcelona: UPC, 2009).

"1983-1990 Miralles/Pinós". (Madrid: *El Croquis*)

The Architecture of Enric Miralles & Carme Pinos. Peter Buchanan, Dennis Dollens. (Santa Fe: Lumen Books, 1992)

A conversation

I explained to C that we were doing a research on public spaces where we studied how some elements of a minor scale or light actions are capable of transforming a place and of constructing a new space of relation. I explained that the project in Parets' Square done in 1985 with E is probably an example that would help us demonstrate our thesis very much. C reacted spontaneously with few desire of remembering the projects realized with E, as she usually did. Then, after a while, she C sat affectionately and started to explain the project, just like she always does. C never likes to draw on white papers where her new lines are the only drawings that stand out alone. So she suddenly took an old green carton box that was on the table beside us and started to draw the Parets' Square overlapping with the commercial texts of the former box.

An Indian market

"We wanted to create a new place. But it had to be a place that did not have anything to do with the context. We had the idea of contstructing a new foreign geometry to the emplacement. We had to jump over the stairs that were crossing the square, we had to ignore the strange form of its perimeter that limited it ... "The drawings that C realized while she explained the project on the commercial texts of the green box seemed to reproduce the same intentions of the Parets' Square. To jump over the existing stairs and to construct a new place...

"I remember that in that epoch we had a photo of a few covers of an Indian market. Looking at that photo, we discovered that what we wanted was to reproduce the effect of those fragile covers, capable of constructing a place. We took those covers and stretched them until the limits of the square to construct a shade that would

define a new place in the square. After that, the only strong idea of the project was to construct a few decks that would not be supported by four pillars."

BALANCED SHADES

In the conferences of the CCCB about Enric Miralles' life and work, organized by the department of composition of the ETSAB, the teacher Enrique Granell was explaining the difference between the shade created by a cloud and the one created by a tree. For Granell, and surely also for C and E, the shade of a tree always turns around the trunk and, therefore, it is always a shade that has a reference point, and that with its immobile position, is able to construct a place.

The covers the Parets' Square are placed on one side of the square and jump over the

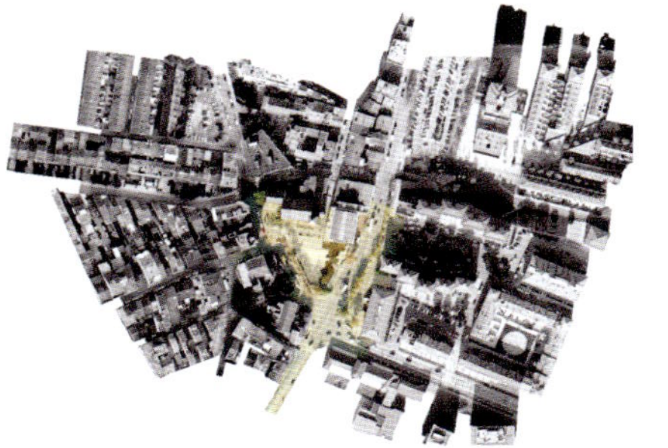

Site plan / Parets del Vallès, Barcelona.

stairs. The sloping position of the wooden covers, each of which is supported only by pillar, provokes the worrying appearance of a precarious balance about to break.

The area constructed by the covers and their pillars is indeed a place, a shade in permanent balance, a shade drawn by the perfect balance of a few covers strategically and finely placed on a Z-shaped beam, a stable equilibrium that constructs the space in shade in one of the three sides that define the square. The other two sides of the square are limit through a row of trees that help to close and to give dimension to the place for that C and E were looking for.

The precise and delicate study of the exact position of each one of the covers makes the Parets' Square turn into a public space constructed between action and drawing, a square between the public constructed space and the public not constructed space, a shade in balance is the catalyst of the space.

+ ACTIVITY

.o1 Citizens — The shade allows the citizens to inhabit the place. A kid rides his bike, just like at the Sants station square.

+ COMFORT

.o2 Shade — The shade built by the canopy creates a new inhabital place.

.o3 Temperature — The shade helps to change the environment.

+ MINUTE o.oo

.o4 Major Plaza — The plaza is the roof of an existing parking lot without trees.

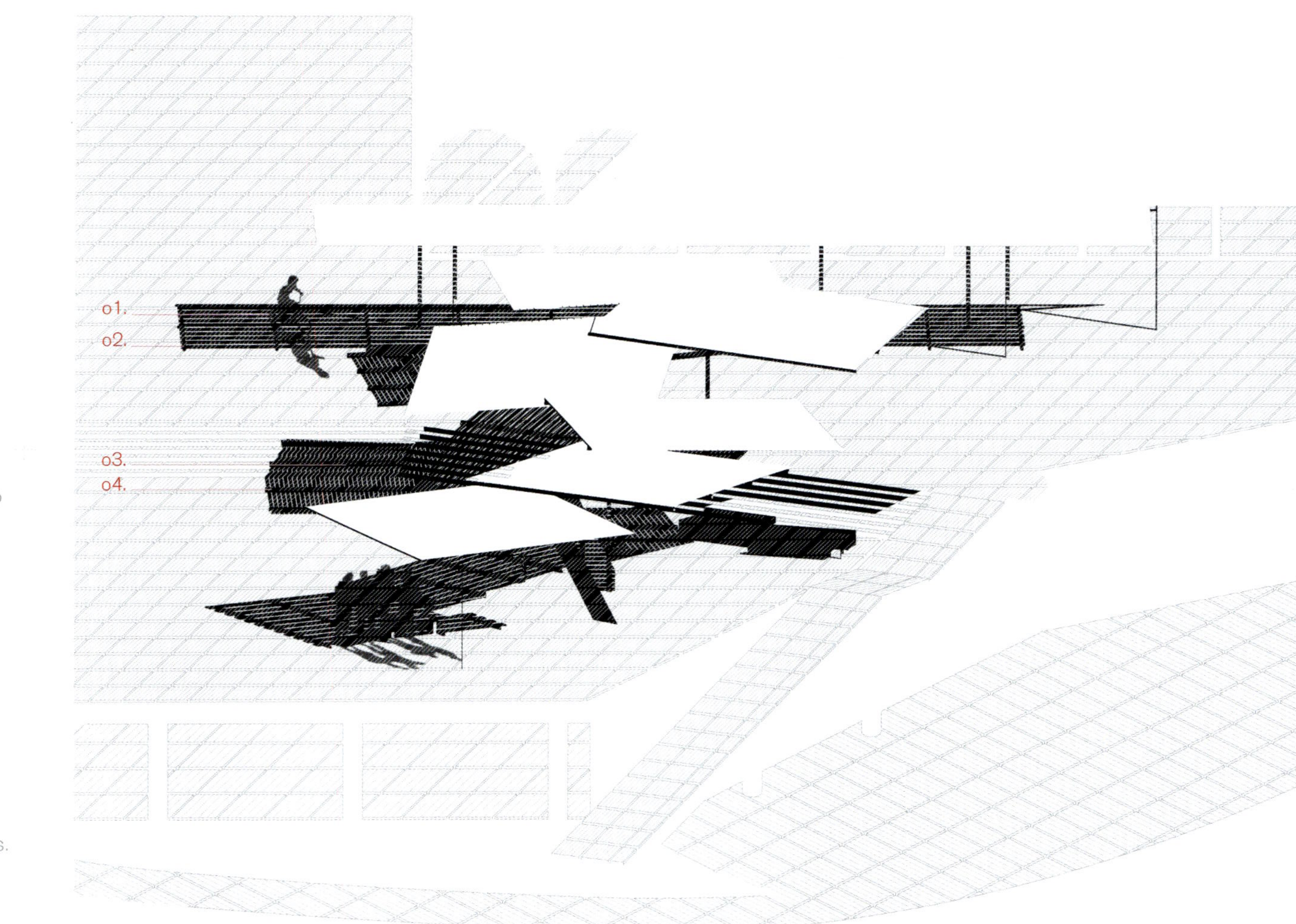

o1.

+ACTIVITY

.o1 Citizens

The shade allows the citizens to inhabit the place. A kid rides his bike, just like at the Sants station square.

o2.

o3.

+COMFORT

.o2 Shade — The shade built by the canopy creates a new inhabital place.

.o3 Temperature — The shade helps to change the environment.

+ MINUTE o.oo

.o4 Major Plaza The plaza is the roof of an existing parking lot without trees.

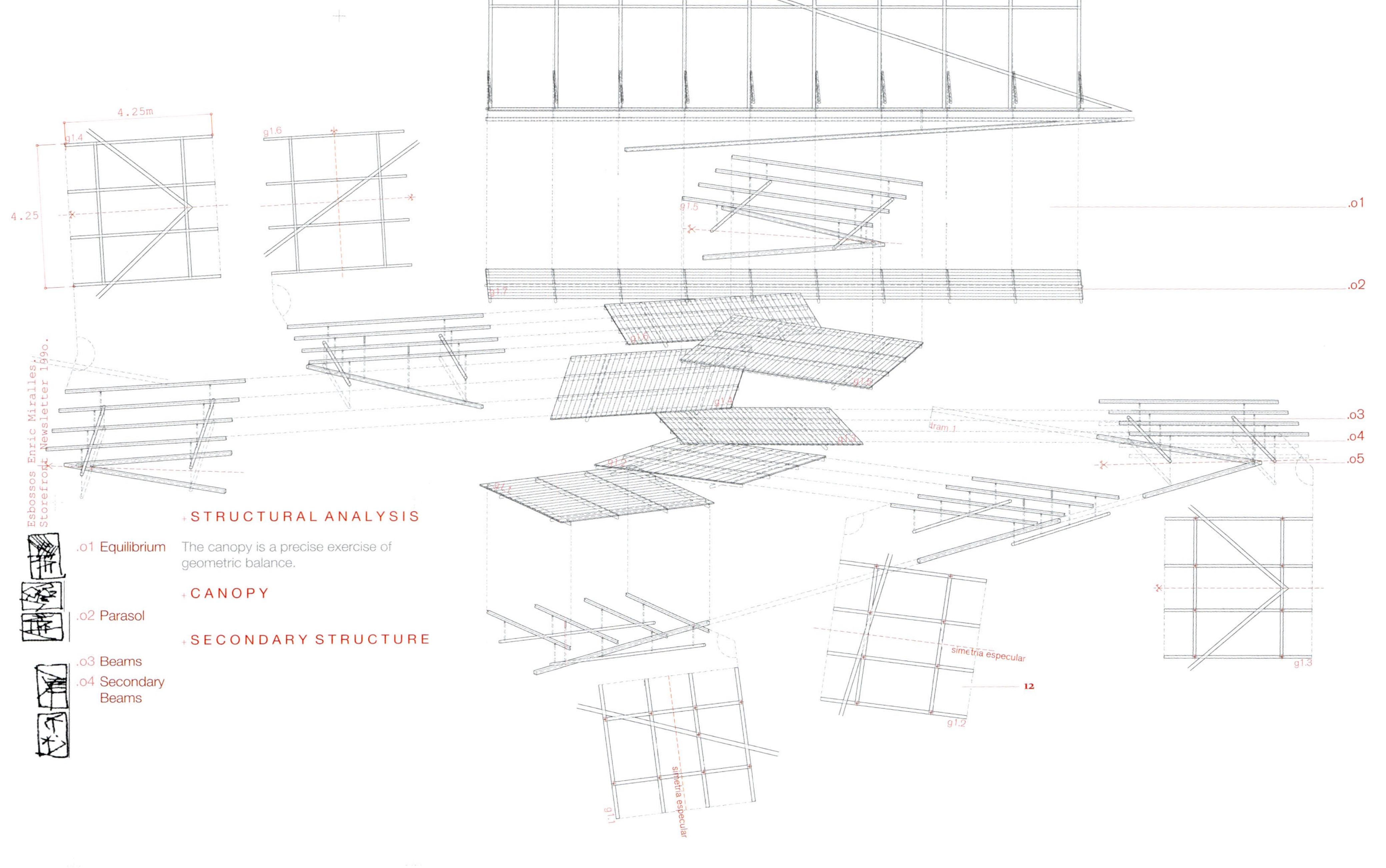

STRUCTURAL ANALYSIS

.o1 Equilibrium

The canopy is a precise exercise of geometric balance.

.o2 Parasol

CANOPY

SECONDARY STRUCTURE

.o3 Beams

.o4 Secondary Beams

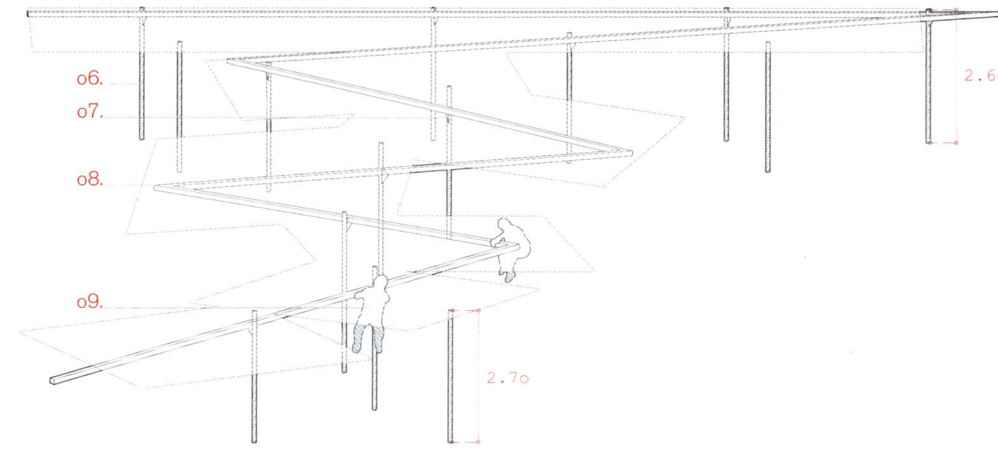

PRIMARY STRUCTURE

.o5 Attachments	
.o6 Columns	
.o7 Plates	Piece for hanging the main beam.
.o8 Main Beam	The main beam has a zig zag shape perfectly balanced with the perfect position of the columns.
.o9 Hammer Man	

Lisses, France

Photography David Belle.

CASE STUDY #13

PARKOUR. THE PRACTICED CITY

cataloging	
.04	*Artistic intervention*
catalyst	SLIGHT URBAN TOPOGRAPHIC ACCIDENTS
example	Urban action sport. Lisses, France.
date	1995 - today
author	David Belle.
address	Urban spaces with slight topographic accidents.

description

PUBLIC
PRIVATE

The Parkour, also known as the art of moving, is a discipline or philosophy that consists of moving from a place of the city to another, in the fastest way possible, using only the human body skills.

CASE STUDY #13

PARKOUR

Bibliography

El animal Público. Manuel Delgado. (Barcelona: Alianza Editorial)

http://es.wikipedia.org/wiki/Parkour

http://kyzr.free.fr/davidbelle/

Politicized city or practiced city

The Parkour might be the most similar image that would graphically exemplify the transformation that the contemporary city is suffering, that the anthropologist Manuel Delgado explains in his book *The Public Animal.* For Delgado, modern urbanism is killing the city. The politicized modern city is turning into the new model of city. Regular cities, smooth cities, Utopian cities, calm, tidy, understandable cities; controlled by night and by day, to prevent any contingency from altering the perfect quietude.

The practiced city

A planned modern city opposite to the practised city (a fully urbanized one) – not in the sense of a city fully submissive to the urbanism laws, but in that of a city abandonned in all the aspects related to urban planning – a complicated human community, formed by a society that produces something and then undoes it again and again. A city that understands urban things as fluctuating, random and casual, that is opposed to any final structural crystallization. A city formed by the multiple crossing of transitory situations.

The traceur David Belle (1973, Fécamp, France, inventor of the parkour), could easily be the main character of a movie called *The Public Animal*, written and directed by Manuel Delgado, interpreting his script: David Belle "it's the ordinary pedestrian who re-invents the planned spaces, and uses them his own way, imposing his tours to any previous politically-determined formalization".

Body and city

The Parkour, also known as the art of moving, is a discipline or philosophy that consists of moving from a place of the city to another, in the fastest way possible, using only the human body skills. It consists of an urban activity in which once a distance has been defined, it is a question of jumping over all the obstacles that you find on your way: fences, rails, walls, covers, etc.

The traceuers run, jump, climb, fly, and keep in balance, practising the Parkour and fundamentally developping a better self confidence, checking if they are capable of overcoming the obstacles and accidents that they have found.

URBAN TOPOGRAPHIC ACCIDENTS

David Belle, gymnast and actor, is an explorer of the differences of the politicized city. The traceurs of the current Parkour, as well as the skaters, have turned into expert scanners, capable of discovering the accidents of the smooth indifferent contemporary cities.

Urban actors sensitive to the prominences of the city's skin, suitable to recognize the tangible and visible condition of the surface and to make ourselves conscious of the world in which we live. They are, as Ignasi de Solà Morales would say, experts that are capable of letting the subject know what surrounds it, through a sensitive way, experiencing it in space and time.

Urban accidents

The Parkour demonstrates how the difference can construct an urban identity formed by weak, casual and transitory references. An identity of misunderstandings, of double meanings of transfers and accidents. Maybe a way of understanding today's public spaces is by means of accidental catalysts. Catalysts that discover the discontinuities to activate the space.

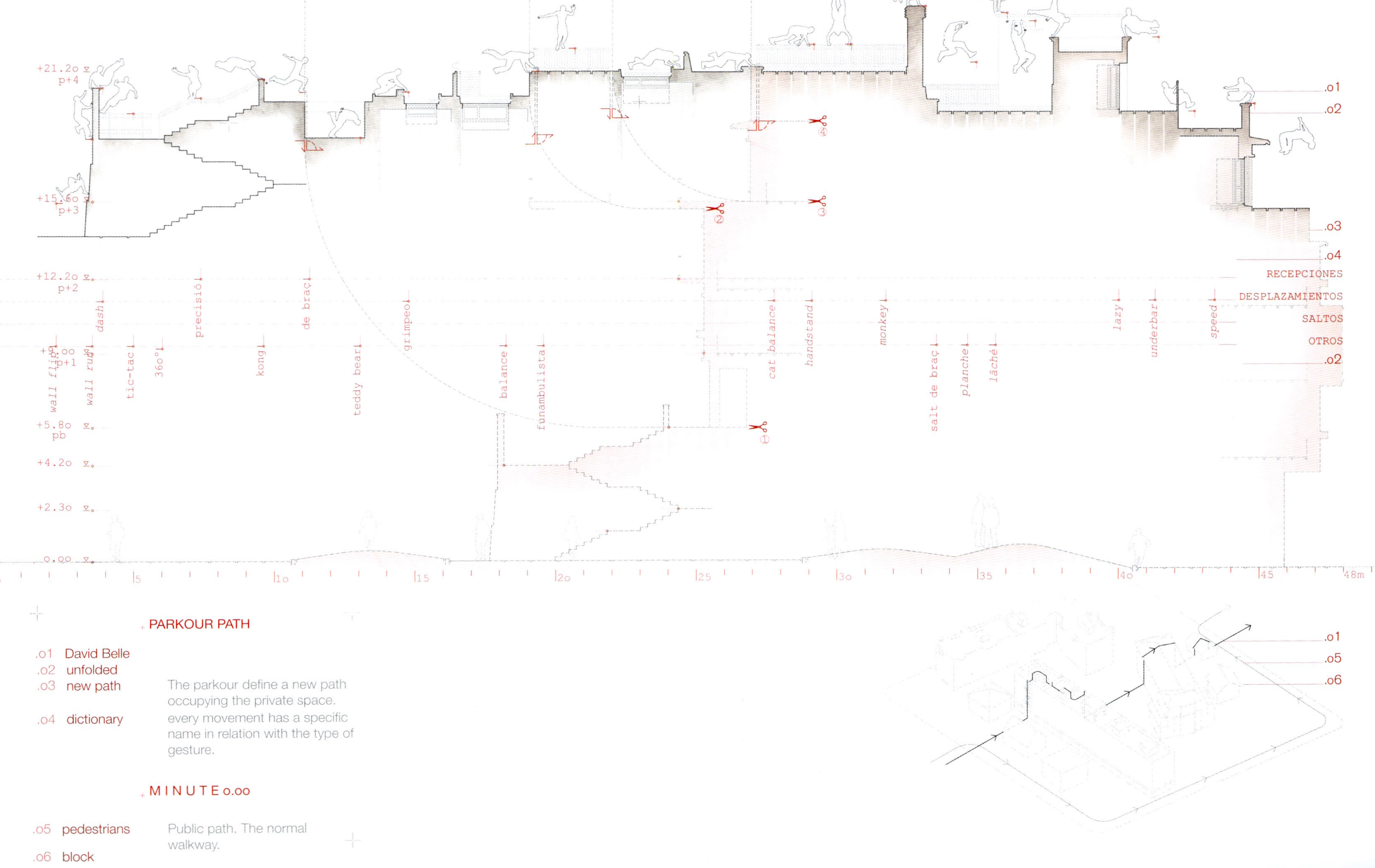

PARKOUR PATH

.o1 David Belle
.o2 unfolded
.o3 new path
.o4 dictionary

The parkour define a new path occupying the private space. every movement has a specific name in relation with the type of gesture.

MINUTE o.oo

.o5 pedestrians
.o6 block

Public path. The normal walkway.

PARKOUR PATH

.o1 David Belle
.o2 unfolded
.o3 new path
.o4 dictionary

The parkour define a new path occupying the private space. every movement has a specific name in relation with the type of gesture.

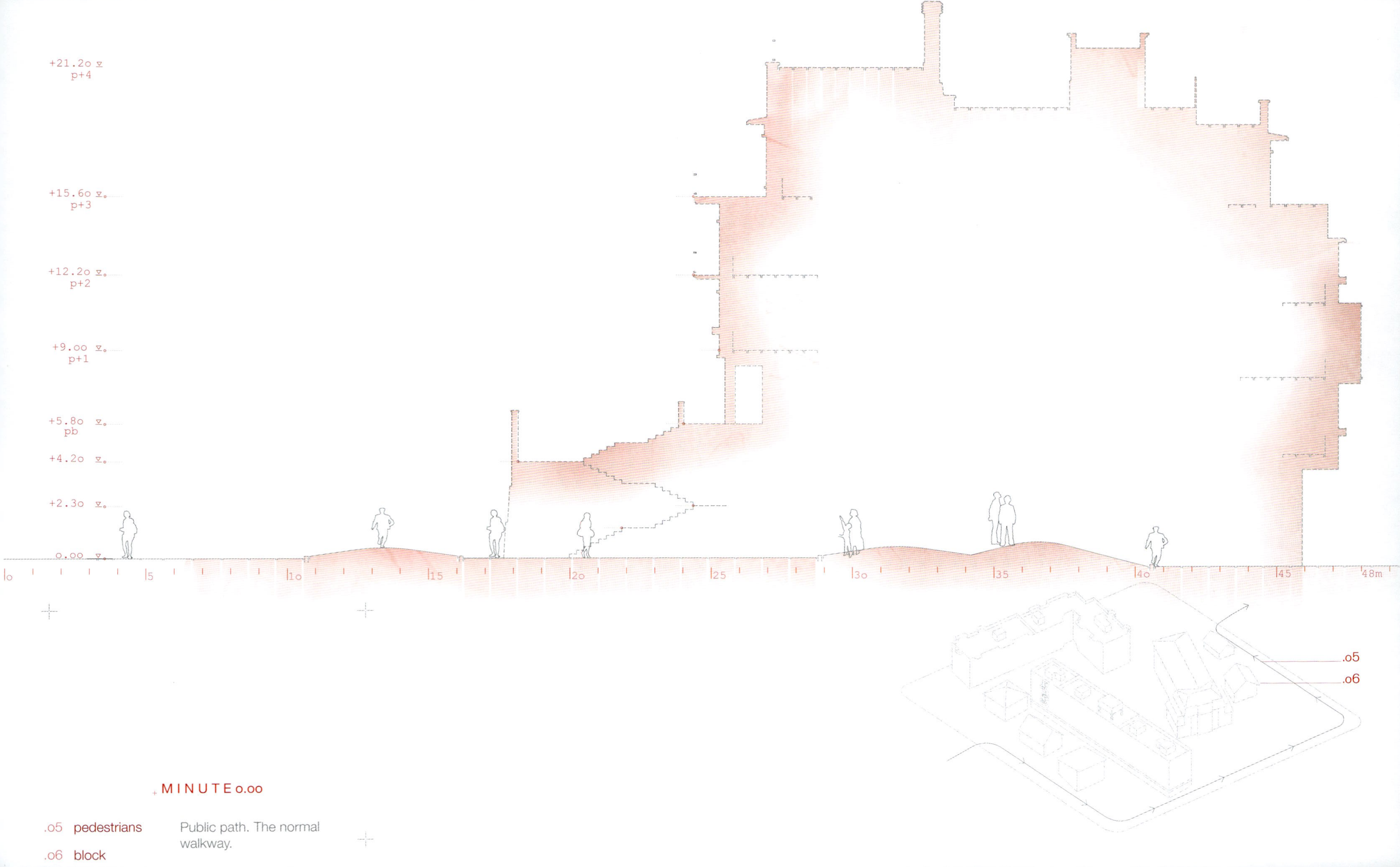

MINUTE o.oo

.o5 pedestrians

.o6 block

Public path. The normal walkway.

CASE STUDY #14

SAO PAULO. PIXAÇAOS IN THE SKY

"Pixadores" painting a façade

Photography CHOQUE

cataloging	
.04	*Artistic intervention*
.05	*Scale mediation*
catalyst	PIXAÇAO
example	Vandalism to stretch the public space. Sao Paulo.
date	2000 - Nowadays.
author	Pixadores.
address	Sao Paulo.

description

TO OCCUPY GRAFFITI LANDSCAPE

The pixades are codified messages with a strong geographic condition. Graffitis are normally executed at the eye level of the people that walk by. However, the pixades change the scale and situate themselves in relation with the city and the landscape.

CASE STUDY #14

SAO PAULO

Bibliography

De rolê pela cidade: os pixadores em Sao Paulo.
Alexandre Barbosa Pereira 2005.
PhD dissertation.

Pichaçao carioca: etnografia e uma proposta de entendimimento.
David da Costa Aguiar de Souza 2007.
PhD dissertation.

A consolidated local action

The phenomenon of the Pixadors in Sao Paulo is not an artistic ephemeral and not transcendental manifestation. Several studies realized by different anthropologists, as Masimo Canevacci, as well as some recent thesis, like *De rolê pela cidade: os pixadores em Sao Paulo* from Alexandre Barbosa Pereira in 2005; *Pichaçao carioca: etnografia e uma proposta de entendimimento* from David da Costa Aguiar de Souza in 2007; they all support the importance of the Pixadors as urban actions that are nowadays already consolidated.

Property invasion

Massimo Canevacci defines the Pixadors as "an already classic phenomenon of urban communication in Sao Paulo, a style that has turned into something really typical of the ca-

pital" (1993). The Pixades are realized by urban bands formed by young people from the periphery of the city that
move to the center of Sao Paulo to realize their actions. These groups of young boys wait and look for the suitable moment. Then, they enter some private property, walk up to the last floor and paint their Pixaçaos, struggling and hanging from the façades, when the security team of the building does not see them.

The skill used by the Pixadors to execute their interventions is similar, but at the same time very different, to the one used to create graffities. The Pixadors also use painting spray, but normally only one color: black. The paintings are never figurative, but they seem to be rather hieroglyphic or trimmings. Inscriptions, Arabic signs - deformed and personal Gothics, realized with a lot of precision and decision; executed, normally, in the cornices of the buildings.

The pixaçaos are more like written messages realized with a coded language practically only to be understood by those who participate in the different Pixadors bands of Sao Paulo; they are not at all like virtuous and ingenious drawings with colors.

PIXADES IN THE SKY

The pixaçaos do not want to be confused with the pichaçaos. Even though the correct way to write it in portuguese would be with the letter "ch", the pixaçaos want their name to be written with "x". They think that the use of this letter becomes a more honnest way to explain what they are really interested in when they take part in their actions: to leave a print on the city. Even though the meaning of the word pichaçao in portuguese is a graffiti painting, it is funny that in catalan, there is a coincidence between the meaning of the word pixaçao – to leave a sign to define the appropriation of a space – with the kind of intervention that they are realizing.

Pixaçaos body and city

The pixaçaos are codified messages with a strong geographic condition. Graffitis are normally executed at the eye level of the people that walk by. However, the pixades change the scale and situated in relation with the city and the landscape.

The pictures of the pixadors doing their dangerous actions in height are always taken with the city as the background. So there is a clear relation between the paintings and landscape.

The pixades transform the public space of the center of Sao Paulo. The dimensions of the public spaces of the streets and squares are extended and stretched until the cornises, due to the dialog established between the different groups of pixadors of the city, and through their paintings found in the last floors of the building; revelling and emphasizing the last conquered building, through the drawings.

Pixades from the top

One day, Sao Paulo wakes up with a new pixaçao saying "ancima de nous deus" (God above all of us); a few days later, there is a response from another pixaçao in a higher building saying

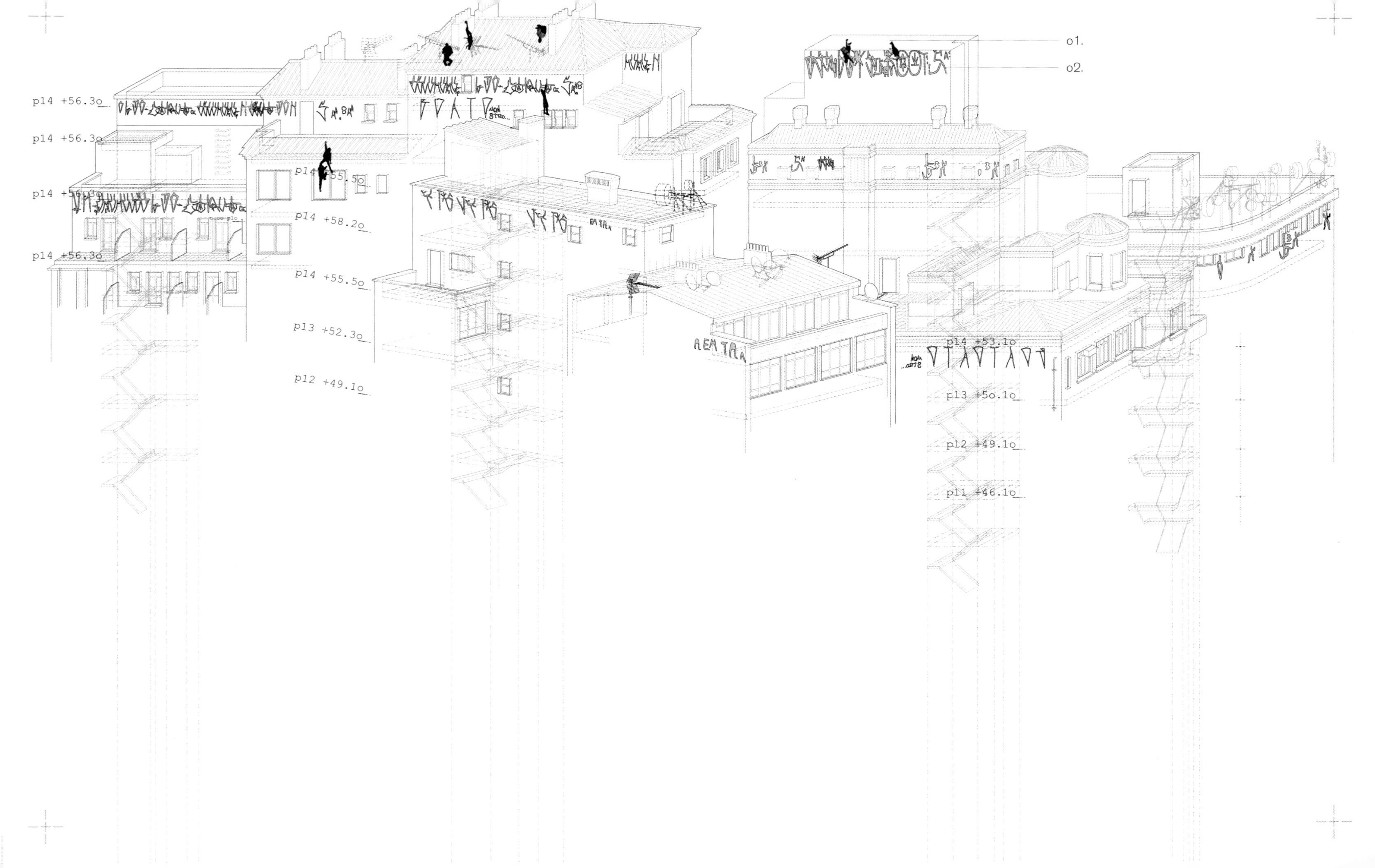

p14 +56.3o
p14 +56.3o
p14 +56.3o
p14 +56.3o
p14 +55.5o
p14 +58.2o
p14 +55.5o
p13 +52.3o
p12 +49.1o
p14 +53.1o
p13 +5o.1o
p12 +49.1o
p11 +46.1o
o1.
o2.

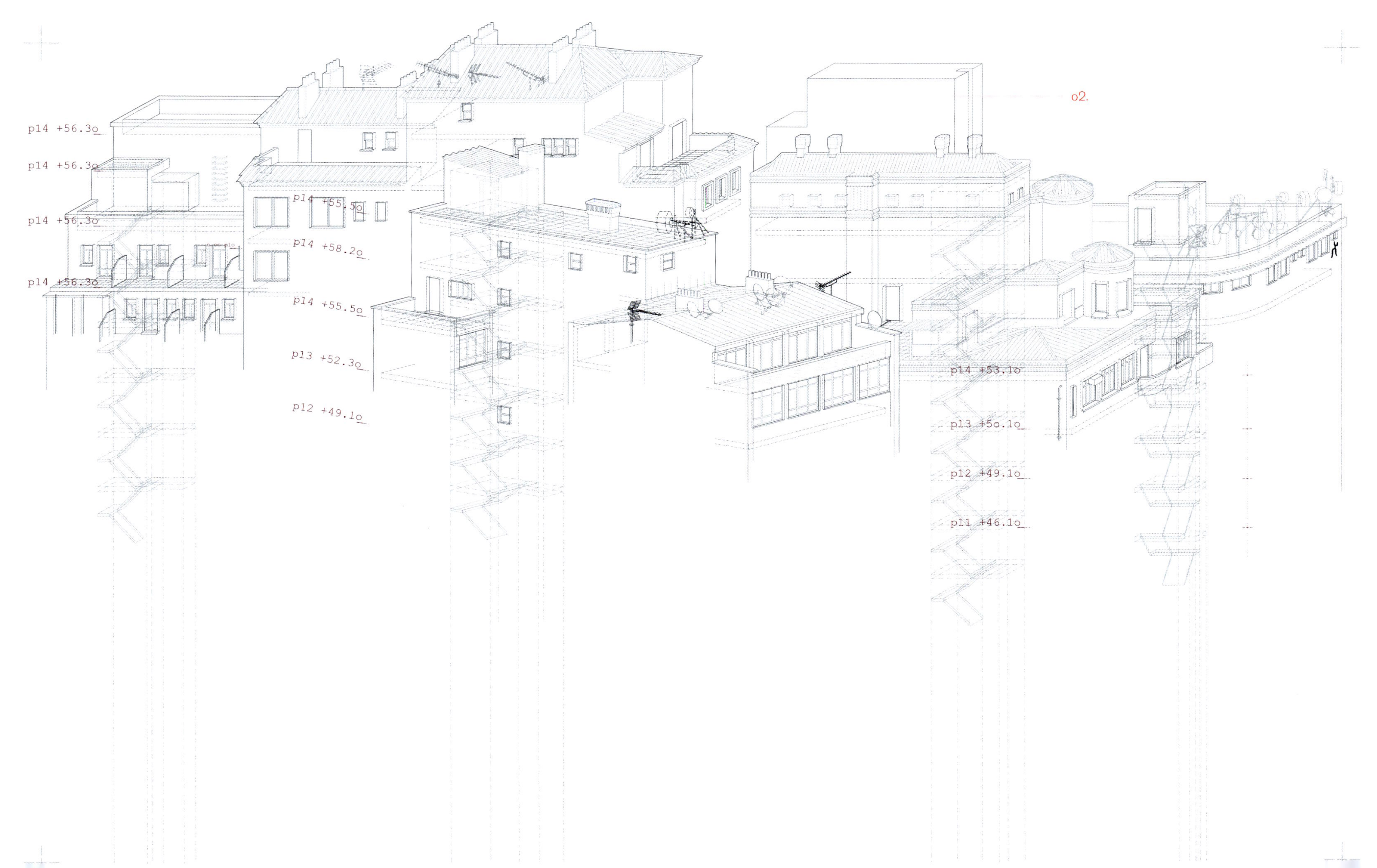
o2.
p14 +56.3o
p14 +56.3o
p14 +56.3o
p14 +56.3o
p14 +55.5o
p14 +58.2o
p14 +55.5o
p13 +52.3o
p12 +49.1o
p14 +53.1o
p13 +5o.1o
p12 +49.1o
p11 +46.1o

01.

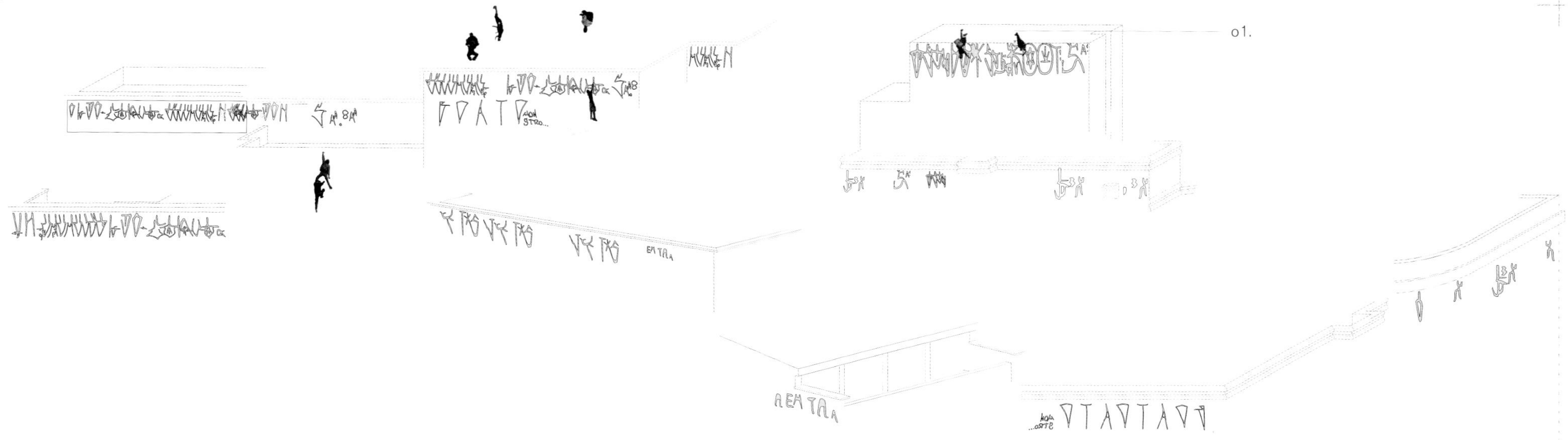

o1.

+OPERATOR
.o1 Pixador
Brazillian artist group that goes inside of the private building to paint their signs.
+CATALYST
.o2 Pixada
Paintings at the top of the building. The pub c space is extended from the walkway to th moldings of the buildings.
+MINUTE o.oo
.o3 Historic Center
Sao Paulo 1.5 million of inhabitants.
20 millino in all of the Metropolitan zone.
o3.

Sketch by Mies van der Rohe
Seagram Square. New York

Photography Kathryn Dean

CASE STUDY #15

SEAGRAM BUILDING. 50cm VS 15.700cm

cataloging	
.05	*Scale mediation*
.03	*Construction of trading and leisure infrastructures*
catalyst	STEPS
example	Leveling that synthesizes ard catalyses the public space. Seagram Plaza.
date	1954-58
author	Ludwig Mies van der Rohe.
address	375th Park Avenue. Between 52nd and 53nd Street. New York City, NY / Zip Code: 10152.

description

STEP
URBAN INTENSITY

Despite the moment that has become the most significant urban intervention of the Seagram Building is the square in front of it, another pretty intense instant are the steps that separate the square from the street. Small steps that distract the attention of the pedestrian seconds before facing the volume of the building. Tall and slender, as if before seeing it they wouldn't need to focus on going up the 50 cm of the stairs.

CASE STUDY #15

SEAGRAM BUILDING

bibliography

Mies van der Rohe: A Critical Biography. Franz Schulze. (Chicago: University of Chicago Press, 1995).

Mies Van Der Rohe. David Spaeth. (New York: Rizzoli, 1988).

Against Hugh Ferrys' imaginary

In 1950, when Phyllis Lambert, Samuel Bronfman's daughter, the president and owner of the Joseph E. Seagram Company, found out that her dad wanted to construct a singular building in New York's Fifth Avenue, she started to look into the projects done so far, to be able to intervene and advise in the development of the project.

Bronfman had initially given the project of the Seagram Building to Khan & Jacobs architects. Lambert's interest in realizing an innovative and special building in New York started to make him doubt on the project realized until then. According to Lambert, Khan & Jacob's project was simply a known design that was limited to the Zoning laws, with solutions that were very current and used.

Lambert wanted the Seagram Building to become a new type of office building, that would not be the heritage of the imagination of the architect and drawer Hugh Ferrys, the responsible of the carbon drawings applying New York's insolation laws of "step by step" in 1922.

Mies van der Rohe choice

Lambert, advised by Philip Johnson, had interviews with different architects, such as Le Corbusier or Wright, until she finally met Mies. Mies' interest in investigating a new way of approaching architecture through new constructive solutions and his capacity of specifying his ideas towards the construction helped Lambert decide that she would definitively give the Seagram project to Mies.

One of the most special monographies of the PaperBack collection is the one about Mies van der Rohe, in which each project is catalyzed through a construction detail. There is no other book such as this one in this great collection, in which the architect's projects are resumed by a construction detail.

MIES STEP BY STEP

Mies' proposal for the Seagram Building was not only an elegant piece of modern architecture, but also an urban decision, and this is what made it become an exceptional masterpiece. Even Phyllis Lambert said so in one of her letters in the 1st of December of 1954: "The solution for the building contains many extraordinary aspects; if you walk up or down the avenue, it will be almost impossible to see it, because it is placed behind the alignment of façades of the street; but once you get there, you get an almost baroque sensation, you can't understand what that is. And then you see it, with its magnificent square, it does not fall on you, for you are able to contemplate it without feeling oppressed or needing to cross the street to have enough perspective. In front of you, there is a great entrance for a great building. I get emotional, just from the thought of it".

Mies managed to understand and condense all the history of the city, through a subtle movement, by emplacing the building in a new urban space. It was an intelligent way of giving importance to the building: by offering the city of New York a new public space; exactly the contrary than what Gropius' PANAM building offered a few years later, placing the building over the Fifth Avenue, occupying the street.

Drawing and step

Lambert's initial idea was to run from Hugh Ferriss' carbon drawings of the step-shaped skyscrapers for the Seagram building; and casually, Mies finally synthesized his project with a carbon drawing. It is a handmade sketch in which Mies explains how the building is placed in the city, with a square in front of it; a drawing in which, Mies clearly explains the importance

of the new public space, by cutting off the Seagram's volume. It's a project that uses the topography to construct a new place for the building; a sketch in which Mies emphasizes the most important moment of the project, the moment of entering the square.

With a very marked and deep line, Mies knows that in the moment when you pass the first stair and enter the square, you raise your view to observe an impressing building. At that moment, Mies decided that he would not stair the building, but that it would be the Seagram that would terrace the public space of the city.

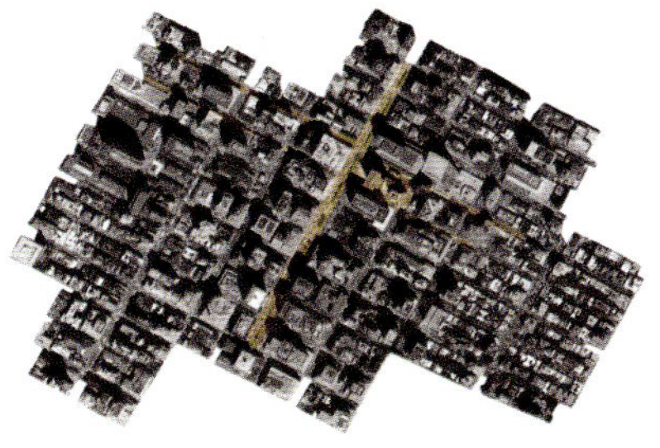

Site plan / Park Avenue. NY.

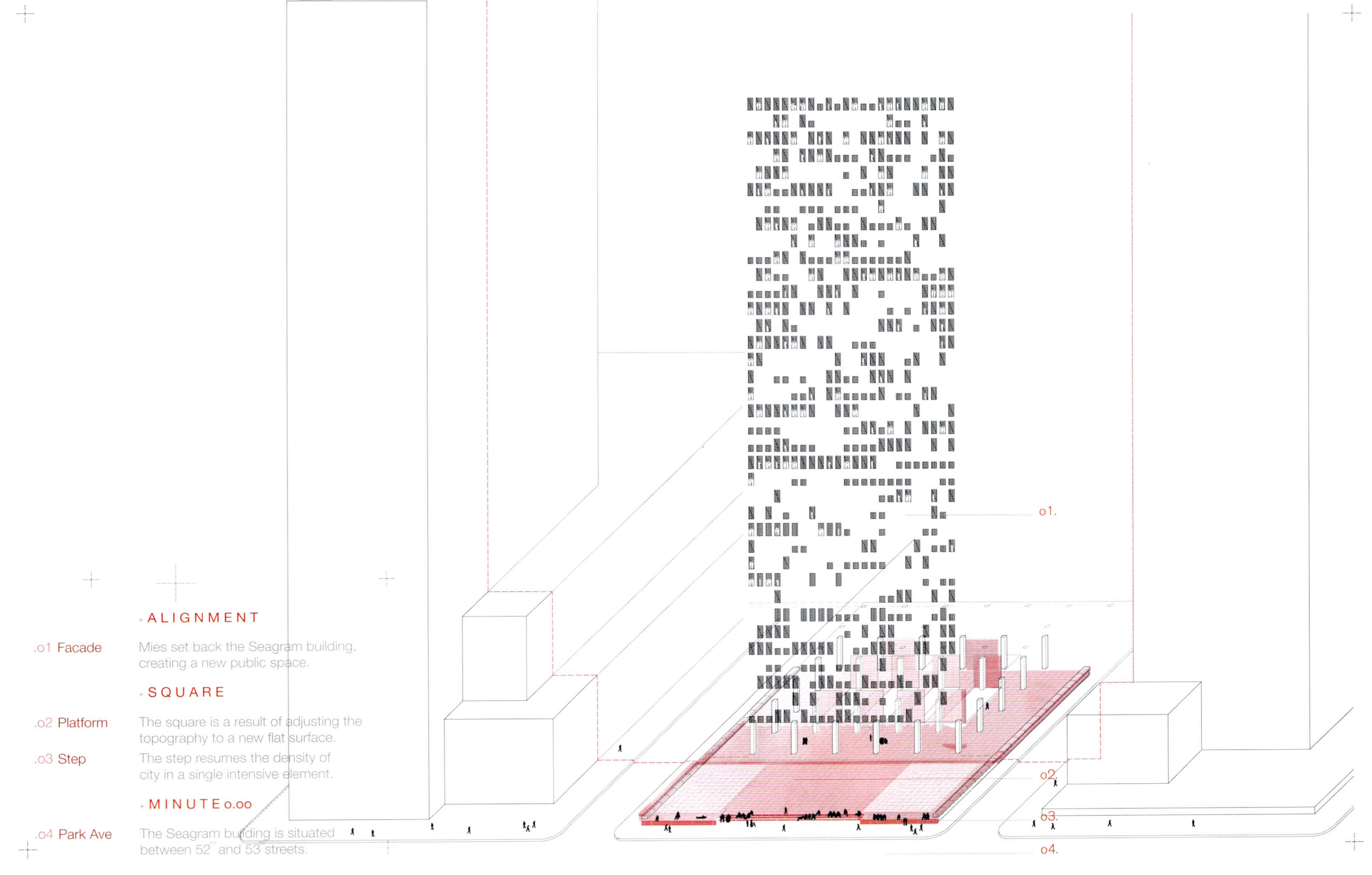

+ALIGNMENT

.o1 Facade — Mies set back the Seagram building, creating a new public space.

+SQUARE

.o2 Platform — The square is a result of adjusting the topography to a new flat surface.

.o3 Step — The step resumes the density of city in a single intensive element.

+MINUTE o.oo

.o4 Park Ave — The Seagram building is situated between 52nd and 53rd streets.

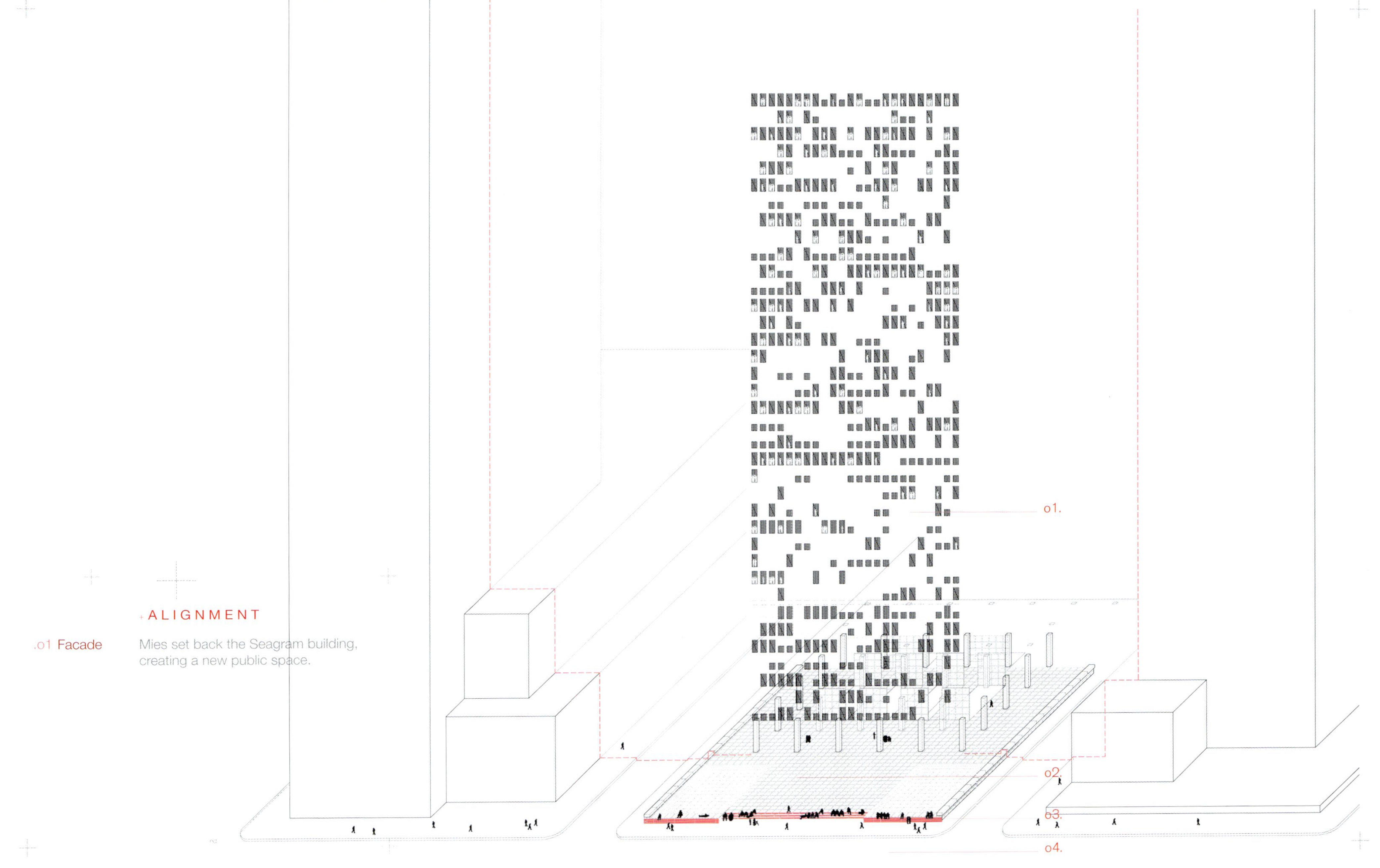

+ALIGNMENT
.o1 Facade
Mies set back the Seagram building, creating a new public space.
o1.
o2.
o3.
o4.

+ SQUARE

.o2 Platform — The square is a result of adjusting the topography to a new flat surface.

.o3 Step — The step resumes the density of city in a single intensive element.

+ MINUTE 0.00

.04 Park Ave

The Seagram building is situated between 52 and 53 streets.

Journaux
PAPET
TABAC
Bière de luxe
Chez Margot
CAFÉ
Bière de luxe

Photogram of the movie
Mon Oncle, by Jacques Tati.

CASE STUDY #16

TATI. PUBLIC GARBAGE

cataloging	
.05	*Scale mediation*
.03	*Construction of trading and leisure infrastructures*
catalyst	MOUNTAIN OF GARBAGE
example	Qualify the space by means of a casual object. Street cleaner in the movie *Mon Oncle*
date	1958
author	Jacques Tati.
address	French city with an industrial neighborhood under development.

description

NATURAL
ARTIFICIAL
CASUAL
TO GO FOR A
WALK

Monsieur Hulot shows us two opposite worlds, while having a walk and whistling. The strict, sterile and perfect order of a modern zone of the city meets the casual, disorganized, imperfect but rich life of an old French neighborhood. The garbage from the local market that the sweeper has collected qualifies the space and becomes the focus of attraction for the pedestrians.

CASE STUDY #16

TATI

Bibliography

Wasting Away. Kevin Lynch.
(San Francisco: Sierra Club Books, 1990).

Theory of the derive and other situationist texts.
Libero Andreotti, Xavier Costa.
(Barcelona: Actar, 1996)

http://www.tativille.com/

Hubiera preferido invitarles a cenar. Elia Torres Tur.
(Barcelona: Pre-Textos)

Dibujos de Enric Miralles y Elias Torres en la India. 1992.
Ed Massilla

Architecture with music

I discovered Jacques Tati in his classes of architecture and landscape, with the professor E.T – one of the most important ones that the ETSAB has had-. E.T. was not only a provocative and stimulating teacher during our student phase, but he was also and is still nowadays an architect that shows that architecture can also be pleasure. It is very hard to think of the movie *Mon Oncle* without thinking about its music. And Monsieur Hulot's whistle while he is randomly having a walk with his bicycle through the streets? ET also taught us how architecture is also music and that there is also some existing architecture without strength.

In the 50s, Tati became a comic capable of continuing the old movie comedy and visual gags without sacrificing the arsenal of music and comedy from the suggestive world of noises.

The six films produced and directed by him follow a process to develop an increasingly refined criticism towards the city and modern architecture. In the film *Mon Oncle*, Tati contrasts the abstract, aseptic functional and perfect world of modern architecture from the Arpel family with Monsieur Hulot's real, dirty and spontaneous life. The only son of the Arpel marriage, Gérard, always waited impatiently to go for a walk with his dreamy, absent-minded and spontaneous uncle; in his ridiculously functional house.

Monsieur Hulot was like a guide to his nephew, showing him superfluous and trivial things of everyday life, accompanying him on walks in which the child discovered many things that you can not find at home and that are in some way essential to feel alive and happy.

E.T. and noise

In the movie, Tati finely uses noise as a fundamental tool to qualify spaces of opposite conditions. In the mute scenes without words,

the mockings and noises critically communicate the inability to live in an ultra designed modern space.

In many of his few articles, E.T normally fills the images with noises. Drawings, handmade collages, pieces of vegetal paper and notes at the margin of the page, all qualify his writings. Personal attempts full of what he would call architecture without strength. All these things seem superfluous and accessory but are actually indispensable to help projects become real architecture.

URBANISM WITHOUT STRENGTH

In the market scene of the movie Mon Oncle, a peasant who sells lettuces, tomatoes and vegetables weighs his clients' orders with a balance placed in a badly parked van with a punctured wheel. The unbalanced balance does not weigh correctly and so the farmer carelessly charges more than it costs.

Garbage

A road sweeper that walks around the market square gathers the garbage of the stallholders from the market. He strolls up and down the valley displacing the mountain of garbage around

the whole square and makes the garbage become the element that qualifies this space; as the noise does in many other scenes.

A mountain of garbage turns into the real catalyst of the square. It is an area of attraction that acts as a magnet, catching the people who walk around the square and gathering around the garbage. A collection of the remains of the market ends up converting that space into a civic place of relation.

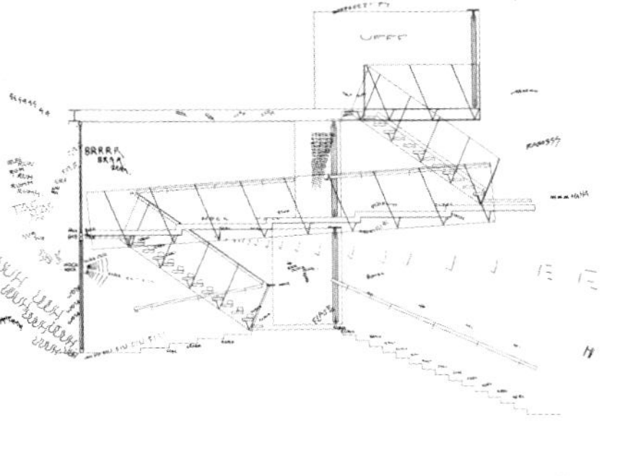

+CHARACTERS

.01 Monsieur Hulot
.02 Neighbor
.03 Sweepers

+CONTEXT

.04 Cafe Chez
.05 Access
.06 Market

+CATALYST

.07 Trash — The trash becomes an attraction that everybody stands around.

+FRAMES

.08 minute 53 — In the 52ND minute the sweeper did not collect the trash and the characters are at the cafe plaza.

.09 minute 55 — In the 55TH minute the trash is collected in a mound and the people have moved around it.

A. feathers
B. cardboard bag
C. flask
D. eggs
E. sheet of newspaper
F. glass bottle
G. broken bowl
H. paper bag
I. piece of cloth
J. tree leaves
K. banana skin
L. glass can
M. lettuce leaves

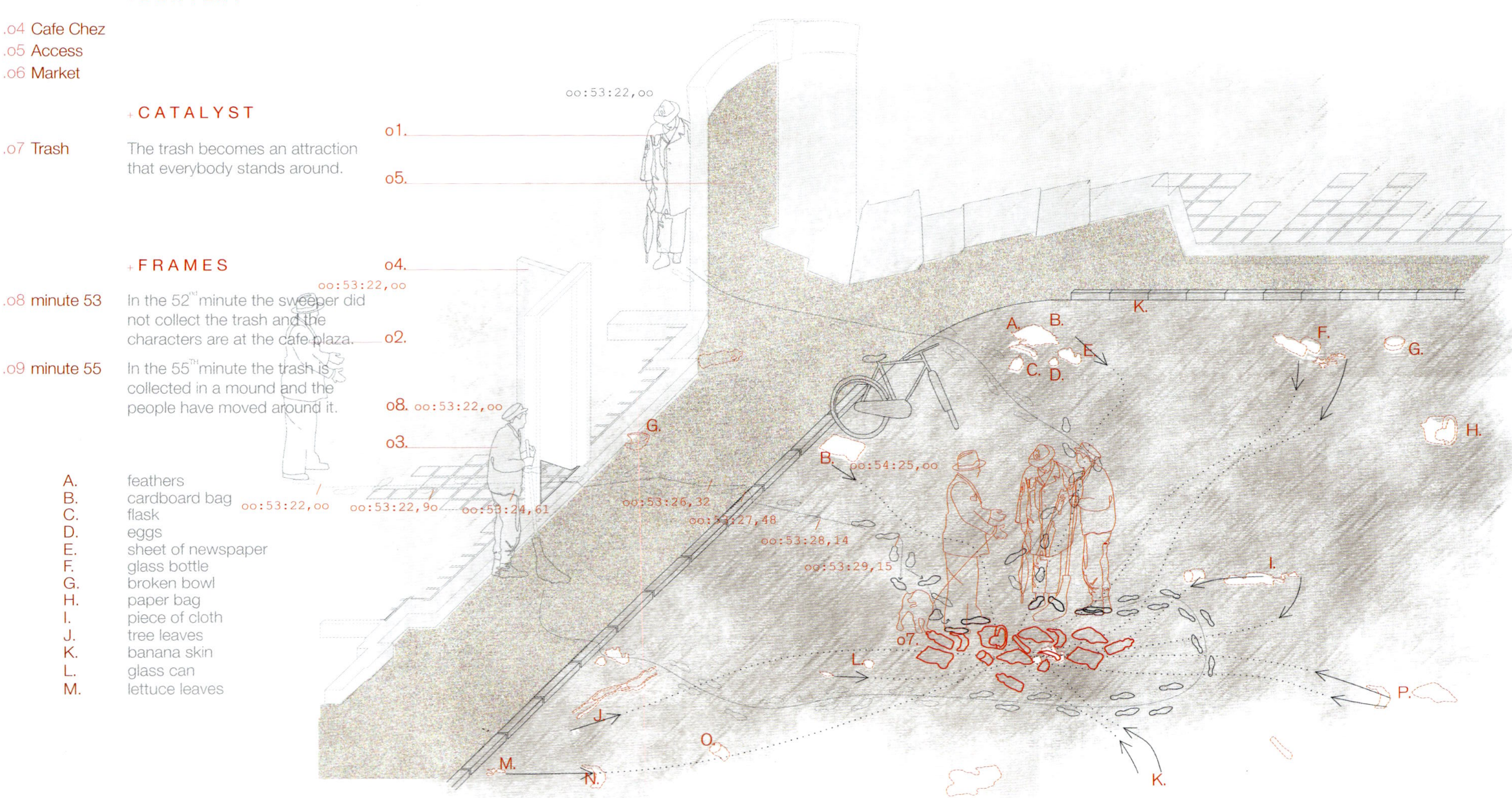

+ FRAMES

.08 minute 53 — In the 52nd minute the sweeper did not collect the trash and the characters are at the cafe plaza.

.09 minute 55 — In the 55th minute the trash is collected in a mound and the people have moved around it.

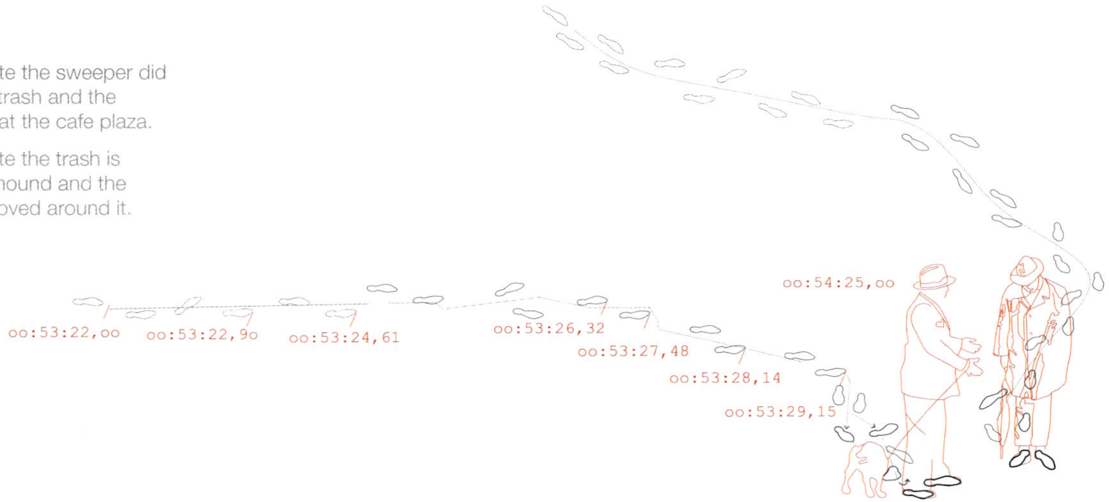

oo:53:22,oo

oo:53:22,9o

oo:53:24,61

oo:53:26,32

oo:53:27,48

oo:53:28,14

oo:53:29,15

oo:54:25,oo

+ CATALYST

.o7 Trash

The trash becomes an attraction that everybody stands around.

- A. feathers
- B. cardboard bag
- C. flask
- D. eggs
- E. sheet of newspaper
- F. glass bottle
- G. broken bowl
- H. paper bag
- I. piece of cloth
- J. tree leaves
- K. banana skin
- L. glass can
- M. lettuce leaves

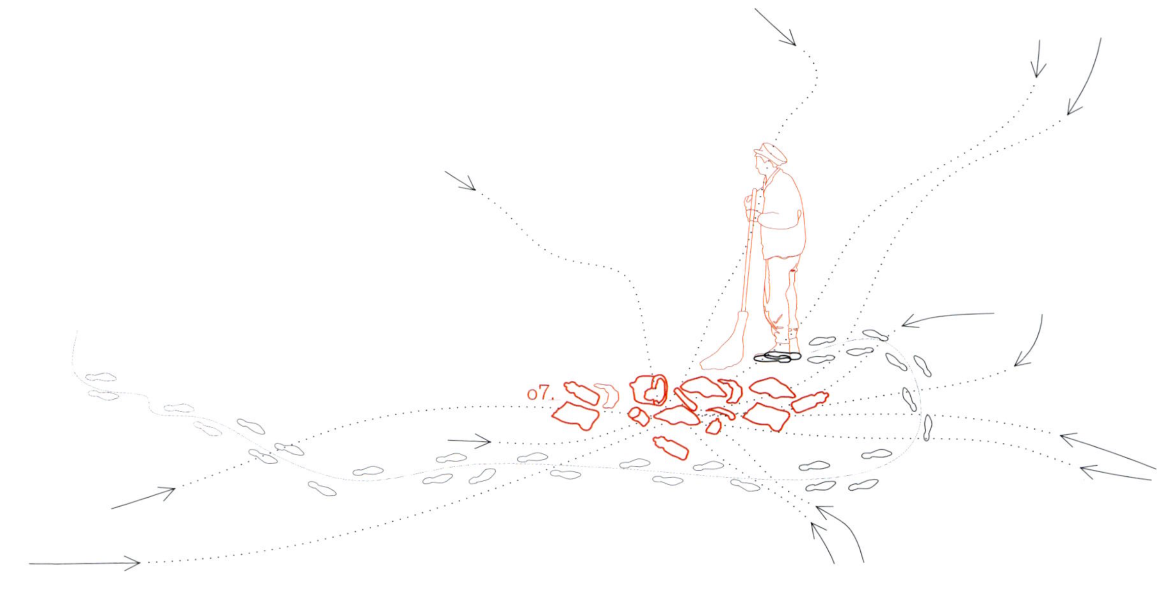

+ CHARACTERS

.o1 Monsieur Hulot
.o2 Neighbor
.o3 Sweepers

+ CONTEXT

.o4 Cafe Chez
.o5 Access
.o6 Market

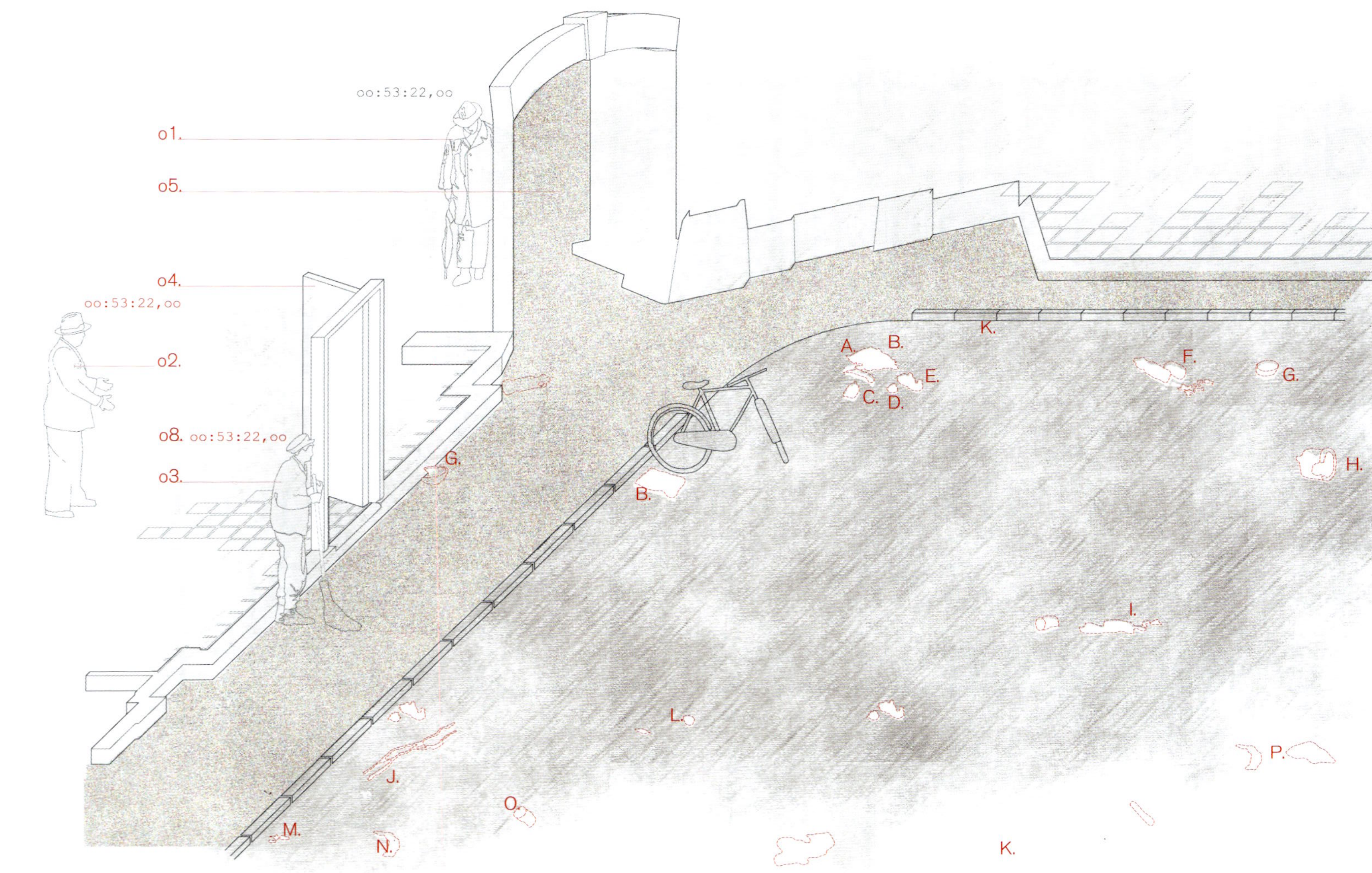

Colin, standing in the corner of the square, was waiting for Chloe. The square was round and there was a Church, Pigeons, a Garden, benches, and, in front, cars and buses on macadam. The sun, too, was waiting for Chloe, but it could have fun making shadows, or helping wild beans sprout in convenient cracks; it could fling open shutters and shame a street lamp still lit because of the recklessness of an electric company technician. Colin rolled up the ends of his gloves and prepared his first sentence. As the hour approached, the modification of its structure steadily intensified

CASE STUDY # 17

VIAN. PINK CLOUD

Bourbon Street, New Orleans.

cataloging

.01 *Environmental modification*

.03 *Construction of trading and leisure infrastructures*

.05 *Scale mediation*

catalyst

CLOUD

example

Construction of a place in a public space occupied by many people. *L'écume des jours.*

date

1947

author

Boris Vian.

address

Street similar to Bourbon Street in New Orleans.

description

TRANSPARENT
COMFORT
SUGAR

The pink cloud that surrounds and walks with Chloe and Colin is the real catalyst of the street that we walk in, an urban cloud that helps them feel and experience the public space in a singular and intimate way.

CASE STUDY #17

VIAN

bibliography

Froth on the Daydream. Boris Vian.
(London: Quartet Books, 1988).

De lo mecánico a lo termodinámico. Javier Garcia-German.
(Barcelona: Gustavo Gili)

He did not know what to do with Chloe. Perhaps bring her to a tearoom, but the atmosphere is usually more or less depressing, and piggish forty-year-old women who eat seven cream cakes while lifting their pinkies, he could not stand that. He could only imagine piggishness for men, for whom it takes on all its meaning whereas natural dignity is retained. Not to the movies, she won't accept that. Not to the deputydrome, she won't like that. Not to the calf races, she'll be scared. Not to the Hospital Saint-Louis, it's illegal. Not to the Louvre, there are satyrs behind the assyrian cherubs. Not to the Saint-Lazare train station, where only wheelbarrows remain, and not a single train.
-Hello!...
Chloe had just come up from behind. He quickly took off his glove, got tangled up in it, punched himself in the nose, yelled "Ouch!..." and shook her hand. Chloe was laughing.
- You seem pretty nervous!...
A long fur coat, the same color as her hair, a fur hat and little fur-lined boots.
She took Colin by the arm.
- Give me your arm. You're not really on the ball today!...
- I felt better the last time, admitted Colin.
She laughed again, looked at him and laughed more and even better.
- You're making fun of me, said Colin, pitiful. That's not very nice.
- Are you happy to see me? – said Chloe.
- Yes!... said Colin

They were walking, following he first sidewalk they found. A little pink cloud descended from the sky and approached them.
- Shall I? it proposed.
- Go ahead! said Colin, and the cloud shrouded them. Inside, it was warm and smelled of sugary cinnamon.
- No one can see us now! Said Colin... But we can see them.
- It's a little transparent, said Chloe. Be careful.
- That doesn't matter, it feels better just the same, said Colin. What would you like to do?...
- Just go for a walk, would that bore you?

- Then tell me things...
- I don't know good enough things, said Chloe. We can look at the store windows. Look at this one!... It's interesting.
In the window, a pretty woman was lying on a matress. Her chest was bare and a device brushed up her breasts, with fine, long, silky white bristles. The sign read: Make your shoes last longer with the Antipode, by Reverend Charles.
-That's a good idea! Said Chloe.
- But that's got nothing to do with it!... It's much more pleasant with the hand.
Chloe blushed.
- Don't say things like that. I don't like boys who say dreadful things in front of girls.
- I'm sorry! Said Colin, I didn't mean to...
He seemed so sorry that she smiled and shook him a little to show him that she was not angry.
In another window, a fat man with a butcher's apron was slitting the throats of little children.
It was a propaganda window for the Public Assistance.
- Look where the money goes, said Collin. That must cost them a bundle to clean that every evening.
- They're not real! said Chloe, alarmed...
- How can we tell? said Colin. They get them for nothing at the Public Assistance.
- I don't like that, said Chloe. Before, there weren't propaganda windows like that. I don't think that's progress.
- It's of no importance, said Colin. It only works for those who already believe in those idiocies.
- And that?... said Chole.
In the window, there was a stomach, mounted on rubber wheels, good and round and bouncy. The ad read: Yours won't crease either if you iron it with the Electric Iron.
- But I know that stomach!... said Colin. It belongs to Serge, my old chef!... What could it be doing there?
- It doesn't matter, said Chloe. You're not going to go on about this stomach. It's much too fat, anyway...
- That's because he really knew how to cook!...
- Let's leave, said Chloe. I don't want to look at store windows anymore, I don't like it.
- What are we going to do? said Colin. Shall we have tea somewhere?
- Oh!... it's not the right time of the day.. and then, I don't really like it.
Colin breathed out, relieved, and his suspenders cracked.
- What made that sound?
- I stepped on a dead branch, explained Colin, blushing.
- How about taking a walk in the Bois de Boulogne? Said Chloe.
Colin looked at her, delighted...
- That's a very good idea... There won't be anyone. She blushed.
- That's not why. And besides, she added for revenge, we won't leave the large walkways. Otherwise we'll get our feet wet.
He tightened the hold on the arm he felt under his.
- We'll take the underground passage, he said.
The two sides of the passage were lined with prodigiously dimensioned aviaries in which the Urban Arrangers stored Spare Pigeons for the Gardens and Monuments. There was also the nursery for sparrows and the nursing of little sparrows. People did not often go down in there because the wings of all these birds made for a terrible wind in which minuscule white and blue feathers flew about.
- They never stop, said Chloe, securing her hat so it would not fly away.
- They're not always the same ones, said Colin.
He was struggling with his coattails.
- Let's hurry to get past the pigeons. The sparrows make less wind, said Chloe, cuddling up to Colin.
They hastened and came out of the dangerous zone. The little cloud had not followed them. It had taken a shortcut and was already waiting for them on the other side.

Dialog from the novel "L'écume des jours", from Boris Vian (extracted from Brian Harper's english traduction).

Urban clouds

Vian's sad and tender novel, led by two friends, Colin and Chick, and their two girlfriends, Chole and Smooth, reports a love story in a surrealistic environment. Their delicate, innocent and pure characters face the hardness of a hostile world.

This brief fragment of Vian's novel allows to raise not only the need to think about the relation between fear, public contemporary space and the need to construct places of concentration; but it also makes us think about how the city must be thought with a more atmospheric and sensory urbanism, a less geometric and compositive one. As Manuel de Solà Morales or Bruno Latour would say, nowadays, it makes us think on how necessary it is to project the public spaces by listening to the urban things, to be able to confront the climatic landscapes, capable of being identified with their own proper smell. Mirko Zardini observes that every city, and every place has its own perfume: the smell of London, the smell of Russia, the smell of Istanbul...

The pink cloud that surrounds and walks with Chole and Colin is the real catalyst of the street that we walk in, an urban cloud that helps them feel and experience the public space.

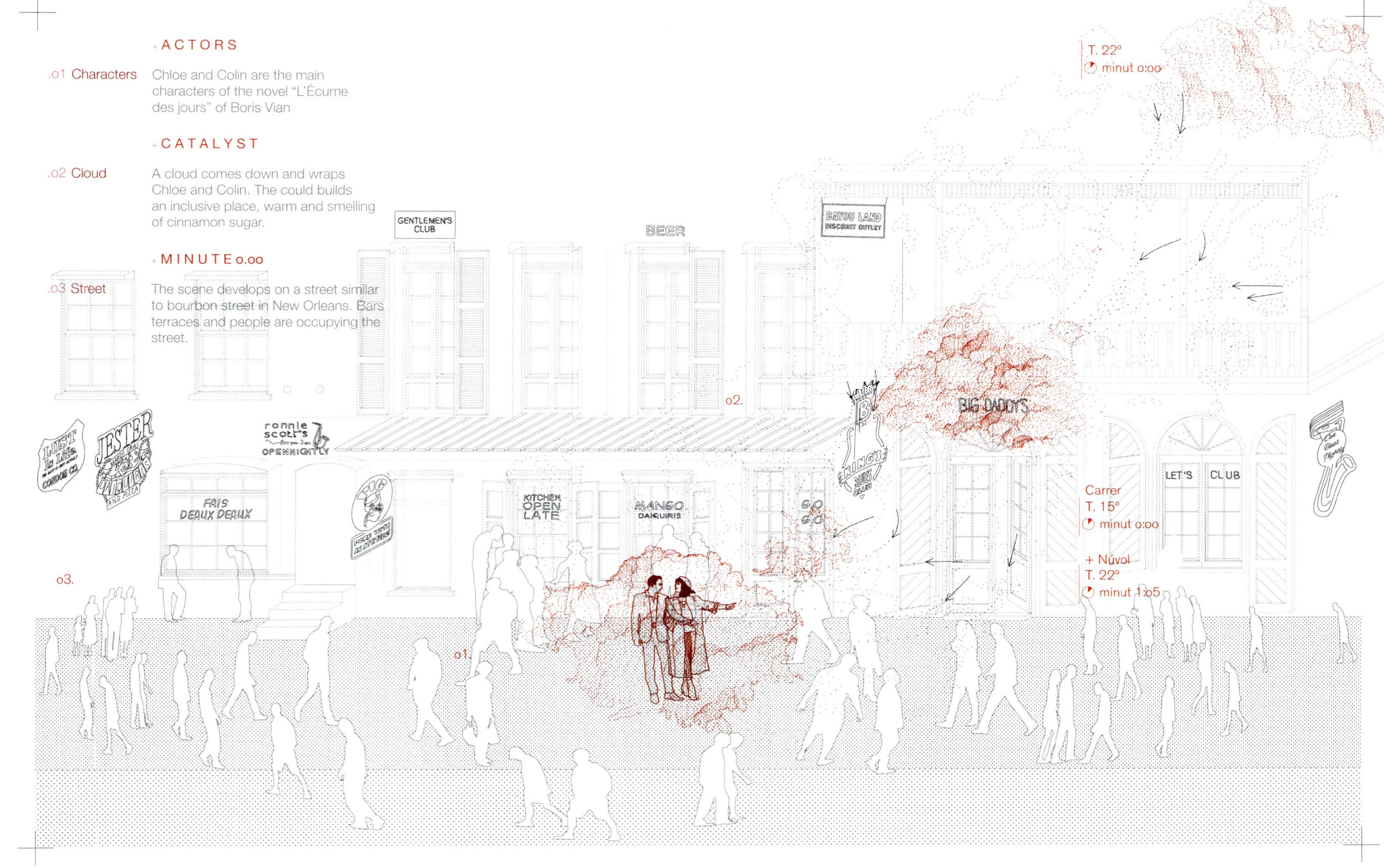
+ ACTORS
.01 Characters
Chloe and Colin are the main characters of the novel "L'Écume des jours" of Boris Vian
+ CATALYST
.02 Cloud
A cloud comes down and wraps Chloe and Colin. The could builds an inclusive place, warm and smelling of cinnamon sugar.
+ MINUTE o.oo
.03 Street
The scene develops on a street similar to bourbon street in New Orleans. Bars terraces and people are occupying the street.
GENTLEMEN'S CLUB
BEER
BAYOU LAND DISCOUNT OUTLET
ronnie scott's
OPENNIGHTLY
FAIS DEAUX DEAUX
KITCHEN OPEN LATE
MANGO DAIQUIRIS
GO GO
BIG DADDY'S
LET'S CLUB
JESTER
LUST
o1.
o2.
o3.
T. 22º
minut o:oo
Carrer
T. 15º
minut o:oo
+ Núvol
T. 22º
minut 1:o5

+ ACTORS

.o1 Characters Chloe and Colin are the main characters of the novel "L'Écume des jours" of Boris Vian

+CATALYST
.o2 Cloud
A cloud comes down and wraps
Chloe and Colin. The could builds
an inclusive place, warm and smelling
of cinnamon sugar.
o2.

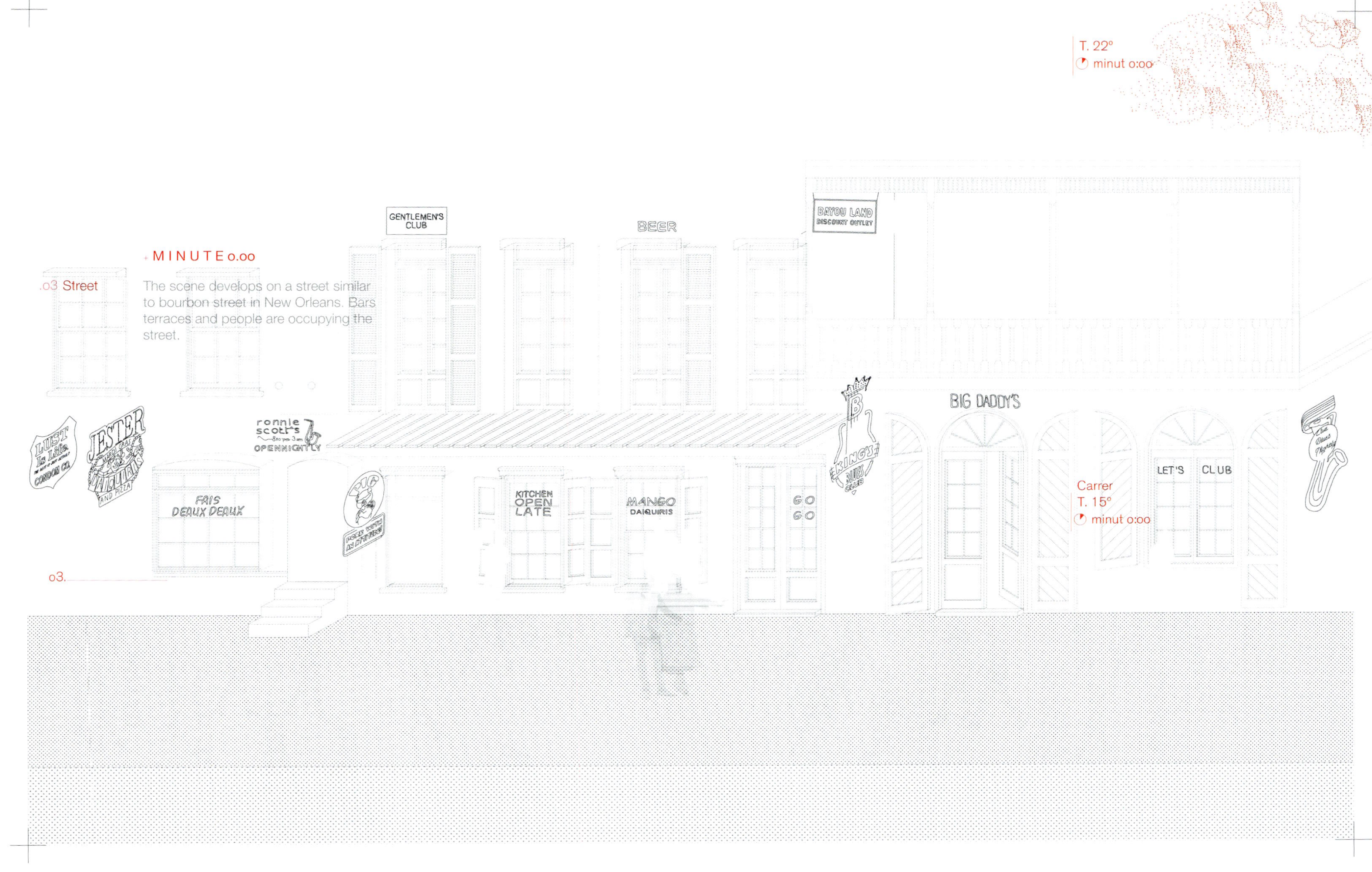

T. 22º
minut 0:00
+ MINUTE 0.00
.03 Street
The scene develops on a street similar to bourbon street in New Orleans. Bars terraces and people are occupying the street.
03.
GENTLEMEN'S CLUB
BEER
BAYOU LAND
DISCOUNT OUTLET
ronnie scott's
OPENNIGHTLY
JESTER
FRIS DEAUX DEAUX
KITCHEN OPEN LATE
MANGO DAIQUIRIS
GO GO
BIG DADDY'S
LET'S CLUB
Carrer
T. 15º
minut 0:00

CASE STUDY # 18

VISTABELLA. AND TALK TO SHELVES

Vistabella Church and its location.
J.M. Jujol

Photography Lluis Alexandre Casanovas and MBE.

cataloging	
.03	*Construction of trading and leisure infrastructures*
.01	*Environmental modification*
.05	*Artistic intervention*
catalyst	SHELVES AT THE ENTRANCE PORCH
example	Catalyst executed with minimum resources. Església del Sagrat Cor de Vistabella.
date	1923
author	Josep Maria Jujol.
address	Plaça de l'Església La Secuita Tarragona / CP: 08029.
description	*Jujol executes a complex geometry exercice by placing the church in a 45° angle, turning the structure. This way, the architect converts a simple crossroad into a square, a meeting spot...*

POOR
MODERNISM
ACTION
STONES
PALM TREES
LAND

CASE STUDY # 18

VISTABELLA

Bibliography

Josep Maria Jujol. Josep Llinàs.
(Koln: Taschen, 2007).

Jujol: Jujol's Universe. Dennis Dollens, Juan José Lahuerta.
(Barcelona: Actar and COAC, 1999).

Ludwig Jujol: Què és el collage, sinó acostar soledats?: Lluis II de Baviera, Josep Maria Jujol. Perejaume.
(Barcelona: La Magrana, 1989).

Jujol. Ignasi de Solà Morales.
(New York: Rizzoli, 1991).

Jujol today

The architecture of Josep Maria Jujol is nowadays a strong influence on many recent catalan projects; thanks to the studies done by Josep Llinàs during the 90's, which tried to rediscover a forgotten architect from the late catalan modernism; and also thanks to the interest that Josep Lluís Mateo had in this architect during his period as director of the Quaderns magazine.

A natural way

The wise, opportunist and direct attitude of Jujol, that takes advantage of any small opportunity to construct an intense project of architecture with the minimum means, has turned into an indispensable lesson for many architects.

It's nice to imagine Jujol speaking with his peasant friends, occasionally turned into construction workers during the weekend; deciding how they would continue the works of Vistabella's church, commenting in what way they could use the stones of the margins of the vineyard fields that surround the village to do a necklace of stones in the church, of how the wood scaffolding at the exterior façade could be used to do the structure and the interior ceiling of the chapel, of how they might re-use the frames of the windows to do the interior lamps, of how the beautiful skittles from the children that play in the square might magically turn into the chandeliers of the altar.

Jujol and the urban context

Even though nowadays people have talked and written a lot about Jujol, in very poor occasions anyone has ever thought about how his work relates with the context. Probably, the small scale of his work, the site plan of his projects, found normally in rural backgrounds, and the fresh virtuosity of his details has naturally lead us to study his works in a more urban way.

TALKING IN CHAPEL

Vistabella's church is located in a typical street in a structure of suburban growth, in a village of 150 inhabitants. The church is keenly placed right in the point of inflexion where the Major street changes direction and a small street appears, leading to the vineyards. This slight turn of the Major Street, in which the structure of the suburban buildings remain interrupted, represents the opportunity for Jujol to construct the main square of the village.

Often they affirm that the plans of the church correspond to a complex arbitrary overlapping of two 45° turned squares, but this is the result of a superficial analysis that only values the church as an isolated element and without context. The plan that Jujol proposes simply introduces the turn of 45 ° from the Major Street in the geometry of the church.

Geometry and public space

The geometric construction of the plan, that synthesizes this fragile condition of urban inflexion and the decision to locate to the church at the end of the lot, permits Jujol to create a slight tension at the Major street, sufficient to form the village square. In this widening of the street, one of the corners of the church stretches obliquely continuing the axes of the turned 45 ° to construct the porch of access and to spatially qualify the plaza. The church opens to the square.

Shelves for ttalking

Shelves for talking I'm sure that Jujol liked to imagine his peasant friends continuing to talk about the church once the construction

had already been finalized. He probably wanted the church to participate in the social activity of the village. It's possible that this is the reason why the three stone pillars that hold the front porch that gives acces to the church are transformed in three simple places that glance at each other, to be able to continue the chat there.

Site plan / Vistabella. La Secuita.

+PARISHONERS

.01 Conversation The distance between the stone seats is perfect for having a conversation.

+IN-BETWEEN

.02 Geometry Jujol takes advantage of the geometry of discontinuous streets to create a hall to the church.

.03 Porch Through a porch, Jujol a space of intermittent scale between the exterior and the chapel.

.04 Bench The columns of the porch have a base made of stone that allows the parishoners to sit and talk before entering the ceremony.

+MINUTE o.oo

.05 Square The intersection of different geometries of the streets creates a small widening which Jujol uses as a tiny plaza.

+PARISHONERS

.o1 Conversation The distance between the stone seats is perfect for having a conversation.

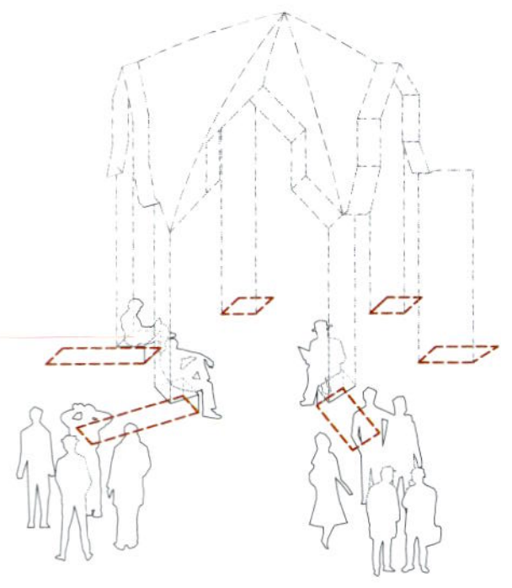

o1.

+ IN-BETWEEN

.o2 Geometry Jujol takes advantage of the geometry of discontinuous streets to create a hall to the church.

.o3 Porch Through a porch, Jujol a space of intermittent scale between the exterior and the chapel.

.o4 Bench The columns of the porch have a base made of stone that allows the parishoners to sit and talk before entering the ceremony.

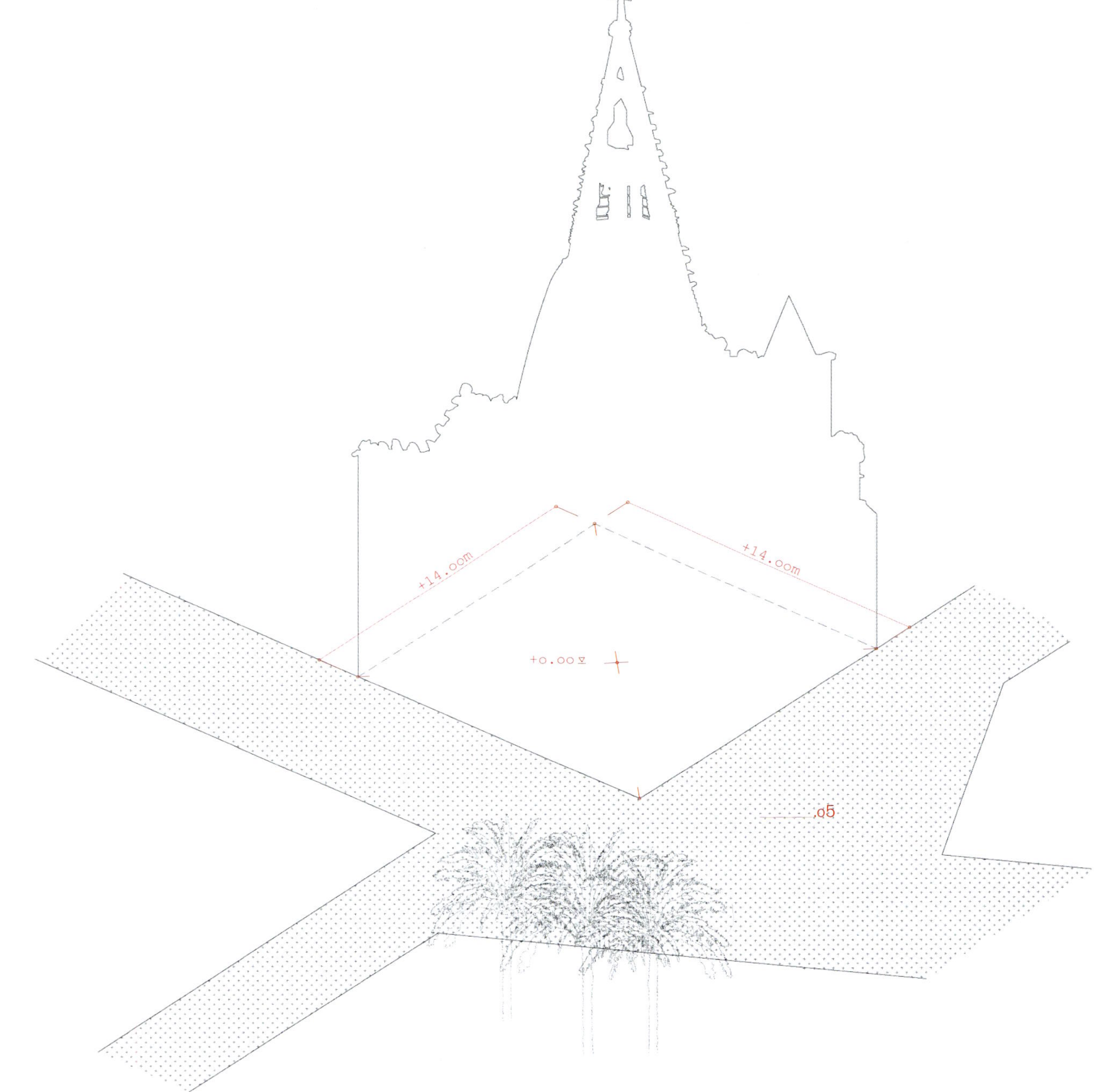

+ MINUTE o.oo

.o5 Square

The intersection of different geometries of the streets creates a small widening which Jujol uses as a tiny plaza.

CASE STUDY # 19

XAVIER RIBAS AND ACTIVE LEISURE

Picture n°13, **Sundays** (BCN Pictures) (1994-1997) 26 C-Type print 120 x 140 cm. Edition of 6.

cataloging

.05 *Artistic intervention*

.01 *Environmental modification*

.03 *Construction of trading and leisure infrastructures*

catalyst

FOLDING TABLES AND CHAIRS

example

Identification and temporary appropriation of an ordinary place. Picture nr 13. Sundays (BCN)

date

1994-97.

author

Xavier Ribas (www.xavierribas.com).

address

Santa Coloma de Gramenet . Barcelona's Metropolitan Area.

description

LEISURE
PLEASURE
IDENTITY

The technology that allowed tables and chairs to be fold was a revolution into the leisure field. It makes possible to scale any landscape to a size that allows us to experience it as if we [were/would be] at our own dining room.

CASE STUDY # 19

XAVIER RIBAS

Bibliography

Xavier Ribas. Ramon Esparza.
(Salamanca: Universidad de Salamanca, 2008)

Santuario. Xavier Ribas.
(Barcelona: Gustavo Gili, 2005)

"Perfecta distracción" (1994-1997). Xavier Ribas.

"Sundays" (1994-1997). Xavier Ribas.

"Flowers" (1998-2000). Xavier Ribas.

The anthropologist photographer

In 1998, the photographer and anthropologist Xavier Ribas realized the photo collection called Sundays (BCN). As the artist himself clearly explains in the text "Perfect distraction", that accompanies the images, the idea of this project is to show many spaces of leisure that arise spontaneously in the periphery of Barcelona during weekends.

According to Ribas, we live in an active society, that has finished constructing and promoting the active leisure and has isolated the traditional relaxing leisure towards the periphery of the city. "So then the person that spends the whole day at the office is recommended to practice

paintball, bungee jumping or rafting; and the construction man is advised to go away to Port Aventura to see the world".

The active leisure

Ribas turns his focus to catch the real leisure, the spontaneous and not planned leisure, that escapes from the business of leisure.

For Ribas, the periphery turns into a true place of freedom, a residual place in which relaxed leisure can be expressed more impulsively on Sundays.

The collection Sundays shows a delicate point of view that intensely expresses how

inhospitable places can be transformed into places of comfort. Ribas' photos explain how the periphery is modified by means of the simple occupation of residual spaces by collapsible Sunday furniture.

CHAIRS, COLLAPSIBLE TABLES AND TABLECLOTH

A pleasant family Sunday can be started by opening all the picnic equipment, the collapsible chairs and tables, the tablecloths, and to set them up under the shade of a pine, next to the Renault 12, with views to the three chimneys of the Besòs' incinerator.

The dog lies down on his mat, under the shade, and drinks water from the plastic Tupperware. There is a ball beside the aluminum table prepared to play a good game before or after eating. The gentleman, already without a shirt, moves trusting and satisfied as if it was his house.

Occasional peripheral occupation

To occupy this inhospitable space with their homes' chairs, tables and tablecloth allows them to transform the space into a familiar one.

The use of these catalysts harmonizes the difference of scales between an immense landscape and the feeling of shelter that is necessary to happily enjoy a Sunday leisure.

+USERS

.o1 Man	The man is not wearing a shirt, so he can better enjoy the sun.
.o2 Car	It helps to bring the chairs, table and all the camping tools.
.o3 Dog	The dog is laying over his blanket with his meal.

+LANDSCAPE & SCALE

.o4 Man	The man is not wearing a shirt, so he can better enjoy the sun.

+ACTION

.o5 Chairs	Folding chairs. Light aluminum tubular structures with fabric.
.o6 Table	Folding table. Light aluminum tubular structure with wood base, for 6 people.
.o7 Volume	The folding picnic furniture allows them to create a domestic space easily.

+MINUTE o.oo

.o8 Periphery	Future occupiable domestic places are normally situated outside of the dense city.

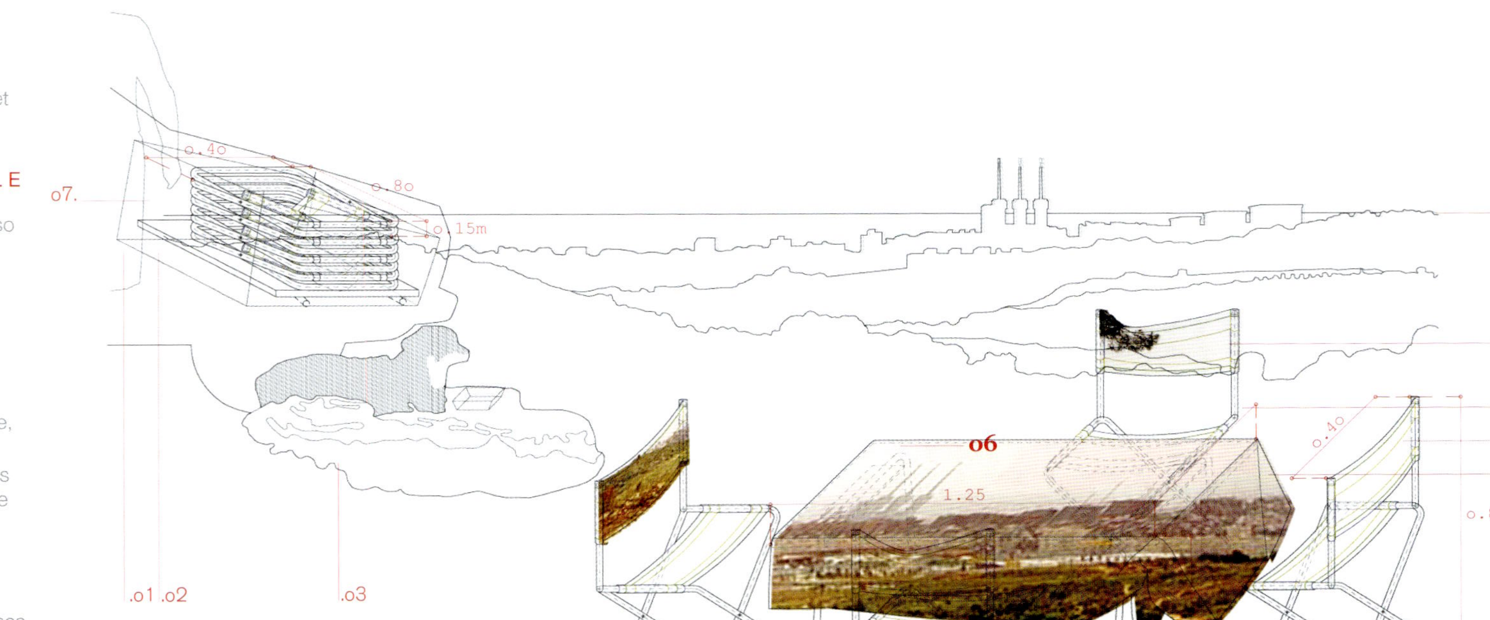

+ USERS

.o1 Man	The man is not wearing a shirt, so he can better enjoy the sun.
.o2 Car	It helps to bring the chairs, table and all the camping tools.
.o3 Dog	The dog is laying over his blanket with his meal.

LANDSCAPE & SCALE

.04 Man — The man is not wearing a shirt, so he can better enjoy the sun.

ACTION

.05 Chairs — Folding chairs. Light aluminum tubular structures with fabric.

.06 Table — Folding table. Light aluminum tubular structure with wood base, for 6 people.

.07 Volume — The folding picnic furniture allows them to create a domestic space easily.

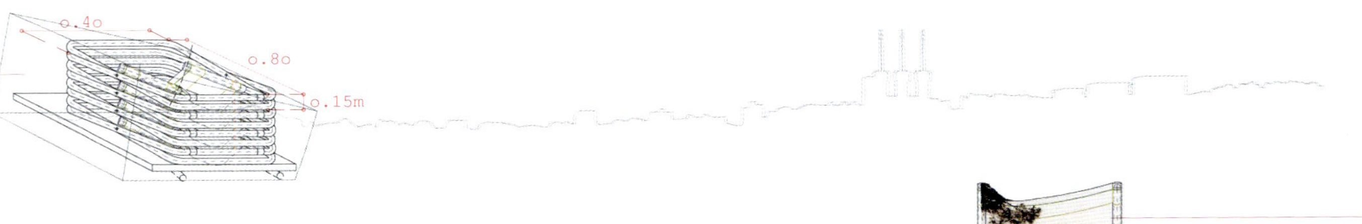

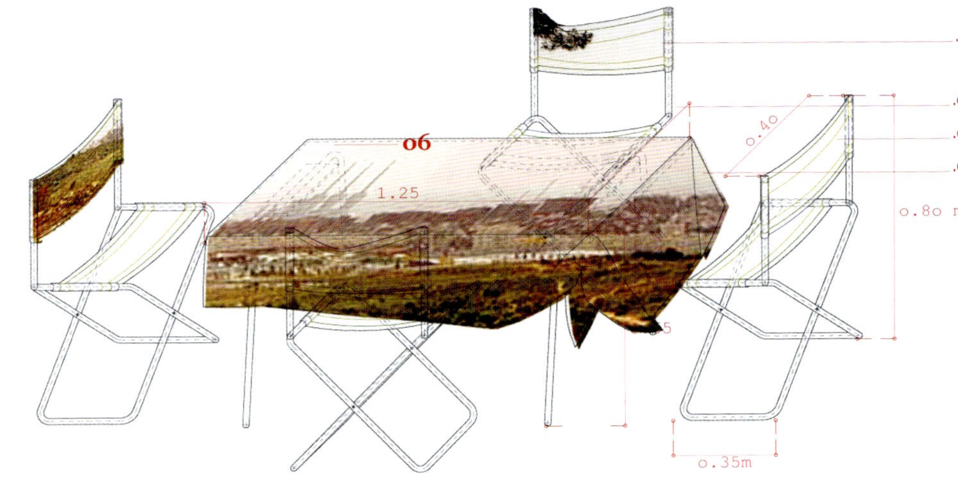

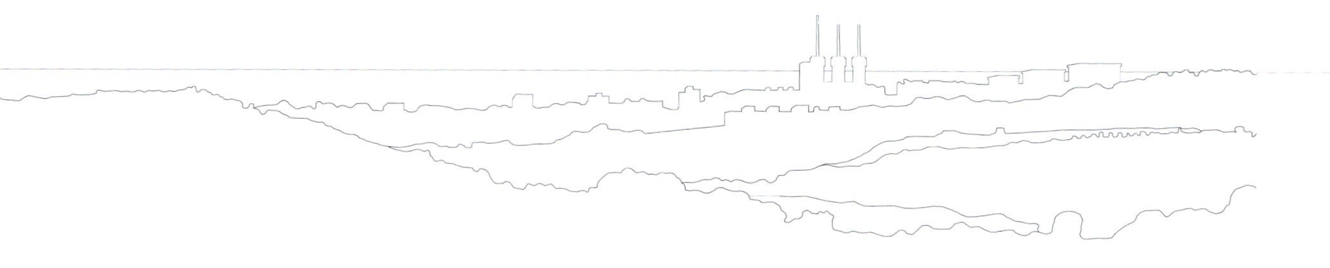

+ MINUTE o.oo

.o8 Periphery

Future occupiable domestic places are normally situated outside of the dense city.

CASE STUDY # 20

ZOCALO. A VERY THIN SHADOW

Plaza del Zocalo **Mexico DF**

Photography MBE

cataloging	
.01	*Environmental modification*
.03	*Construction of trading and leisure infrastructures*
.05	*Artistic intervention*
catalyst	SHADE
example	The effect of a non-predicted catalyst. Zocalo Square of Mexico DF.
date	1999
author	Monumental Flags program, president Ernesto Zedillo
address	Plaza de la constitución. Mexico DF.

description

CHANGE
SUN
THIN

The casual effect of a shade over an asymmetric square converts a cold place into a space of gathering.

CASE STUDY # 20

ZOCALO

Bibliography

Francis Alÿs: http://www.francisalys.com/

Installation: "Paseos por la ciudad". Francis Alÿs.

Film: *Zocalo, May 20 1999*. Running time: 12 hours. Francis Alÿs.

Plaza de la Constitución el Zocalo: http://es.wikipedia.org/wiki/Plaza_de_la_Constituci%C3%B3n_(Ciudad_de_M%C3%A9xico)

Banderas Monumentales: http://es.wikipedia.org/wiki/Banderas_monumentales_de_M%C3%A9xico

La Bandera de México:http://es.wikipedia.org/wiki/Bandera_de_M%C3%A9xico

Mexicans at the Zocalo

I approach a Mexican man who is waiting in row to buy some entrances, and I ask him what he's doing in that particular place, since he is standing right under the thin flagpole's shadow at the Zocalo Square of Mexico DF.

The Mexican man was surprised by my question, and gave me a simple response, that made me understand the curious popular phenomenon of the shade of this immense square.

The Plaza of Constitution, also known as the Plaza of the Zocalo, is a hard public space, paved with a few big porous dark slabs, undressed, without vegetation. A place in which

the silent sun fills an empty urban space of unusual proportions (195mx240m). A public space that has gradually, with the time, turned into the center of the historical center of Mexico DF; concentrating the most important religious and political buildings of the city. A place in which they have developed most cultural events and the most relevant social concentrations of the history of this country.

A vacant space

The Zocalo square has had different types of pavings during the past years, usually combining areas of park and leafy vegetation with some harder pavings, for about 400 years, it has had numerous offers and reforms, that combined different solutions, it was only in the last one that it obtained this singular, unoccupied aspect.
Among many of the projects designed for the square, Luis Barragan's offer from 1953 that had been seduced by this deserted and monumental character of the space is probably the one in charge of its empty appearance without trees or any vegetation.

Barragan's offer, which was never constructed, consisted of not occupying the space but of only constructing an invisible underground, which would improve the accessibility of the pedestrians to the middle of the square.

From 1950 up to the present, the only important action that has been realized in the Zocalo has been the raising of the Mexican flag in the center of the square. This element, of giant proportions, forms a part of the program of Monumental Flags initiated in 1999 by the president Ernesto Zedillo with the aim of promoting the culture and the patriotic Mexican spirit.

A VERY THIN SHADOW

When I visited the square and observed with interest the row of people waiting under the shade of the flagpole, I was very surprised to discover that all the individuals were of Mexican origin. Till then, in all the images that I had seen of the square, I had only concentrated on the curious effect of the shade and I had never paid attention on the persons that were there. Very enlightened by my finding, I approached the Mexican man and asked him the question, hoping to find a response to understand the reason of this local custom. His answer was very clear: " I stand here because this way I can rest under the shade of the flagpole when I cross the square".

An asymmetric square

The path that this man continued is a very common one: people arrive to the corner of the square through the Pino Suarez street, and then go to 5 de mayo street. So I guessed that was the common way to cross the Zocalo.

His comment allowed me to discover the asymmetry of the square and that the shaded arcaded façades are exactly not the sunny ones, and the flat south façades are precisely the worse for the pedestrians that pass through the Metropolitan Cathedral and the National Palace, since they are the sunnier ones.

In conclusion, all the people that arrive to the Zocalo square through Pino Suarez street avoid to walk beside the perimetral façades, because of their orientation and heat; so they choose to cross the square diagonally, realizing a shorter path, and stopping under the shade of the flagpole.

A civic shade

Even though this flag appeared in the square for a political purpose, its thin shadow constructs the only space of relation that this monumental but minimalist square really has.

Site plan / Plaza del Zocalo. Mexico DF.

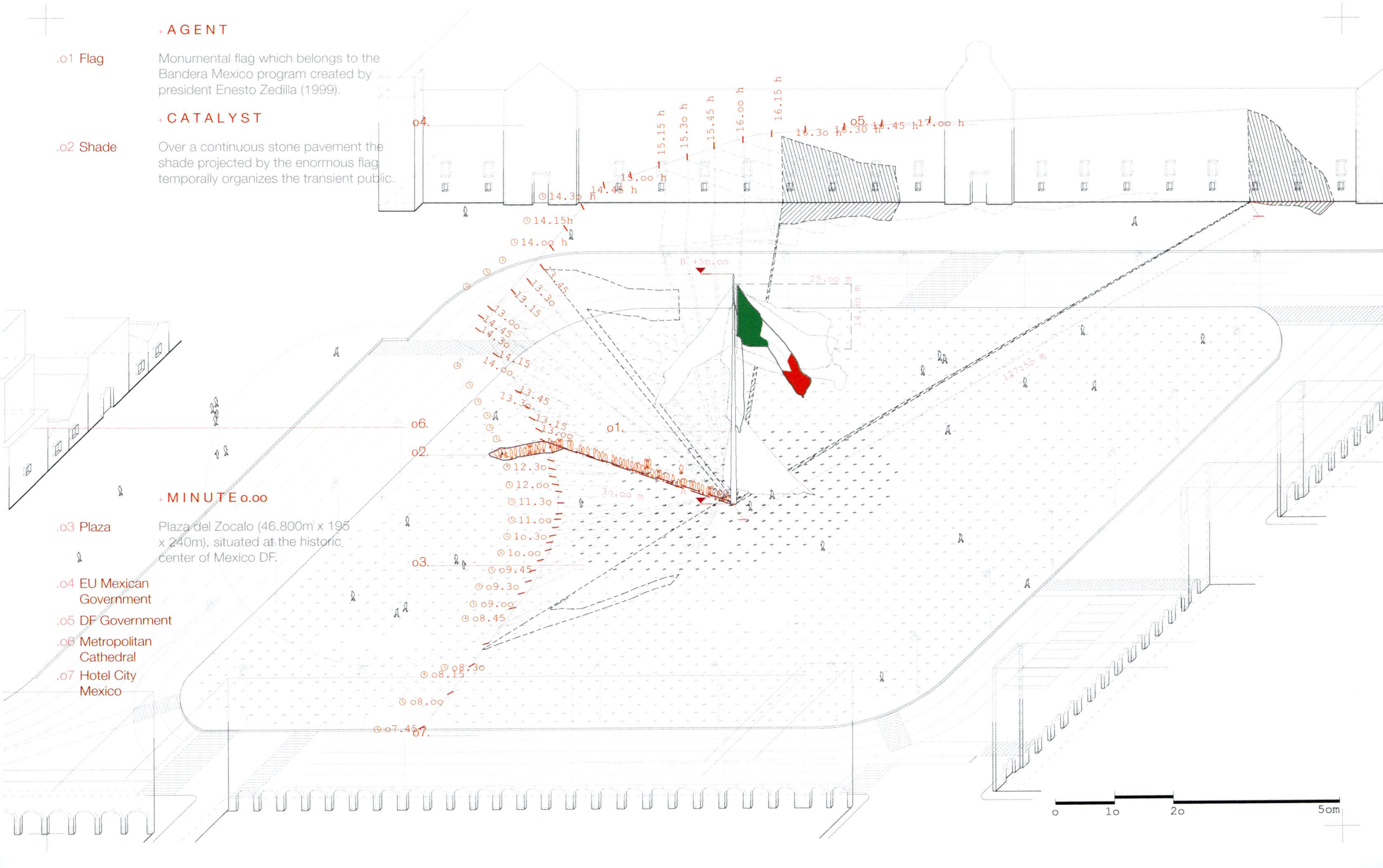
+AGENT
.o1 Flag
Monumental flag which belongs to the Bandera Mexico program created by president Enesto Zedilla (1999).
+CATALYST
.o2 Shade
Over a continuous stone pavement the shade projected by the enormous flag temporally organizes the transient public.
+MINUTE o.oo
.o3 Plaza
Plaza del Zocalo (46.800m x 195 x 240m), situated at the historic center of Mexico DF.
.o4 EU Mexican Government
.o5 DF Government
.o6 Metropolitan Cathedral
.o7 Hotel City Mexico
o1.
o2.
o3.
o4.
o5.
o6.
o7.
o7.45
o8.oo
o8.15
o8.30
o8.45
o9.oo
o9.3o
o9.45
1o.oo
1o.3o
11.oo
11.3o
12.oo
12.3o
13.oo
13.15
13.3o
13.45
14.oo
14.15
14.3o
14.45
14.oo h
14.15h
14.3o h
14.45 h
15.oo h
15.15 h
15.3o h
15.45 h
16.oo h
16.15 h
16.3o h
16.30 h
16.45 h
17.oo h
30.oo m
25.oo m
14.5o m
127.5o m
B +5o.oo
o
1o
2o
5om

+ CATALYST

.o2 Shade

Over a continuous stone pavement the shade projected by the enormous flag temporally organizes the transient public.

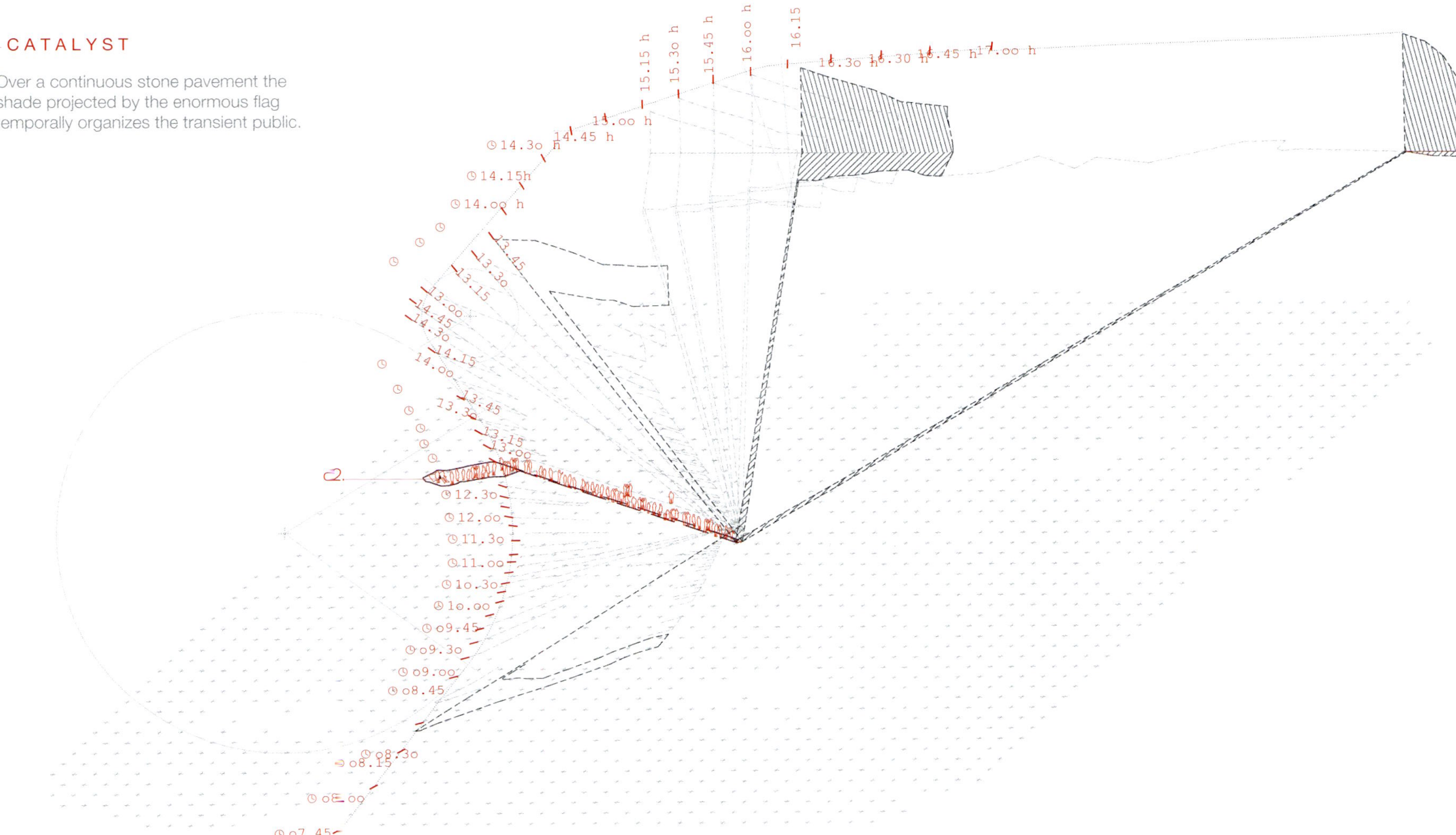

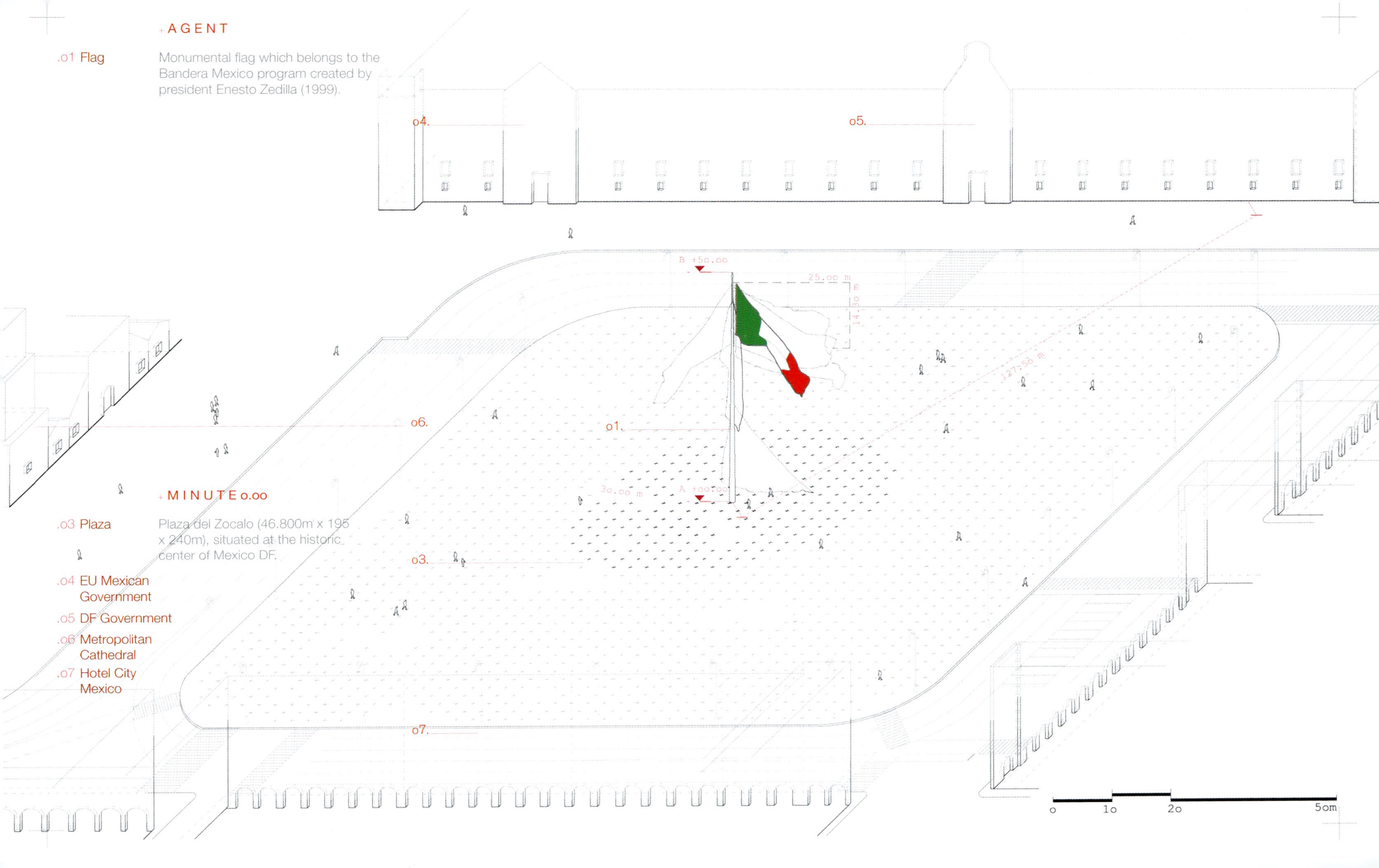
+AGENT
.o1 Flag
Monumental flag which belongs to the Bandera Mexico program created by president Enesto Zedilla (1999).
o4.
o5.
B +50.00
25.00 m
14.30 m
127.50 m
o6.
o1.
+MINUTE o.oo
30.00 m
A +00.00
.o3 Plaza
Plaza del Zocalo (46.800m x 195 x 240m), situated at the historic center of Mexico DF.
o3.
.o4 EU Mexican Government
.o5 DF Government
.o6 Metropolitan Cathedral
.o7 Hotel City Mexico
o7.
o
1o
2o
5om

3. AGAINST INDIFFERENCE:
NOTES ON THE DRAWINGS OF MANUEL BAILO

This book is called "Urban Catalysts" because it is intended to provoke thought about ways to reinvent the modern city. In so many cities today public spaces often seem disused or forgotten. The cities seem almost indifferent to social life. Manuel Bailo shows us that this indifference is only superficial.

Bailo's exquisite drawings reveal to us that there is a vibrant and often secret urban life that is unfolding before our eyes. It may not be exactly what architects had in mind when they designed these urban spaces, but life and even some unusual communities are nevertheless thriving in our contemporary cities in surprising and vivid ways.

Depicting scenes of public life on four continents, from snake charmers in a Moroccan city square to New Yorkers spilling out of their office buildings during a power outage to Italians congregating on a low bench outside a huge palace, the drawings of Manuel Bailo speak to what seems a universal human need in today's sprawling cities: to be outside and in the company of others.

Architect Manuel Bailo traveled the world for five years observing and documenting these urban scenes. He synthesized his observations as a series of exquisite line drawings that depict inventive ways in which people resist the alienating force of the contemporary city.

"Nowadays the architecture of our cities is somewhat generic," writes Professor Bailo. "It doesn't put down roots in the place it is built, and as a result many of the cities we live in are composed of very neutral abstract spaces. My work looks at how people seek to construct new spots of identity for themselves in these rather impersonal cities."

Currently on view in the Dean's Gallery are large drawings inspired by scenes of urban street life Bailo observed and analyzed in Brazil, Italy, Spain, Morocco, and New York. Two additional Bailo drawings in the exhibit were inspired by the world of film and photography.

Bailo brings an imaginative perspective to the world of architecture and urbanism, along with a deep concern for the place of free, outdoor public life in the modern city.

Sanda Iliescu
Associate Professor of Art and Architecture
The University of Virginia at Charlottesville